GARDNER'S
guide to

Interr Multimedia & Animation Studios

Garth Gardner, Ph.D.

GG
C

GGC Inc. / Publishing

Fairfax, Virginia

Production Team

Editor: Garth Gardner, Ph.D.
Associate Editor: Bonney Ford
Assistant Editors: Florissa Reynoso, Benesia Babb, and Sandy Skipper
Researcher: Andrew Johnston
Research Assistants: Casey Noble, Carene Clark, Tom Brooks, Wendell Howard, and Pat Riley.
Associates: Jenny Arata
Art Director: Nic Banks

Disclaimer

After publication of this manuscript, changes may occur. Such changes administered by the individual studios should take precedence over the information in this book. While reasonable effort will be made to update changes in subsequent editions, the reader is encouraged to seek current information from appropriate offices at the companies.

Editorial inquiries concerning this book should be addressed to:
The Editor, Garth Gardner Company, Inc., 4602 John Hancock Court. Suite 302, Annandale, VA 22003.
E-mail comments and corrections to: gardner@ggcinc.com.
Visit our website: http://www.gogardner.com

Library of Congress Cataloging-in-Publication Data

Gardner, Garth
    Gardner's guide to internships at multimedia and animation studios/ Garth Gardner.
      p. cm.
    Includes index.
    ISBN: 1-58965-000-X
      1. Multimedia systems--Vocational guidance. 2. Computer graphics--Vocational guidance. 3. Computer animation--Vocational guidance. 4. Internship programs--United States--Directories. I. Title: Guide to Internships at multimedia and animation studios. II. Title: Internships at multimedia and animation studios. III. Title.

QA76.575 .G35 2001
006.7'023'73--dc21

2001016027
CIP

Printed in the United States of America
10 9 8 7 6 5 4 3 2 1

About the Editor
Garth Gardner, Ph.D.

Dr. Gardner is a graduate of the Ohio State University's Advanced Computing Center for the Arts and Design and Department of Art Education. Dr. Gardner is currently an Associate Professor of Multimedia at the New Century College, George Mason University. Before his appointment at GMU, Dr. Gardner was an Assistant Professor at William Paterson University where he co-directed the Center for Computer Art and Animation. A member of William Paterson University's proposed MFA degree committee, in the Spring of 1996 Dr. Gardner chaired a subcommittee responsible for developing the proposed MFA degree concentration in Computer Art and Design.

As a consultant, Dr. Gardner has advised various colleges and universities in structuring their curricula for teaching computer graphics and animation. He is a member of the Professional Advisory Board for the development of a BFA degree program in Computer Graphics and Multimedia at the Fashion Institute of Technology.

His research has focused on computer-art education and he is considered one of the nation's experts in this area. Dr. Gardner has presented papers at several universities including the University of California Los Angeles' Animation Workshop, the University of Southern California, Florida A&M University and the Fashion Institute of Technology. He has been a contributing author to several national and international animation magazines and professional journals. His computer fine art images have been published and exhibited in galleries and museums nationally and in China.

Dr. Gardner founded and chaired the DECATA Animation Festival 1996, a college animation festival that was linked to other universities through interactive distance learning technologies. Dr. Gardner is the President and Publisher at GGC, Inc., A Computer Graphics, Publishing, Animation and Consulting firm. The Company's clients include: Universal Records, Air Jamaica, B.A.D., and Florida A&M University. His most recent publications are *Gardner's Guide to Computer Graphics, Animation and Multimedia Schools*, and *Gardner's Guide to Internships in New Media*, the number one resource for finding an internship in computer graphics, animation and multimedia. In addition Dr. Gardner is the executive producer of *Gardner's Great Animation Show*, a video that showcases 3D animation from some of the best animation schools in North America.

Acknowledgments

I thank the many people who have helped create, produce, and review the materials in this book, which has been a learning experience for us all. In particular I am especially thankful to Bonney and Nic for their loyalty to this project. I wish to express gratitude to the magazines and advertisers who continue to support this guide. In addition, I thank the associates of GGC Publishing for their invaluable help, support, and devotion in researching this subject. —G. Gardner

About This Book

This book is written for the college student who wishes to pursue a career in the field of multimedia which, for the purpose of simplifying this book, we have defined as the following areas: pre-production, computer graphics, computer animation, traditional animation, web design, video production, digital imaging studios, visual effects, post production, and sound. In short, it is written for the person who dreams of joining the ranks of an elite group of creative artists and scientists that are in the business of creating multimedia and animation projects. This reference guide is also created for those who seek the services of an animation or multimedia studio.

Gardner's Guide to Internships at Multimedia and Animation Studios is designed to assist prospective interns of the industry to locate a specific studio that may be in search of their talents. This book will help people interested in employment or employing the services of a computer graphics studio to answer the following questions:

• What studios may potentially be a source of employment?

• What is the size of the studio; what is the number of employees?

• What are the studio's areas of specialization?

• What services does the company provide?

Gardner's Guide is the first step to answering these questions and many others. The Guide is designed to be used to quickly reference information on multimedia and animation studios. Please be advised that our objective in creating this guide is to provide you with a starting point. For the most accurate and up-to-date information, please contact the studios directly.

Profiled Categories

The studios that are profiled in this book offer services in Computer Graphics, Animation, or Multimedia. The studios are listed alphabetically within three geographic areas in the US: east coast, west coast, central and a general category for Canada. For each profiled studio, the following facts are presented: Area of Specialization; Number of Employees; Description of Studio; Contact Information, and Web Address, when available.

Table of Contents

9   Introduction

11   Where to Start

11   When to Apply for an Internship

13   G.P.A. Requirements

13   Payment Issues

13   Foreign Students

14   Résumés and Cover Letters

14   Multimedia Résumé Recommendations

18   Five Basic Resume Designs

23   Web Résumé Sample

25   Sample HTML Script for Creating Résumé on the Web

27   Cover Letter

27   A Winning Cover Letter

30   Interviewing

31   Interview Questions

32   Things to Take to the Interview

33   Interview Thank You Letter Sample

37   East Coast

101   Central

127   West Coast

227   Canada

239   Index listed by State or Province

248   Index listed by company name

Introduction

Perhaps one of the most important decisions one must make in their academic career is finding the right major, a major area of emphasis, a major that best fits your personality and one that prepares you to attain your goals in a changing work-force. Though most academic programs in multimedia have some kind of internship course in the curriculum, others still rely on the student to do this work as an extra curriculum activity. Regardless of your school's policy regarding internships, note that an internship is a very important experiential learning opportunity. Internships serve as a means to bridge the gap between academia and the professional world. They serve as the means to continue where your school may have fallen short or to solidify the theories you have learned. Internships give you the opportunity to "test drive" a career. They can give you the opportunity to earn extra academic credit. They allow you to see from the inside, to test whether a particular career is right for you. Beyond being real world experience, it also provides students with a venue for networking with professionals in their areas of emphasis. In the case of the multimedia student then an internship opportunity can also be an opportunity to work on professional projects that may lead to an improved demonstration reel and portfolio. Finally an internship often offers students a chance to work on a production team where all members are well established in their areas of specialization. Internships add practical experience to your résumé.

This book is designed to equip students with the necessary knowledge for finding an internship in the field of new media, computer graphics, animation, web page design, television production, graphic design and many other areas. The primary purpose of this book is to guide students in the area of multimedia to various internship opportunities available to them. There are various other steps a student must take beyond the initial search for internship, some of which may be: submitting a résumé and portfolio, arranging for a phone interview, interview in person. Taking these steps into consideration, this book will offer basic guidelines to assist students through these subsequent procedures.

This is truly a great field to be a part of; there is no other field like it that offers such excellent opportunities for artists and scientists. With the Internet market

on a constant incline, career opportunities for practitioners in this field are endless. Today trained web artists and programmers are commanding salaries that rival that of doctors and lawyers, and trained graphic designers and animators are working more efficiently with the aid of the computer.

Where to Start

Start by making an appointment to speak with a career counselor at your school to discuss your career goals and objectives. You must first figure out what area of new media most intrigues you. Explore the options on paper. When you have decided on an area or combination of areas, begin the search. Look first at the major companies that specialize in your area of interest. Select at least 20 primary companies that you would like to target. Visit the web sites of these companies to get a general understanding of what they do, available internships, deadline information and requirements for applying for an internship. In most cases they simply need to have a cover letter and résumé. E-mail the director or coordinator of the internship program and get a general feel for the ratios of acceptance. Do not be intimidated by the large pool of applicants to the internship program. Do make sure that you have

fulfilled the requirements necessary for an internship at the company and that you are working within the deadline. Be practical about your decision. Remember that some internships require an in-person interview. Be realistic and plan ahead. It is not unusual for students to already have dozens of leads for a summer internship by mid-fall of the previous year.

When to Apply for an Internship

Although students who are seniors in high school to college seniors are eligible to apply for internships at a new media company, the most commonly acceptable group are students at the college junior and senior level. Interns must be returning to college at the end of the internship program. This is a requirement at most companies. Students may apply for an internship as early as a year in advance. In fact the most common deadline for internships is mid-November of the preceding year for summer internships. Other internships are rolling and accept for an average period of three months all year round. Others are very loose and accept on an as-needed basis, without any deadlines. Therefore you must start in your freshman year to find an internship for your sophomore year. The is advisable for students in the animation, web design

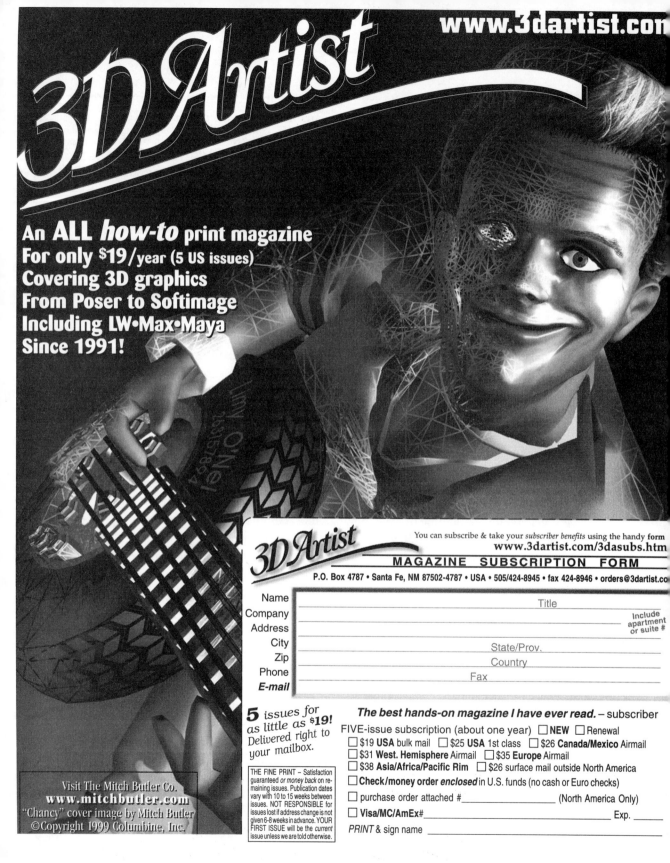

and other areas that are extremely competitive. This way if you are not successful in finding an internship in your sophomore year, you can try for your junior year.

G.P.A. Requirements

Although the acceptable grade point average (G.P.A.) for internships can vary, I have yet to come across an internship program that accepts students below a 2.5 G.P.A., and these are rare. The average G.P.A. for most internship programs is 3.0 and above, 3.5 for the most competitive internship programs at popular companies. Other companies may look at the G.P.A. from the major subjects only, and may not consider such subjects as Mathematics, and the Sciences to be relevant. Though most are looking at the package deal, i.e. the personality, educational rank, and interest in the subject area, it often the G.P.A. that is considered the first criteria for evaluating prospective interns.

Payment Issues

Yes it is a fact that most companies do not pay interns for their time, and also they do not charge interns either. The internship program is a learning experience for the students and a primarily teaching one for the company. Every intern hired must be trained and that is a costly undertaking for the company. According to a visual effects supervisor at a major California company "we had an intern that would walk in front of the set at times when we were shooting and we would have to re-shoot the entire scene." It is a fact that inexperienced individuals can be costly to a company. But not all are non-paid internships; some companies provide interns with a travel allowance for travels to and from work. Others pay a monthly stipend and some pay a minimum wage. Keep your eyes on the larger picture; you are not there to get a salary; you are there primarily for the experience and to make meaningful connections, and most importantly to learn more about the field that excites you. If you are one to say "no pay no way" you will be looking at a limited pool of possibilities.

Foreign Students

Foreign students may obtain an internship in the US. but must comply with the regulations of the Immigration and Naturalization Services (INS). Often prospective employers welcome these students but do not welcome the documents that are necessary for them to gain employment in the US. Usually an issued letter of acceptance from the employer is the key document for the foreign student to file through their school for an off-campus internship. In most cases if the internship is a part of the academic requirement for obtaining a degree at the school, the permission is granted. In this case the student is also free to accept monetary compensation if applicable. Foreign students' seeking an internship must first see the foreign students advisor at their school for detailed advice on these and other procedures relating to employment in the US.

Résumés and Cover Letters

Before you are called for your first interview, you must first attract your employer with your résumé and cover letter. Whether you are applying for an entry level position or Vice-President, your résumé and cover letter should stand out above the rest. Résumés are an outline, briefly yet concisely describing your educational history, work experience and computer skills. Be brief and to the point, highlight things in bold, and use bullets when necessary. Try to avoid getting personal, such as including hobbies. Focus on your employment strengths and skills. With modern technology, résumés can journey to the attention of a potential employer with the click of a mouse. Résumés can be sent through e-mail, snail mail, fax, and posted on the Internet. If you have

difficulty writing your own résumé, there are services available for résumé writing.

Multimedia Résumé Recommendations

Perhaps you are all prepared for the new century and you have put together a résumé that has the look and feel of the year 2000 and beyond, one that is on-line, designed for interaction, and accessible through your web site. Presenting such résumé may not be such a good idea, especially when you are dealing with an established media company which has just embarked on the area of new media and may be apprehensive or simply not equipped to view disk or interactive versions of your résumé. To them, anything beyond print sends off a red light. As a prospective intern, stick to the traditional one page printed résumé. If you wish, create an interactive résumé as a secondary option. Most companies today receive at least 10 résumés for every one position available. Most do not accept attached e-mail résumés. Your prior education and employment history are the prime factors used by prospective employers for selection.

Here are some tips on preparing for and handling a prospective employer if you have a résumé that shows a variety of experiences:

Put your new media experience at the top. Throw out that idea that your résumé needs to be in chronological order. Don't make them search for your new media experience when that's what they're most interested in. This goes for your portfolio as well. Make sure everything in your portfolio is prominently displayed. Only include new media projects and drawings if they are incredible, or help to explain some aspect of the project. Such drawings may be incorporated in a story board for a future or present project.

Delete the jobs that do not relate to your goals today. It is always tempting to include the waitstaff job that you did at the fast food restaurant, but before you do so, think twice. If you have not had any experience in the field of new media and you are just breaking ground, that job as a waiter should stay. It will work for you. It shows the prospective employer that you have worked on a professional team and with a great reference, it can help to establish that you work well with others. Remember that the new media environment is very much team-oriented. On the other hand, if you have experience working on a multimedia project, and you are simply

looking to get an internship to get in the door of a major company, delete the waiter position. In this case the information will help to establish that you are focused and goal-oriented. If you are in a position where you have interned in different areas of media, for instance, and you have got a super-résumé and cannot decide whether or not you should cut out your awards, toss your TV news experience first. Most newspaper employers do not think much of this medium, and you would not have any clips from it anyway. Some prospective employers might even look down on you for it, and it is not worth the risk. People in television want to see television experience on your résumé and those in web design want to see web design experience and that is the bottom line.

Praise your medium. Though you are only looking for an internship it is not to early too present yourself with a certain degree of confidence and loyalty to the field you have chosen to study. You may not be totally convinced which area of new media you would like to pursue; however, in the world of big business and large corporation, division of the various areas of new media has led to specialization. If your intention is to eventually work at a large multimedia corporation, you may want to start today to develop a commitment for an area of new media. Prospective employers want to know that as an intern you will continue to develop in an area of new media. Know the facts and speak knowledgeably about an area of new media that you enjoy. Discuss some advantages of this area on traditional media.

Chris Jones

123 Main Street Anytown USA 55555 · (555) 555 5555
E-mail: chris@anywhere.com · URL: http://www.anything.com

software knowledge

Flash (2 yrs), Lightwave (2 yrs), Composer (6 mo's), Adobe Illustrator (1yr), Adobe Photoshop (learning), Windows NT, Mac OS

experience

Yapping Pup Productions
June 1998 - Feb. 1999
Technical director
Worked on corporate logos including "WCAT" in Baton Rouge, and "Here's Your Mattress" for The Mattress Warehouse in Murfreesboro.

Gogardner.com
July 1997 - Dec. 1998
Animation assistant
Assisted with web-based animation for corporate websites.

education

George Mason University, Any City
1998-present

State College or University, Any City
attended 1992-1994

relevant coursework

1 semester CAD, 2 semesters shell scripting in C++, 2 years Light wave training. 8 semesters traditional painting, 8 semesters computer animation, 6 semesters traditional cell animation.

other

I own a PC and love coming up with my own animation. I am currently working on a 30-minute 3D animation about snowboarding which I have scripted and storyboarded.

chris jones

123 Main Street Anytown USA 55555 · (555) 555 5555
E mail: chris@anywhere.com · URL: http://www.anything.com

software knowledge	Flash (2 yrs), Lightwave (2 yrs), Composer (6 mo's), Adobe Illustrator (1yr), Adobe Photoshop (learning), Windows NT, Mac OS
experience	Yapping Pup Productions June 1998 - Feb. 1999 Technical director Worked on corporate logos including "WCAT" in Baton Rouge, and "Here's Your Mattress" for The Mattress Warehouse in Murfreesboro. Gogardner.com July 1997 - Dec. 1998 Animation assistant Assisted with web-based animation for corporate websites.
education	George Mason University, Any City 1998-present State College or University, Any City attended 1992-1994
relevant coursework	1 semester CAD, 2 semesters shell scripting in C++, 2 years Light wave training. 8 semesters traditional painting, 8 semesters computer animation, 6 semesters traditional cell animation
other	I own a PC and love coming up with my own animation. I am currently working on a 30-minute 3D animation about snowboarding which I have scripted and storyboarded.

chris jones

123 Main Street Anytown USA 55555 · (555) 555 5555
E-mail: chris@anywhere.com · URL: http://www.anything.com

software knowledge

Flash (2 yrs), Lightwave (2 yrs), Composer (6 mo's), Adobe Illustrator (1yr), Adobe Photoshop (learning), Windows NT, Mac OS

experience

Yapping Pup Productions
June 1998 - Feb. 1999
Technical director
Worked on corporate logos including "WCAT" in Baton Rouge, and "Here's Your Mattress" for The Mattress Warehouse in Murfreesboro.

Gogardner.com
July 1997 - Dec. 1998
Animation assistant
Assisted with web-based animation for corporate websites.

education

George Mason University, Any City
1998-present

State College or University, Any City
attended 1992-1994

relevant coursework

1 semester CAD, 2 semesters shell scripting in C++, 2 years Light wave training. 8 semesters traditional painting, 8 semesters computer animation, 6 semesters traditional cell animation

other

I own a PC and love coming up with my own animation. I am currently working on a 30-minute 3D animation about snowboarding which I have scripted and storyboarded.

Chris Jones

123 Main Street Anytown USA 55555 · (555) 555 5555
E-mail: chris@anywhere.com · URL: http://www.anything.com

software knowledge
Flash (2 yrs), Lightwave (2 yrs), Composer (6 mo's), Adobe Illustrator (1yr), Adobe Photoshop (learning), Windows NT, Mac OS

experience
Yapping Pup Productions
June 1998 - Feb. 1999
Technical director
Worked on corporate logos including "WCAT" in Baton Rouge, and "Here's Your Mattress" for The Mattress Warehouse in Murfreesboro.

Gogardner.com
July 1997 - Dec. 1998
Animation assistant
Assisted with web-based animation for corporate websites.

education
George Mason University, Any City
1998-present

State College or University, Any City
attended 1992-1994

relevant coursework
1 semester CAD, 2 semesters shell scripting in C++, 2 years Light wave training. 8 semesters traditional painting, 8 semesters computer animation, 6 semesters traditional cell animation.

other
I own a PC and love coming up with my own animation. I am currently working on a 30-minute 3D animation about snowboarding which I have scripted and storyboarded.

Chris Jones

software knowledge

Flash (2 yrs), Lightwave (2 yrs), Composer (6 mo's), Adobe Illustrator (1yr), Adobe Photoshop (learning), Windows NT, Mac OS

experience

Yapping Pup Productions
June 1998 - Feb. 1999
Technical director
Worked on corporate logos including "WCAT" in Baton Rouge, and "Here's Your Mattress" for The Mattress Warehouse in Murfreesboro.

Gogardner.com
July 1997 - Dec. 1998
Animation assistant
Assisted with web-based animation for corporate websites.

education

George Mason University, Any City
1998-present

State College or University, Any City
attended 1992-1994

relevant coursework

1 semester CAD, 2 semesters shell scripting in C++, 2 years Light wave training. 8 semesters traditional painting, 8 semesters computer animation, 6 semesters traditional cell animation.

other

I own a PC and love coming up with my own animation. I am currently working on a 30-minute 3D animation about snowboarding which I have scripted and storyboarded.

123 Main Street
Anytown USA 55555
(555) 555 5555

E-mail: chris@anywhere.com
URL: http://www.anything.com

Web Résumé Sample

ANY PERSON
1111 Main Street
City, State 12345
Phone: 123-456-5555
Fax: 987-654-5555
E-mail: anyperson@address.com

SUMMARY OF QUALIFICATIONS
Animation student with extensive traditional animation experience. Expertise includes developing and
implementing characters. Excellent storytelling and oral communication skills.
Applications: Maya; 3D Studio Max; Macintosh design software applications.
Program Languages: C, C++, UNIX and HTML coding.

KEY ACHIEVEMENTS
Teaching Assistant for Animation Course, Fairfax, VA 1999-present
George Mason University
Worked with the faculty and assisted with the evaluation of students' performance in the course.
Reviewed papers and animation projects. Took daily attendance.

Assisted the students to achieve the course objectives. Lead individual sessions with students to review
the technical aspects of the course. Taught animation software, and reviewed animation techniques.
Assisted students with drawing tools on the computer. Organized group activities and field trips.
Maintained relations with the students through office hours.
Director, Animated Film for MTV- 1998-1999
Independent Project.

Wrote and proposed film concept to MTV. Created animation storyboard and wrote script. Organized
presentation and proposed budget for the film.
Managed all functions of the animation production, organized staff, lead daily discussion with the
animation team. Managed an animation budget
of $30,000.

Worked with recruitment firm to select qualified staff members for the project. Reviewed portfolios/
resumes and hired the management staff for the film.

EDUCATION
M.F.A. Computer Animation, 1998-expected in 2001
B.A. Multimedia, New Century College, George Mason University, 1998

Feel free to e-mail me any question: anyperson@address.com

Sample HTML Script for Creating Résumé on the Web

```
<HTML>
<HEAD>
<TITLE>Any person résumé</TITLE>
</HEAD>
<BODY BGCOLOR="#ffffff">
<TABLE WIDTH="450" BORDER="0" CELLSPACING="2" CELLPADDING="0">
<TR>
<TD WIDTH="100%"><P ALIGN=CENTER>RÉSUMÉ OF ANY PERSON</P>
<P>ANY PERSON<BR>
1111 Main Street<BR>
City, State 12345<BR>
Phone: 123-456-5555<BR>
Fax: 987-654-5555<BR>
E-mail: anyperson@address.com<BR>
<BR>
<B>SUMMARY OF QUALIFICATIONS </B><BR>
<BR>
Animation student with extensive traditional animation experience.  Expertise
includes developing and implementing characters. Excellent storytelling
and oral communication skills. </P>
<P>  Applications: Maya; 3D Studio Max; Macintosh design software applications.</P>
<P>  Program Languages: C, C++, UNIX and HTML coding. <BR>
<HR ALIGN=LEFT></P>
<P><B>KEY ACHIEVEMENTS </B></P>
<P><B>Teaching Assistant for Animation Course</B>, Fairfax, VA 1999-present</P>
<P>George Mason University</P>
<P>  Worked with the faculty and assisted with the evaluation of students' performance in the course.  Reviewed papers and
animation projects. Took daily attendance.</P>
<P>  Assisted the students to achieve the course objectives. Lead individual
sessions with students to review the technical aspects of the course.  Taught
animation software, and reviewed animation techniques. Assisted students
with drawing tools on the computer. Organized group activities and field
trips.</P>
<P>  Maintained relations with the students through office hours.<BR>
</P>
<P><B>Director, Animated Film for MTV</B>- 1998-1999 </P>
<P>Independent Project.</P>
<P>  Wrote and proposed film concept to MTV. Created animation storyboard
and wrote script. Organized presentation and proposed budget for the film.</P>
<P>  Managed all functions of the animation production, organized staff, lead daily discussion with the animation team. Managed
an animation budget
of $30,000. </P>
<P>  Worked with recruitment firm to select qualified staff members for the project.  Reviewed portfolios/resumes and hired the
management staff for the film.<BR>
<HR ALIGN=LEFT></P>
<P><B>EDUCATION </B></P>
<P>M.F.A. Computer Animation, 1998-expected in 2001</P>
<P>B.A. Multimedia, New Century College, George Mason University, 1998 </P>
<P><HR ALIGN=LEFT></P>
<P>Feel free to e-mail me any question: <A HREF="mailto:%22anyperson@address.com">anyperson@address.com</A></P>
<P><BR>
</TD></TR>
</TABLE>
</BODY>
</HTML>
```

SUBSCRIBE

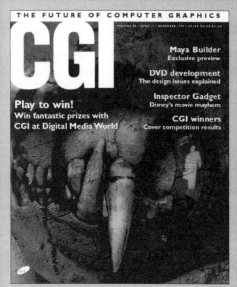

C3

C3 is the only dedicated monthly technology and business magazine for professional users of 3D design and visualisation software and hardware.
USA: $72 for 12 issues

DESIGN4

Design4 is the exclusive magazine for users of Discreet software and provides exclusive and unrivalled advice to professional animators and 3D artists worldwide.
USA: $60 for 12 issues

CGI

CGI is the leading business and technology magazine for professionals working in film, TV, video, games development, multimedia, web design and broader uses of animation and computer graphics.
USA: $72 for 12 issues

Cover Letter

Cover letters can help you express your interest in the employer, your qualifications, requirements, and your availability for an interview. The cover letter allows you to include information not stated in the résumé. Cover letters are sometimes overlooked, but it is still essential to include one with your résumé. The cover letter should be written with conciseness and clarity. Remember you are a professional, and your cover letter represents you. Résumés and cover letters are your first step in the door, followed by the interview. However, before you can get to the interview, you must be able to sell yourself in writing.

A Winning Cover Letter

The fact that most internships are highly competitive means that the intern applicant must pay closer attention to the cover letter. Put yourself in the employer's position for a minute, with over 10-100 applicants competing for every available internship position, each with similar backgrounds. How would you make the choice; what would be the deciding factors? Your cover letter is your first written contact with the company, and it may well be your only chance to convince them that, of the hundreds of applicants that they may have reviewed recently, you are a strong contender for the position. In a pool of résumés that sounds and looks similar, a well-constructed cover letter can give you the edge. The following template concepts are based on approaches recommended by Joe Grimm, recruiting and development editor of the Detroit Free Press.

Be original not bland

Though it may be tempting and more straight forward to go with the traditional bland cover letter, this will not help to get the attention of the employer. For example, come up with some creative ways of introducing yourself. Remember that you are applying for a creative position in a new media. Try to avoid opening your cover letter with one of the following phrases.

• I am applying for a summer photo internship with the Daily Tidings because I know I can do the job well.

• I currently am a senior majoring in journalism and minoring in psychology at Party Tech. In addition, I…

• My name is Slim Shady, and I am a sophomore in the process of completing a bachelor's degree in journalism at Ivy League University.

Do not get wordy

Get to the point quickly. Avoid these approaches:

• I am currently looking for a summer internship in the new media industry and would like to be considered for such a position at your newspaper. I am a junior in college pursuing a concentration in print-journalism and would very much appreciate a chance to apply what I have learned to a premiere new media company, such as yours.

• It has come to my attention through an advertisement at George Mason University that intern positions in feature animation are available at your studios.

• I am writing to express my interest in an internship at ILM over the coming summer.

• I would like to use this letter as an opportunity to introduce myself as a qualified candidate for the summer internship program at the Pixar Studios.

Tell a story

New media designers are often expected to produce convincing designs that tell a story about a product. Here is your opportunity to show the company that you can. If you take this approach, say — quickly — what the point of the story is.

• Each day, Barb Shook carried an armful of shirts into the dry cleaners, and picked up a few clean ones, neatly pressed and bagged in plastic. Working the counter to pay for my journalism studies, I was intrigued by the woman with all the shirts. Finally, I just had to ask ...

• It's surprising how quickly you can wear out a pair of shoes on the streets of Chicago...

• When Jim Johnson appeared to chase his family out of the house and then set fire to it, the neighbors thought he was acting crazy again. It turns out, he was a hero.

• My parents told me that if I was going to go out of state to go to school, then I'd have to get there on my own. In a borrowed car that became my living quarters for the next four days, I did.

The experienced approach

Many internship candidates have only slight experience. If you have loads of experience to offer — especially if it's in commercial, multimedia production, let them know.

• In two summer internships, I have assisted in the design and planning of over 10 web sites for companies such as Ford and General Motors.

• As the Webmaster of my department, I am chiefly responsible for designing the department's web site.

• Few animators my age can say that they wrote all of the software used in the creation of an animation.

• I have endured horseflies, poison ivy, angry dogs and downpours to get a good quote or a telling detail for a story…

The direct approach
If you're proud of who you are and a what-you-see-is-what-you-get person, try the fresh and straightforward approach. What would you tell the employer, face to face, games aside, about why they should hire you? Avoid wordy. Be crisp, not bland.

• Please accept my application for a photo internship at the Detroit Free Press. I believe that my experience at school and in a prior internship, as well as my knowledge of the area make me a strong candidate for your newspaper.

• Hire me for a photography internship because I work tirelessly, find excellent photo opportunities everywhere and develop them well.

• My passion is to create animation…

The twist approach
Wake up the reader with a twist or a tease. Play contradiction, irony or the unexpected to maximum advantage. Remember that one of the key things employers want to find in a good cover letter is evidence that you can write.

• Like most student designers, I expected to start at the bottom as the "go for" at an interactive studio, planning getting coffee, answering phones. That's not what I got, though, when I showed up for the first day of work last summer…

• Sometimes, the stories I tell amaze me…

• It's been said that you're only as good as your last animation. Let me tell you what it was…

• I have to admit, I wasn't excited the first time I was asked to create a design for a user interface.

The confident approach
A narrow line to walk, be bold without being brash, assured without being arrogant. Only you can tell whether such an approach is natural to you.

• I am exactly the right person for your sports-writing internship!

• Are you looking for a highly motivated, team-centered, up-and-coming photographer who is hard working and creative? I am that person.

- There are few guarantees in life. I am one. Hire me, and you will not be disappointed.

- The person you have been looking for has applied.

Autobiographical approach

Can you tell a story about yourself that explains why you are an excellent prospective intern? Some people can begin their letters in these ways:

- My family always said I loved to tell stories.

- Perhaps it's my sense of order that led me to newspaper design.

- Since the age of 8, I have known that this was the right business for me.

- Maybe it was destiny, because it sure wasn't heredity.

- As a senior in high school, I swore I'd never leave my home and family. I did, though, kicking and screaming, and it was the best thing I ever did.

Interviewing

A woman walks into an interview wearing a pants suit with her résumé in hand. She carries herself with confidence. Taking a deep breath and with a firm handshake she says, "Hello Mr. Smith, I'm Jane Doe. Pleased to meet you." From the moment Jane walked through the door, the interview had begun. Interviewing is crucial to landing the perfect job, and it is more than showing up and filling out an application. Think of it as going on a first date, where you want to make a positive first impression. During an interview, hopeful applicants are put under the microscope, and evaluated in every way from appearance to skills. You are a product on display, wanting to become an asset to the company. Therefore, you must prepare yourself. In preparation for the interview, know your strengths and weaknesses because you will most likely be asked to analyze those characteristics. Think about what your response will be to questions like "What do you expect from your supervisor?" "Where do you see yourself in five years?" "Why do you think you would be a good fit for this organization?" Answer directly, try not to ramble or reveal negative information about yourself. Write down your answers if you have to, whatever helps to build your confidence for the interview. Get a friend to play-act an interview, so that you can practice. Mannerisms are equally important: relax, sit-up straight and do not slouch or fidget. If you have a tendency to fidget excessively, such as uncontrollable leg shaking or nail biting, try to control it because you might appear less relaxed and confident. Eye contact with the interviewer is considered a sign of confidence. Keep in mind that your employer will expect you to have questions of your own. Some questions you might want to ask: "Is there room for advancement?" "Does Company X have a tuition reimbursement program?" Do not hesitate to ask any other possible questions you might have, and of course, you should remain confident during every aspect of the interview, including when you take the floor. Dress in appropriate business attire, and carry yourself with class and confidence. As we enter the new millennium, employers will continue to require an interview for virtually every job opening. Hopeful candidates will prepare themselves for what can be the difference between employment and an on-going search in the classifieds. An interview can make or break your chances. Good luck!

Interview Questions

• Prepare questions to ask your interviewer. For example:

• What are some of the tasks and projects I will be involved in?

• What are your expectations of an intern who works for your organization?

• What is the dress code of your organization?

• Will I have the opportunity to meet regularly with my internship supervisor?

• What sort of training or orientation with I receive?

• How many hours per week will you want me to work?

• Will there be a salary, stipend or college credits for my work there?

• Will I receive reimbursement for my travel expenses?

• Will I be covered by workers' compensation if I am injured at my internship site?

• What is the duration of the internship?

Be prepared to answer the following questions in your interview, these are some commonly asked questions:

• Are you familiar with our company, services and products?

• Why do you want an internship at this company?

- What objectives do you hope to obtain through this internship?

- What are your career goals?

- What are your greatest strengths and biggest weaknesses?

- Beyond your class projects what meaningful projects have you been involved in? Why was this meaningful?

- Beyond your academic program, have you worked on team projects? Talk about your experience.

- We have several candidates for this internship position, why should we choose you?

- Who is your least favorite manager? Why?

- How would you resolve conflicts between your academic schedule and surprise, rush jobs here?

Things to Take to the Interview

- Copy of your résumé and cover letter.

- Portfolio, sides, video, drawings etc.

- Copy of college transcripts, especially if it has changed since you submitted the internship application.

- Copy of completed application for internship.

- A positive attitude and enthusiasm for the field of New Media.

Interview Thank You Letter Sample

January 12, 2000

1212 Main Street
Fairfax, VA

Ms. Bonney Ford,
Marketing Director
GGC, Inc.
1212 John Doe Lane
Fairfax, VA

Dear Ms. Ford:

Thank you so much for taking the time from your busy schedule last Thursday to interview me for the internship position at GoGardner.com. After our meeting, I am convinced that your company is the best place for me to learn about e-commerce and web design, my long-term career goal.

As you may recall, I have skills in graphic design and would be able to create new logo designs and write articles for the web site. I was pleased with your interest in my ideas for updating the web site. I know I can make a contribution to GoGardner.com while I learn as much as possible about the company and e-commerce.

Please let me know if I can provide you with any additional information about my qualifications or objectives. I look forward to hearing from you soon.

Sincerely,

Mary Going

This form is also available at **http://www.gogardner.com/bizform.html**

Company Name

Areas of Specialization

Number of Employees

Description of Company

Street Address

City, State, Zip Code

Telephone Number

Fax Number

Web Address

Mail to:

GGC publishing

Complementary Listing
4602 John Hancock Ct. Ste.302
Annandale, VA 22003
703-354-8278
703-354-8279 fax

www.gogardner.com

East Coast

3DVisual.com

Area(s) of Specialization: Animation and Visual Effects

Number of Employees: 8

The company can provide photo-realistic, computer-generated animation in any format, including AVI, MPEG, Digital Betacam, DVCAM, MiniDV, Betacam SP, Panavision, HDTV, IMAX, and DVD.

3DVisual.com
15212 Dino Dr.
Burtonsville, MD 20866
Phone: 301 476-9470
Alt. Phone: 301 476-9482
Fax: 301 476-9535
URL: http://www.3Dvisual.com

AARGH Animation, Inc.

Area(s) of Specialization: Traditional Animation

Number of Employees: 6+

The company produces animation for feature films, commercials, TV shows, industrials, laser shows, kiosks, games, and bar mitzvah. They produce turnkey animation, storyboards, animation, and character design. Clients include These Mouse Guys, Hanna Barbera, Golden Books, Kenner Toys, NASA, P&G, and others. One animator, Jeffrey Varab, has animated for Fox, the Mouse Guys, Amblin, Universal, and another animator Don Bluth has created for "Titan A.E.", "Mulan", "Balto", "Ferngully", "The Tigger Movie", and over a dozen others.

AARGH Animation, Inc.
100 Universal Street Plaza #22A
Orlando, FL 32819
Phone: 407 224-5501
Fax: 407 370-2602
URL: http://www.storyboards-east.com/anm-fm.html

Activeworlds.com, Inc.

Area(s) of Specialization: 3D Computer Animation, Virtual Reality

Number of Employees: 23 (+5 consultants)

Activeworlds.com, Inc. provides software products and on-line services that permit users to enter, move about and interact with others in a computer-generated, three-dimensional virtual environment using the Internet. It hosts hundreds of virtual worlds in three-dimensional environments. In addition, Activeworlds.com develops worlds for other companies granting them licenses for the use of the technology. The company also licenses the technology to clients to create worlds.

Activeworlds.com, Inc.
95 Parker Street
Newburyport, MA 01950
Phone: 978 499-0222
Fax: 978 499-0221
URL: http://www.activeworlds.com

AFCG, Inc.

Area(s) of Specialization: CGI, Animation, Film/Video Effects

Number of Employees: 3

AFCG has been creating high-end computer animation and effects for the film and commercial production industries since May 1987. Most work is created using Silicon Graphics workstations running the "Prisms" or "Houdini" software packages from Side Effects Software. The company uses custom-built software tools, as well as the "Amazon" paint packages from Interactive Effects and "RasTrack" from Hammerhead Productions. AFCG's most recent work may be viewed in nationally aired television commercials for Campbells Soup, Duracell, Nasdaq, AT&T, Nissan, Dr. Pepper, 7Up and Motorola.

AFCG Inc.
305 East 46 Street, 14th Floor
New York, NY. 10017
Phone: 212 688-3283
Fax: 212 688-6752
URL: http://www.afcg.com

Amalgamation House

Area(s) of Specialization: Animation and Design for Film/Video

Number of Employees: 5+

Amalgamation House Inc. is a multi-story, multi-disciplinary, multi-faceted, multi-media collective serving creative needs within the commercial, corporate, and independent arenas. Through fifteen-odd years, its areas of expertise include cel and high-end computer animation, special effects and graphics for film/video, interactive, & traditional design for print, as well as website development.

Amalgamation House
1218-20 Shackamaxon Street
Philadelphia, PA 19125-3914
Phone: 215 427-1954
Fax: 215 426-6372
URL: http://www.pixelmixers.com

Animagicians

Area(s) of Specialization: CG Effects, Internet/Intranet, Corporate Graphics, Animation, Architecture, Web Site Graphics

Number of Employees: 500+

Animagicians is a design firm made up of a staff with freelance backgrounds in 3D graphics and web development.

Animagicians
Phone: 617 964-9491
Fax: 617 527-7692
URL: http://www.amagic-inc.com

Animagination, Ltd.

Area(s) of Specialization: Advertising,
Animation, CGI Effects

Number of Employees: 3+

Animagination, Ltd. is a full service
animation production house based in New
York City. The primary product is traditional
hand-drawn cel animation created for the
advertising industry. Cel work is combined
with high-tech effects available through
computer-generated imagery. Work ranges
from adding the small animated effects to
enhance an otherwise totally live action
production, through producing every aspect
of a job starting with a script and handing
back a finished picture.

Animagination, Ltd.
402 Eighth Ave., PH East
New York, NY 10001
Phone: 212 695-1237
Fax: 212 695-1238
URL: http://www.nycartoons.com

Animatic and Storyboards, Inc.

Area(s) of Specialization: Animation,
Storyboards, Promotion

Number of Employees: 4+

Animatics & Storyboards, Inc. creates
productions, presentations, promotions and
websites using graphic art, storyboards, cel
animation, After Effects design and pre-
visualization, conceptual art, creative
character design, and internet animation.
The Orlando, Florida studio employs writers,
artists and voice-over talent, music
composers and performers, and utilizes
multiple high end computers and software,
non-linear editing equipment, and sound
effects.

Animatics and Storyboards, Inc.
8137 Lake Crowell Circle
Orlando, Florida 32836
Phone: 407-370-BORD (2673)
Fax: 407-370-2602
URL: http://www.storyboards-east.com

Animated, Inc.

Area(s) of Specialization: Animation, Digital
Video/Film

Number Of Employees: 3

Animated, Inc. has a 25 year history in both
the film and computer industries.

Beginnings as documentary camera, Oxberry animation camera and optical bench operators led to involvement in every phase of animation and motion graphic special effects for both feature films and commercials. Experienced in motion control via the film industry, the company now uses proprietary camera systems including hardware, software and machinery.

Animated, Inc.
1600 Broadway #301
New York, NY 10001
Phone: 212 265-2942
Fax: 212 265-2944
URL: http://www.animatedproduction.com

Animation NYC

Area(s) of Specialization: Design, Animation, Stop motion, Clay Animation

Number of Employees: 12

Animation NYC is a script-to-screen creative services company. Originally created to produce stop-motion and clay animation using digital capture technology, the company has provided stop-motion animation and consulting for Sesame Street, Calvin Klein and MTV Animation. Animation NYC combines illustration, computer graphics, and stop-motion clay animation to provide content for television, CD-ROM and the Web. The company employs a dozen multimedia artists including 3D

modelers, graphic designers and illustrators from across the country.

Animation NYC
44 W. 24th St.
New York, NY 10010
Phone: 212 229-9449
Fax: 212 229 9445
URL: http://www.animationnyc.com

Animation Technologies

Area(s) of Specialization: 3D Animation, Interactive Programming, Web Design, Consulting

Number of Employees: 25

Animation Technologies is a visual communications company specializing in business-to-business media solutions. The Company uses 3D animation, computer graphics, and interactive media to create visual explanation of complex information. Animation Technologies builds custom interactive 3D applications for the Internet.

Animation Technologies
45 Milk Street
Boston, MA 02109
Phone: 617 423-6040
Fax: 671 423-6044
URL: http://www.animationtech.com

Animators at Law, Inc.

Area(s) of Specialization: Trial Exhibits/ Animation, Jury Research, Web Design, Marketing Design

Number of Employees: 12

Animators At Law develops strategies and designs for visuals in the courtroom. The company's goal is to create visual presentations that can communicate information faster than the spoken word and that will be retained for longer periods of time. Animators work with the personnel in jury research and trial strategy using a team-based approach to developing demonstrative evidence and trial strategy and create using both artistic design and programming. Animators offers full-service 24 hour support for all work, including trial presentation hardware and on-site technicians.

The company creates teaching tools for the legal community - videos for judicial patent tutorials that distill abstract concepts, CD-ROM books and interactive programs that explain complex theories, scientific and medical illustration and animation that educate legal teams.

Animators At Law, Inc.
1423 Powhatan Street, Suite 3
Alexandria, Virginia 22314
Phone: 800 337-7697
Fax: 703 548-5450
URL: http://www.animators.com

Animus Films

Area(s) of Specialization: Animation, stop motion

Number of Employees: 5

Animus Films
2W. 47th St., #1209
New York, NY 10036
Phone: 212 391-8716

AniVision, Inc.

Area(s) of Specialization: CGI, Animation, Film/Video Production

Number of Employees: 55

AniVision is a full service animation & video production company. It produces Sales Promotional Tapes, Interactive CD/DVD Authoring, Sales and Management Training Tapes, TV Commercials and Programming, 3D Modeling and Architectural Flythroughs.

AniVision Inc.
228 Holmes Ave. NE
Huntsville, AL 35801
Phone: 800 793-8601
Alt. Phone: 256 382-8000
Fax: 256 382-8002
URL: http://www.anivision.com

APA Studios

Area(s) of Specialization: Animation, Film/ Video Production for Advertising

Number of Employees: 1+

A full service production company, offering: Computerized Motion Control, Full Production Facilities, Animation, Product Demo Engineering, Live Animation, Stop - Motion, Customized Props, Macro Photography, Time Lapse. With clients such as Pepsi, Nabisco, Ban, Nuprin, and Seiko, the company offers video and animation to the advertising industry.

Bob Self
APA Studios
500 South Lake View Drive,
Lake Helen, FL 32744
Phone: 904 228-2144
Fax: 407 352-8662
URL: http://www.a-p-a.com

APC Studios

Area(s) of Specialization: CGI, Animation, Film/Video Production

Number of Employees: 9+

APC Studios is a full-service facility that can take a project from a thumbnail sketch to production, through the posting process and finally to the mastering, package design and distribution process.

APC Studios
3838 Oakcliff Industrial
Atlanta, GA 30340
Phone: 770 242-7678
Alt Phone: 770 242-9652
Fax: 770 242-0278
URL: http://www.apcstudios.com

Artbear Pigmation, Inc.

Area(s) of Specialization: Animation Character Design and Development. Cel Animation.

Number of Employees: 2+

Artbear Pigmation has been producing animation, from concept through final output for the past 27 years. Specializing in character design, project development, and animation creating combinations of live action, 3D, and/or photo collage with traditional characters. The company produces shorts on video and film for the purposes of educational, instructional videos or television commercials.

Artbear Pigmation, Inc.
415 Elm Street
Ithaca, NY 14850
Phone: 607 277-1151
Fax: 607 277-1166
URL: http://people.clarityconnect.com/ webpages/artbear/artbear.html

Aspen, Inc.

Area(s) of Specialization: 3D Animation, Drafting, Design

Number of Employees: 2

Aspen Inc. is a creative service to provide marketing solutions for businesses by using graphic application programs for high quality design, animation, 3D modeling, photo retouching and pre-press. During the past ten years the company designed many items including TV animation, magazine covers, packages, labels, calendars, business cards, catalogs, and posters. Aspen creates entire visual identities for companies from the company logos, brochures, advertisements and all kinds of printed material to animation and web site design.

Aspen, Inc.
P.O. Box 655
Garfield, NJ. 07026
Phone: 973 772-7526
Fax: 973 772-7413
URL: http://www.aspeninc.net

Association for Independent Video & Filmmakers

Area(s) of Specialization: Publishing, Sponsoring National Media Events

Number of Employees: 10+

AIVF is the national service organization for independent media providing programs and services. They publish a national magazine and several books, maintaining a library of media arts resources, and sponsoring events throughout the country.

Association for Independent Video & Filmmakers
(also the Foundation for Independent Video and Film)
304 Hudson Street, 6th floor
New York, NY 10013
Phone: 212-807-1400
Fax: 212-463-8519
URL: http://www.aivf.org

Atlanta Video

Area(s) of Specialization: CGI, Film/Video Production and Post Production, Animation

Number of Employees: 5+

The Company specializes in graphics, post production, multimedia, and video production. The graphics division offers 2D and 3D animation and graphic services, using such software programs as 3D Studio Max, Fractal Design Painter, Adobe Photoshop, After Effects, Autodesk Animator Studio, Morph, and In Sync Speed Razor. The post production area offers various non-linear editing suites. The multimedia area is equipped to do interactive and web-based projects. Atlanta Video has a large collection of stock footage including Aztec and Mayan sites, peoples, ruins, and art works, all on 16mm film. 3D models are also available.

Atlanta Video
1733 Clifton Rd.
Atlanta, GA 30329
Phone: 404 327-6060
Fax: 404 327-6065
URL: http://www.atlantavideo.com

Atlantic Motion Pictures

Area(s) of Specialization: Film/Video Production and Effects, Animation

Number of Employees: 8+

Atlantic Motion Pictures is a full service production company that specializes in visual fx and high end animation for the television, theatrical and advertising industries. Atlantic began in 1982 as a company specializing in the design and production of film animation and motion graphics, and has expanded its operation to include motion control, stop motion, table top, traditional animation, computer animation and live action photography, allowing for the production of a wide variety of multimedia effects and combinations.

Atlantic Motion Pictures
162 W. 21st St., 4th floor
New York, NY 10011
Phone: 212 924 - 6170
Fax: 212 989-8736
URL: http://www.atlanticmotion.com

AVC

Area(s) of Specialization: Film/Video Production and Post Production: Sound, Editing, Animation, Effects

Number of Employees: 6+

AVC offers clients high quality video production. All field footage is recorded directly to Digital Betacam. The footage is then edited on digital non-linear workstations for a pure Digital Betacam product. AVC post offers everything from a team of professionals, to a top of the line "post Boutique". In addition to a post production facility, AVC offers a ProTools 24 Audio Suite and has both high quality 3D animation and digital effects.

AVC
514 SE. 11th. Court
Fort Lauderdale, FL 33316
Phone: 954 761-1178
Fax: 954 761-1266
URL: http://www.avcvideo.com

Avekta Productions

Area(s) of Specialization: Video, 3D Animation, Multimedia, Website Design

Number of Employees: 7

Avekta Productions specializes in using high-end technology to assist corporate directors in human resources and marketing. The company has worked with Time Warner, and

O'Neil Data Systems and Investor's Business Daily. Avekta runs commercials produced on desktop systems on CNN and CNBC featuring Fortune 500 CEO's like MCI President, Gerald Taylor, Publisher, Steve Forbes, and Jack Kemp. Avekta directs the satellite media tours for Steve Forbes and Forbes Magazine. Avekta produced one of the first American made situation comedies for Russia and CIS countries, reaching 150 million viewers.

Avekta Productions
164 Madison Ave., 4th floor
New York, NY 10016
Phone: 212 308-8000
URL: http://www.avekta.com

Balsmeyer & Everett, Inc.

Area(s) of Specialization: Marketing, CGI, 2D and 3D Animation, Digital Effects, Editing

Number of Employees: 8+

Balsmeyer & Everett, Inc. studio facilities specializes in visual effects technology. Digital effects and 3D animation are created on SGI workstations running Softimage, Cineo, Chalice, and a host of other software packages and are output on a Solitaire Cine III film recorder. Graphics and 2D animation are created on Macintosh workstations running Adobe After Effects, Premier, Photoshop, etc. Balsmeyer & Everett, Inc. has it's own in-house film-editing, screening and non-linear video editing facilities. Their 10,000 sq. ft. studio houses a 2000 sq. ft. stage with a Mechanical Concepts/Cooper Controls motion control system. They also provide a variety of portable motion control systems designed by General Lift for location work.

Balsmeyer & Everett, Inc.
459 W. 15th. St.
New York, NY 10011
Phone: 212 627-3430
Fax: 212 989-6528
URL: http://www.balsmeyer-everett.com

Betelguese Productions, Inc.

Area(s) of Specialization: Editing, Production, CGI, Animation, Sound Composition

Number of Employees: 100

Betelguese is a full service facility housing digital on-line rooms, multi format on-line rooms, AVID on-line/off-line suites, Inferno, Flame, Flinet, Macintosh design suites, interactive design and implementation, digital audio rooms, and tape duplication in every format. Services include digital on-line programming, multiformat editing, non-linear editing, production services, graphic design, digital compositing and animation, interactive systems, media conversions and transfers, digital audio post, sound composition, and all format duplication.

Betelguese Productions, Inc.
44 E 32ND St.
12 Fl.
New York, NY 10016
Phone: 212 251-8600
Fax: 212 251-8633
URL: http://www.Betelgeuse.com

Big Sky Editorial

Area(s) of Specialization: Film/Video
Production, Editing and Restoration

Number of Employees: 7

Big Sky Editorial focuses on editing and
restoration of film.

Big Sky Editorial
10 East 40th St.
Suite 1701
New York, NY 10016
Phone: 212 683-4004
Fax: 212 889-6220
URL: http://www.bigskyedit.com

Bill Feigenbaum Designs, Inc.

Area(s) of Specialization: Animation, 2D and
3D Graphics, Live Action Integration

Number of Employees: 3-12

Bill Feigenbaum Designs Inc. is a company
that specializes in the production of visual
effects that incorporates cel animation, 3D

and 2D computer graphics and live action
integration. The company specializes in
working with other small companies to help
create a project in a reasonable time frame.

Bill Feigenbaum Designs Inc.
15 W. 26th St., #1615
New York, NY 10010
Phone: 212 327-0360
Fax: 212 327-0369

Black Logic

Area(s) of Specialization: 3D animation,
Visual effects

Number of Employees: 40+

Black Logic is a full service production
company. Black Logic offers live action,
graphic design, high-end visual effects and
computer animation for film and television.
Their goal is to create various styles of
digital imagery that will make their clients'
projects unique.

Black Logic
305 East 46th Street
New York, NY 10017
Phone: 212 980-9200
Fax: 212 759-2224
URL: http://www.blacklogic.com

Blue Rock Editing Co.

Area(s) of Specialization: Advertising Editing and Post Production

Number of Employees: 55

Blue Rock Editing represents a portion of the services available under the Palestrini Post umbrella. The company provides the advertising community editing and post production.

The Blue Rock Editing Co.
575 Lexington Avenue
New York, NY 10022
Phone: 212 752-3348
Fax: 212 752-0307
URL: http://www.bluerockny.com

Blue Sky Studios

Area(s) of Specialization: CGI, Computer Animation

Number of Employees: 150+

Blue Sky Studios was founded in 1987 by David Brown, Alison Brown , Chris Wedge, Carl Ludwig, Eugene Troubetzkoy, Ph.D., and Michael Ferraro to produce photo-realistic, high-resolution computer-generated character animation for commercials, feature films and the entertainment industry. Blue Sky's credits include their 1998 Oscar Award-winning short film "Bunny" . The studio has also completed several computer-animated characters for the box-office hit "Star Trek:

Insurrection" (1998 Paramount); the computer-generated aliens in the Twentieth Century Fox feature film release "Alien Resurrection" (1997); numerous characters and special effects for "A Simple Wish" (Bubble Factory/Universal Pictures 1997), and a host of dancing, singing cockroaches for the MTV cult classic "Joe's Apartment" (Geffen Films/Warner Bros. 1986), and "Fight Club" directed by David Fincher. The studio also works with the New York Indie film community completing a number of special effects projects for films such as "Just The Ticket" (1999); "Lulu on the Bridge" (1998), and "Jesus' Son"

Blue Sky Studios
1 South Rd.
Harrison, NY 10528
Phone: 914 381-8400
Fax: 914 381-9791
URL: http://www.blueskystudios.com

BNN

Area(s) of Specialization: Film/Video Production

Number of Employees: 40

A Time Warner's New York Cable News service. Established in 1983, BNN has produced for VH1, Disney, The Travel Channel, NBC, the ASPCA and Scholastic. The company is involved in development in web design and deployment, video journalism, comedy, and feature films. BNN is a television production and program development facility located in New York, NY., which has produced program segments for clients including: MTV, CBS, A&E, VH1, Court TV, The Sci-Fi Channel, Lifetime, Fox Television, ABC, NBC, ESPN, The Today Show, MacNeil-Lehrer Newshour, Entertainment Tonight, Travel Channel and BRAVO.

BNN
253 5th Ave.
New York, NY 10016
Phone: 212 779-0500
Fax: 212 532-5554
URL: http://www.bnntv.com
E-mail: AvaSeave@BNNtv.com

Boca Entertainment

Area(s) of Specialization: Animation, Multimedia

Number of Employees: 2

BOCA Entertainment Ltd. is a full service production entity that conceptualizes, develops, produces and markets animation projects. Its principals have a history in children's entertainment, having created, written and produced series such as Care Bears, teenage Mutant Ninja Turtles, Hot Wheels and Skydancers. Boca Entertainment Ltd. CEO Jack Olesker created the original development work for "Mighty Morphine Power Rangers."

Boca Entertainment
9128 Villa Portofino Circle
Boca Raton, FL 33496
Phone: 561 392-8160
Fax: 561 479-0630

Borris FX

Area(s) of Specialization: Computer Animation, 3D Computer Graphics, Desktop, Production

Number of Employees: 51

Founded in 1995 and based in Boston MA, Borris FX creates in 3D DVE, titling and compositing plug-in technology serving the video, film and multi-media production markets. Its products offer editors and 2D graphic artists software with creative flexibility. The company maintains partnerships with industry companies such as Avid/Softimage, Adobe, Canopus, Discreet Logic, DPS, FAST, in-sync, Media 100, Panasonic, Sony and Ulead.

Borris FX
381 Congress St.
Boston, MA 02210
Phone: 617 451-9900
Fax: 617 451-9916
URL: http://www.borisfx.com

Broadway Video Design

Area(s) of Specialization: CGI, Film/Video Production and Post Production, Interactive Media

Number of Employees: 500

Broadway Video Design is an independent entertainment production company. Founded in 1979 by Lorne Michaels, creator and executive producer of "Saturday Night Live." From creative development and production to editing, design, sound and interactive media, Broadway Video offers technology and expertise across all media. Clients include broadcast and cable networks, advertising agencies, Fortune 500 corporations, independent television producers and major software publishers.

Broadway Video Design
1619 Broadway
New York, NY 10019
Phone: 212 333-0500
Alt. Phone: 212 265-7600
Fax: 212 333-0501
URL: http://www.broadwayvideo.com

Broadcast Video, Inc.

Area(s) of Specialization: Film/Video and Post Production

Number of Employees: 150+

BVI offers complete post-production services for a variety of clients including television networks, advertising agencies, and production companies. Among BVI's services are: on-line editing, off-line editing, film-to-tape transfer, programming, special effects and design, music scoring/composing, audio design and production, language translation and subtitling, sound stage, insert stage, remote video production, duplication, multimedia and network transmission services.

Broadcast Video Incorporated
20377 NE 15th Ct.
Miami, FL 33179
Phone: 305 653-7440
Fax: 305 651-0478
URL: http://www.bvinet.com

Bush Entertainment, Inc.

Area(s) of Specialization: Film/Video Production and Post Production

Number of Employees: 12+

Bush Entertainment is a video and film production company in SW Florida. They provide services from creative concept and field crews to post production editing, design and finishing. The company specializes in 35mm, 16mm film or BetacamSP production and camera crews, Bush Entertainment is located in Fort Myers, Florida.

Bush Entertainment
11000-2 Metro Parkway
Ft. Myers, Florida 33912

Phone: 941 275-9575
Fax: 941 275-8395
URL: http://www.bushentertainment.com

Buzzco Associates, Inc.

Area(s) of Specialization: Animation

Number of Employees: 5

Founded in 1987, Buzzco Associates creates commercial projects. Buzzco Associates is a traditional animation house that has created animation shorts and ID spots for clients such as Nickelodeon, Burger King and several others.

Buzzco Associates, Inc.
33 Bleecker Street
New York, NY 10012
Phone: 212 473-8800
Fax: 212 473-8891
URL: http://www.buzzco.com
E-mail: Info@buzzzco.com

BXB, Inc.

Area(s) of Specialization: CGI, Film/Video, Effects Editing

Number of Employees: 2+

BXB Inc. was created in August 1987 as a design and special effects editing company. Its founders, Henry Baker and Patty Bellucci, started the company as an instrument through which to conduct creative work on film/video and effects editing.

BXB, Inc.
532 La Guardia Pl., #2L
New York, NY 10012
Phone: 212 924-8654
URL: http://www.bxbinc.com

Cabana Corporation

Area(s) of Specialization: Film/Video, Multimedia, Sound

Number of Employees: 15

Designed by architect David Ling, Cabana consists of 18,000 sq. ft. of studio space, and 4,500 sq. ft. of landscaped outdoor space. Cabana's editorial staff uses AVID technology and a completely integrated audio, video and high-speed data network to improve creative control and turnaround time during the editing process. A comprehensive system of tie-lines connects all AVID rooms, graphics rooms, sound studios, business departments and common spaces for communication.

Cabana Corporation
535 Fifth Avenue
New York, NY 10017
Phone: 212 490-9200
Fax: 212 490-9785
URL: http://www.cabana-edit.com

Camp Chaos Animation Studio

Area(s) of Specialization: Web Cartoons, Animation

Number of Employees: 10

Camp Chaos Entertainment creates cartoons and short films for the web and, secondarily, for other media using the current production software. The company has been recognized by "Entertainment Weekly", "US News and World Report", "Yahoo! Internet Life", ZDNet, E! Entertainment Television and leading websites like The Romp, POP.com, RealNetworks' Real.com, Shockwave.com, AtomFilms.com, ZDNet.com. The company licenses one or more original productions, or clients may commission the creation of original animated productions for websites.

Camp Chaos Animation Studio
P.O. Box 2575
West Lawn, PA 19609 2575
Phone: 610 603-0591
Fax:: 425 699-9880
URL: http://www.campchaos.com

The Cartoon Tycoon

Area(s) of Specialization: Cel Animation

Number of Employees: 2

The Cartoon Tycoon produces traditional and non-traditional cel animation for local,

national and international audiences. The company creates TV commercials, show openings, corporate videos, CD-ROMs, series pilots, TV bumpers, or network IDs.

The Cartoon Tycoon
207 Walnut Alley, Suite 250
New Cumberland, PA 17070
Phone: 717 770-2500
Fax: 717 770-2008
URL: http://www.cartoontycoon.com

Century III at Universal Studios

Area(s) of Specialization: CGI, Animation, Film/Video Production and Post Production

Number of Employees: 50+

Century III was established in 1976 for commercial and corporate productions. Century III employs a staff of individuals in project management, location/studio productions, post production, audio design, special effects, computer graphics and animation, engineering design, interactive multimedia development, software development, cost analysis, accounting and marketing. The company has created local, regional, national and international projects for producers, independents, advertising agencies, television stations and broadcast cable networks, as well as government, corporate marketing, communications and training departments.

Century III at Universal Studios
2000 Universal Studios Plaza
Orlando, FL 32819
Phone: 407 354-1000
Fax: 407 352-8662
URL: http://www.century3.com

Charlex

Area(s) of Specialization: 3D Computer Animation, CGI, Multimedia, Film/Television

Number of Employees: 50

Charlex creates design concepts and layouts for clients such as Ford, Fila, Nissan, Lucent Technologies, Qwest, Ryder Trucks, and Budweiser.

Charlex
2W. 45th St., 7th Floor
New York, NY 10036
Phone: 212 719-4600
Fax: 212 840-2747
URL: http://www.charlex.com

Children's Television Workshop

Area(s) of Specialization: Film/Video

Number Of Employees: 500+

CTW and Sesame Street were created as an "experiment" in 1968, and the show debuted on November 10, 1969. Designed to use the medium of television to reach and teach preschoolers skills that provide a successful transition from home to school. The show includes learning the alphabet, numbers, and pro-social skills.

Children's Television Workshop
One Lincoln Plaza
New York, NY 10023
Phone: 212-595-3456
Fax: 212-875-6088
URL: http://www.ctw.org

Cineframe Animation

Area(s) of Specialization: 3D Modeling/ Animation for Broadcast, Games, Theme Parks, Net, and Film

Number of Employees: 1

Cineframe Animation is David Gallagher's freelance 3D animation studio. He specializes in modeling and animating advanced 3D characters for theme parks, games, advertising, internet, and film. Cineframe uses Softimage 3D software on an Intergraph TDZ-2000 workstation.

Cineframe Animation
424 Elm St.
Port Chester, NY 10573
Phone: 914 937-2196
URL: http://www.cineframe.com

Cineric

Area(s) of Specialization: Film Post Production, Restoration, Digital Film Services

Number of Employees: 20

In New York, Cineric provides titles, optical and post-production special effects for feature films. The company utilizes both optical printing and digital imaging. They offer scanning, recording, video to film, and specialized image processing services. In optical printing and film restoration, the company creates a 35mm blow-up from a 16mm or Super 16 negative, also providing blow-up/conversions of a wide range of film formats to standard 35mm including Super 8, VistaVision, TechniScope (2-perf), 3-perf, as well as anamorphic conversion from Super 35mm to 35mm 'Scope. The company developed a variety of processes using both photochemical and digital techniques including a new faded color negative restoration process. Cineric has restored over 200 films including "Jason and the Argonauts", "The Birds", "American Graffiti", "A Man for All Seasons", "The Man from Laramie" and "The Caine Mutiny".

Cineric
630 Ninth Avenue, 5th Floor
New York, NY 10036
Phone: 212 586-4822
Fax: 212 582-3744
URL: http://www.cineric.com

Cinesite Film, Scanning and Recording

Area(s) of Specialization: CGI, Film/Video, Digital Imaging and Effects

Number of Employees: 2

Cinesite is a digital effects studio. The company was founded in 1992 as a wholly owned subsidiary of Eastman Kodak Company. With facilities in both Hollywood and Europe, Cinesite is a full service digital effects company which provides services in digital compositing, 2D & 3D effects, wire and object removal, film stock repair and restoration, and digital film scanning and recording. Cinesite did visual effects work on such films as "Armagedon", "Dr. Dolittle", "Primary Colors", "The Truman Show", "Lost in Space", "Air Force One", "Sphere", "Event Horizon", "Tomorrow Never Dies", "Jerry Maguire", "Space Jam", and "Smilla's Sense of Snow".

Cinnesite Film, Scanning and Recording
360 W. 31st Street
Suite 710
New York, NY 10001
Phone: 212 631-3414
Fax: 212 631-3436
URL: http://www.cinesite.com

City Lights Media Group

Area(s) of Specialization: CGI, Film/Video and Motion Picture/Television Production and Post Production

Number of employees: 30+

City Lights Media Group is comprised of four divisions:

City Lights Editorial is the company's post-production service and facility, which features edit suites containing Avid non-linear editing equipment and software, technical support and a staff of creative editors. City Lights FX is the company's graphics, animation and visual effects division, which features Silicon Graphics and Power Mac workstations, SoftImage and After Effects. City Lights Productions is the company's film and video production unit.

City Lights Media Group
6 East 39th Street
New York, NY 10016
Phone: 212 679-4400
Fax: 212 679-3819
URL: http://www.citylightsmedia.com

Click 3X

Area(s) of Specialization: Digital Effects, Animation, Broadcast Design

Number of Employees: 31

The Click 3X matrix of design studios offers digital effects, animation, and broadcast design for the commercial, film, and television markets. Click 3X is part of the Illusion Fusion! Group of digital media companies which includes: New York-based IF! Interactive and Sound Lounge, an integrated digital studio that creates digital content for both the broadcast and Internet markets. Click 3X specializes in visual effects design and supervision, computer animation, character design and compositing. The studios operate multiple Silicon Graphics 3D workstations, Windows NT, Macintosh platforms and an AVID nonlinear off-line suite, as well as a Henry suite and Inferno/Flame compositing suites running on Silicon Graphics Onyx II super computers.

Click 3X—New York
16 West 22nd Street
New York, NY 10010
Phone: 212 627-1900
Fax: 212 627-4472
URL: http://www.click3x.com

Click 3X-Atlanta
345 Peachtree Hills Avenue
Atlanta, GA 30305
Phone: 404 237-9333
Fax: 404 237-9393

Cole and Company

Area(s) of Specialization: Digital Media Production, Multimedia, Events Management, Sales/Marketing

Number of Employees: 15

Cole & Company specializes in international event management, video production, new product introductions, multimedia and sales and marketing programs. The company provides a full line of digital media production services, and creative services worldwide: video and film production and editing, multimedia, event production and management, public relations, and print support.

Cole and Company
654 Beacon St. Fifth Fl.
Boston, MA 02215
Phone: 617 236-4699
Fax: 617 236-0373
URL: http://www.cole-co.com

Communications Group, Inc.

Area(s) of Specialization: Audio/Video/Film Production

Number of Employees: 4+

The Communications Group, Inc. help people communicate ideas through audio, video and film productions. Since 1983, The Communications Group has produced corporate communications projects, commercials, documentaries and feature films for local, national and international clients. Typical projects involve shooting an interview, crewing a feature film, or producing an interactive CD-ROM project from inception to distribution.

The Communications Group, Inc.
P.O. Box 50157
Raleigh, NC 27650
Phone: 919 828-4086
Fax: 919 832-7797

Continuity Studios

Area(s) of Specialization: 3D animation, computer assisted animation.

Number of Employees: 60+

Continuity has developed various properties, of it's own creation and others including Buckly o' Hare, Skeleton Warriors, CyberRad, Ms. Mystic, Nighthawk, etc. for TV and Comics. Neal Adams: the Sketch Book was compiled by Arlen Schumer from Continuity Studios. It spans Adams' comics career, revealing unpublished works, and Adam's thought process, and storytelling techniques.

Continuity Studios
4710 W. Magnolia Blvd.
Burbank, CA 91505
Phone: 818 980-8852
Fax: 818 980-8974

Continuity Studios
62 W. 45th Street, 10th Floor
New York, NY 10036
Phone: 212.869.4170
Fax: 212.764.6814
URL: http://www.nealadams.com
URL: http://www.nealadamsentertainment.com
E-mail: nadams@earthlink.net

Corey Design Studios, Inc.

Area(s) of Specialization: 2D Character
Animation

Number of Employees: 5

Corey Designs Studio Inc. creates, communicates, inspires, and entertains viewers with interactive animation and graphics. Coreytoons specializes in 2D broadcast animation, web design, and interactive services. Clients have included Fox Television and Nickelodeon.

Corey Design Studios Inc.
27 Chestnut Oval
Orangeburg, NY 10967
Phone: 914 365-1619
Fax: 914 365-3077
URL: http://www.coreytoons.com

Cosmic Blender

Area(s) of Specialization: Film/Video
Production- Coordination and Management

Number of Employees: 35

Cosmic Blender provides shooting and broadcast-quality production gear for local, national and international productions. Cosmic Blender offers professional shooting for both video and film, full digital Beta, Beta, and DV shooting packages. CB also offers production coordination and management, from solving equipment issues to securing location permits, etc.

Cosmic Blender
44 Pleasant St.
Watertown, MA 02472
Phone: 617 924-3737
Alt Phone: 800 240-3734
Fax: 617 924-3373
URL: http://www.cosmicblender.com

Crawford Digital

Area(s) of Specialization: CGI, Multimedia,
Animation

Number of Employees: 300+

Atlanta-based Crawford Communications, Inc. was established in 1981 and remains privately held by President Jesse Crawford. The company provides services for domestic and international clients involved in all facets of television, film, audio, Internet and satellite communications. Crawford

Communications has evolved with technology to comprise film transfer, digital and HD post production, sound design and mixing, 5.1 surround sound, DVD authoring, standards conversion, streaming media/webcasting, on-line services, satellite transmission, television network origination and playback and transportable satellite truck services.

Crawford Digital
3845 Pleasantdale Road
Atlanta, GA 30324
Phone: 404 876-7149
Alt Phone: 800 831-8027
Fax: 404 892-3584
URL: http://www.crawford.com

Creative Time

Area(s) of Specialization: Multimedia Production .

Number of Employees: 6+

Founded over 13 year ago Creative Time produces visual arts exhibitions, theater, performing arts and music. Creative Time/DNAid is a series of public art projects that address the implications of today's genetic research on the global futures.

Creative Time
307 7th Ave., Suite 1904
New York, NY 10001
Phone: 212 206-6674

Fax: 212 255-8467
URL: http://www.creativetime.org

Crush Digital Video

Area(s) of Specialization: Digital Video Disc (DVD) Production and Services

Number of Employees: 15+

Crush Digital Video is a DVD Authoring Studio in New York City. Crush uses digital technology in the fields of entertainment, publishing and business. Crush Digital Video is an independent facility in existence to create DVD products for commercial use.

Crush Digital Video
147 West 25th Street, 4th fl.
New York, NY 10001
Phone: 212 989-6500
Fax: 212 645-9093
URL: http://www.crushdv.com

Curious Pictures

Area(s) of Specialization: CGI, Design, Animation, Television Production, Effects

Number of Employees: 50+

Curious Pictures is an international design and television production company producing comedy, graphically inspired live-action, special effects, graphics and animation of all types. The staff of directors, designers, artists and animators produces TV commercials, on-air graphics/titles and television programming. The company was founded in early 1993 as a division of Harmony Holdings, Inc.; there are branches in New York and San Francisco.

Curious Pictures
440 Lafayette Street
New York, NY 10003
Phone: 212 674-1400
Alt Phone: 212 674-7600
Fax: 212 674-0081
URL: http://www.curiouspix.com

Curious Pictures San Francisco
1360 Mission Street Suite 201
San Francisco, CA 94103
Phone: 415 437-1400
Fax: 415 437-1408

Cutting Vision, Inc.

Area(s) of Specialization: Production and Post Production

Number of Employees: 10

Cutting Vision Inc. creates full resolution editing, graphic design and custom visual effects, as well as sound design with a fully digital record and mix suite. The company redigitizes clients' source material for an exact uncompressed on-line conform in both NTSC and PAL. The company's Audio Suite works the same way so that edits are instantly read by a 16 track AMS Neve Audiofile for accurate and fast loading to accommodate record and mix sessions.

Cutting Vision, Inc.
665 Broadway Suite 1201
New York, New York 10012
Phone: 212 533-9400
Fax: 212 533-9463
URL: http://www.cuttingvision.com

Cyclotron

Area(s) of Specialization: Visual Effects for Advertising and Broadcast

Number of Employees: 15+

Cyclotron is a design and visual effects group working with advertising and broadcast communities.

Cyclotron
220 East 42nd Street
New York, NY 10017
Phone: 212 687-8989
Fax: 212 818-0655
URL: http://www.strangequark.com

Data Motion Arts

Area(s) of Specialization: Animation

Number of Employees: 15

Data Motion Arts has been creating computer animation and imagery for more than a decade. The company's mission is to create animation that involves the blending of emerging technologies with art to create productions that are humorous, entertaining and informative.

Data Motion Arts
89 Fifth Ave.
Suite 501
New York, NY 10003
Phone: 212 463-7370
Fax: 212 463-7820
URL: http://home.dti.net/dma/

Deep Blue Sea

Area(s) of Specialization:, Film/Video Visual Effects and Animation

Number of Employees: 15+

Deep Blue Sea is a design, visual effects and animation house servicing national and international networks, advertising agencies and production companies. In addition to 3D animation, 2D animation and compositing, Deep Blue Sea also features a cel Animation department which has created spots for MTV, Pollo Tropical, Banesco Banks of Venezuela in addition to the Florida Lottery, McDonalds and Kmart.

Deep Blue Sea
2850 Tigertail Ave.
Miami, FL 33133

Phone: 305 857-0943
Fax: 305 856-3692
URL: http://www.deepbluesea.com

Digital Animation Corporation

Area(s) of Specialization: Animation and Computer Graphics

Number of Employees: 2

Digital Animation Corporation is an animation and graphics development company that creates broadcast animation and graphics for corporate producers worldwide. DAC produces collections of animation and graphics for the Cable/Broadcast, Corporate and Independent Video Production. It is also the producer of broadcast animation collections serving Cable, Broadcast, Entertainment and Fortune 500 Companies such as CNN, Disney Studios, General Motors, Intel Corp. and the US Government. DAC also has clients in over 30 foreign nations.

Digital Animation Corporation
920 Lakecrest Dr.
Seneca, SC 29672
Phone: 864 710-5979
URL: http://www.graphicsdac.com

Digital Bunker

Area(s) of Specialization: CGI, Multimedia Design

Number of Employees: 2+

A graphic and multimedia design firm located in the Washington, DC area established in January, 1999. Their designers have over six years of designing for the Internet.

Digital Bunker
14001-C Saint Germain Drive #347
Centreville, VA 20121
Phone: 703 578-8581
URL: http://www.digitalbunker.com

Dynacs Digital Studios

Area(s) of Specialization: Engineering Design and Analysis, Multimedia Digital Services, Marketing

Number of Employees: 15

Dynacs Digital Studios specializes in modeling the motion of flexible craft in space, designing flight decks for the latest supersonic transports, developing cryogenic test facilities, and restoring vintage film footage. Dynacs has a number of different locations: Houston, TX; Los Angeles, CA; Seattle, WA; KSC, FL; Cleveland, OH; Albuquerque, NM; Bangalore, India.

Dynacs Engineering Co., Inc.
35111 US. Highway 19 N., Suite 300
Palm Harbor, FL 34684
Phone: 727 787-1245
Fax: 727 787-2503
URL: http://www.dynacs.com

Dzignlight Studios

Area(s) of Specialization: Film/Video Digital Effects, CGI, Animation

Number of Employees: 3+

Founded in 1995 in Atlanta, GA, Dzignlight Studios offers digital special effects and computer graphics solutions to film and video professionals.

Dzignlight Studios
800 Forrest St.
Atlanta, GA 30318
Phone: 404 355-0755
Fax: 404 892-8991
URL: http://www.dzignlight.com

Eagle Films

Area(s) of Specialization: Traditional Animation, Stop-motion, Animation, Film/Video

Number of Employees: 2+

Eagle Films specializes in video production, visual effects, and animation for the corporate-industrial, commercial, entertainment-gaming, and feature film markets. Techniques include: photorealistic computer animation as well as traditional methods such as matte painting, miniatures, stop motion animation, and pyrotechnics. Eagle Films is owned by producer/director/writer Philip Cook and is affiliated with professional associates covering film, video, and graphic production.

Eagle Films
2809 Marshall Street
Falls Church, VA 22042-2004
Phone: 703 237-8160
Fax: 703 237-8160
URL http://www.eaglefilms.com

The Effects House Corporation

Area(s) of Specialization: Film/Digital Post Production

Number of Employees: 6

The Effects House Corp. is a fully integrated post-production facility, incorporating film and digital technology, designed to provide optical effects, 16 mm to 35mm blow-ups, anamorphic and vista vision photography, title design, computer animation, film scanning and recording. Digital effects include wire removal, insert compositing, and 3D animation.

The Effects House Corporation/New York
7 West 36th Street
3rd Floor
New York NY. 10018
Phone: 212 564-9022
Fax: 212 564-9081
URL: http://www.effectshouse.com

The Effects House Corporation/New Jersey
37 Edward Hart Dr.
Liberty State Park
Jersey City, NJ. 07305
Phone: 201 309-1292
Fax: 201-309-1392

Empire Video, Inc.

Area(s) of Specialization: DVD and CD-ROM, Audio/Video Editing, Web Site Design

Number of Employees: 6+

Empire Video, Incorporated is a full service film, video, interactive media, still photography and graphics design and production company. The company was founded on the premise that video provides the most effective means of conveying complex technical concepts or procedures. Initially concentrating on technical training productions shot in video, the company has diversified to include corporate promotional, direct marketing, training and public relations oriented projects, some of which have been shot in 16mm film. Empire continues to produce film and video for the public as well as the private sector. Projects have included programs directly for the office of the Secretary of Defense, and 2 one-hour documentaries for the U.S. Navy (through the Navy League of the United States) and the Arleigh Burke Leadership Foundation.

Empire Video, Inc.
7406 Alban Station Court
Suite A-118
Springfield, VA 22150
Phone: 703 866-1934
Fax: 703 866-1936
URL: http://www.empirevideo.com

Engineered Multimedia, Inc.

Area(s) of Specialization: Interactive Multimedia and Web Development

Number of Employees: 24

Engineered Multimedia Inc. (EMi) develops web and interactive media in science, engineering and instruction design. The company utilizes technologies such as: streaming content, Flash and 3D animation, on-line collaboration, virtual reality, and interactive product simulation.

Engineered Multimedia, Inc.
333 North Point Center East
Suite 250
Alpharetta, GA 30022
Phone: 770 475-1978
Fax: 770 475-4220
URL: http://www.engmm.com

The Envision Group

Area(s) of Specialization: 3D Animation, Imaging for Architecture, Broadcast Television

Number of Employees: 4

The company produces interactive design with a vision for new multimedia, serving clients such as Dell, Time Warner and Picture Television

The Envision Group
19 San Hope St.
Suite 2B
Boston, MA 02116
Phone: 617 266-0222
Fax: 617 266-01111
URL: http://www.envision3d.com

EPI

Area(s) of Specialization: Multimedia Development/Production/Marketing

Number of Employees: 100+

EPI Communications is a full service integrated marketing and graphics firm specializing in the use of both new and conventional communications media. Creative services include the design and development of websites, multimedia presentations, corporate and training videos, broadcast spots, print advertisements, brochures, direct mail, annual reports, corporate identification, trade show exhibits and event staging. Services include high-end prepress, photographic laboratory, digital output, exhibit and video production. EPI Systems offers digital graphics systems integration, technical support and onsite installation.

EPI Communications
6116 Executive Boulevard, Suite 210
Rockville, MD 20852
Phone: 301 230-2023
Fax: 301 468-2060
URL: http://www.epi-net.com

F-Stop Studio

Area(s) of Specialization: Traditional Animation

Number of Employees: 1

F-Stop Studio creates various types of animation that can be applied to areas including: cel animation, motion graphics, feature titles, photo projections, 2D & 3D computer animation, and music videos.

F-Stop
231W. 29th St., #203
New York, NY 10001
Phone: 212 239-8010

Fablevision Animation Studios

Area(s) of Specialization: Animation, Story-based Multimedia, CGI

Number of Employees: 8

FableVision Studios creates positive programming and story-based media for children and adults. Working closely with sister-company Cosmic Blender, a high-end script-to-finish production facility, FableVision creates stories using animation and multimedia.

Fablevision Animation Studios
44 Pleasant St.
Watertown, MA 02472
Phone: 617 924-3737
Alt. Phone: 800 240-3734
Fax: 617 924-3373
URL: http://www.fablevision.com

Fantasimation Classic Animation

Area(s) of Specialization: 2D Animation

Number of Employees: 7

Fantasimation Animation Studios is a full service animation production facility specializing in classic style cartoon animation. Located on Long Island, NY, employees write, board, animate, paint and edit productions in house. Fantasimation is a self-contained company that works on Development, Pre-pro, track breakdown, ink and paint, editing, compositing and web design and web cartoons.

Fantasimation Classic Animation
3601 Hempstead Turnpike
Levittown, NY 11756
Phone: 516 579-0609
Fax: 516 579-9409
URL: http://www.fantasimation.com

Fathom Studios

Area(s) of Specialization: Film, Television, and Computer Animation

Number of Employees: 120

The company creates visual imagery to add impact to presentations, broadcast spots, television shows, movies, and video games.

Fathom Studios
1800 Peachtree Street NW
Suite 250
Atlanta, GA 30309
Phone: 404 554-4050
Fax: 404 554-4001
URL: http://www.fathomstudios.com

Film East

Area(s) of Specialization: Film, Effects, Broadcast Design

Number of Employees: 6

With facilities in Marlton, New Jersey, Film East is a visual effects, broadcast design, and film services company.

Film East
115 West 30th St.
Suite 304
New York, NY 10001
Phone: 212 760-1596
Fax: 212 563-9390
URL: http://www.filmeast.com

Film/Video Arts

Area(s) of Specialization: Film/Video, Editing, Multimedia Education, Equipment Rental

Number of Employees: 10

Founded in 1968, Film/Video Arts is a nonprofit media arts center in the New York region. Film/Video Arts provides an environment for courses, rents production equipment and edits projects to encourage interaction between producers - whether working on narrative features, documentaries, experimental work, shorts, industrials, cable programs, music videos or student projects.

Film/Video Arts
50 Broadway, 21st Fl.
New York, NY 10004
Phone: 212 673-9361
Fax: 212 324-3318
URL: http://www.fva.com

Fire Mist Media

Area(s) of Specialization: Logo Animation, 3D Illustration, Simulations, Medical, Animation, Program Openers

Number of Employees: 1

Fire Mist Media, located in Philadelphia, PA, is an animation and graphics company owned by Jeff Brown who has had over 10 years experience in digital animation, photography, theatrical design (lighting and projections) and video. Customers speak directly to the animator. It is a resource for the small to medium sized production company or post house.

Fire Mist Media
Upper Darby, PA
Phone: 800 580-0701
Fax: 610 734-0705
URL: http://www.firemist.com

Finish

Area(s) of Specialization: Film/Video Editing, Post Production

Number of Employees: 20

Founded January 1st, 1994, Finish Digital Editing Arena is a full service post production facility for high end digital editing in Boston along with random access off-line capabilities, plus supervision and coordination of any project including production graphics, audio, and film transfer.

Finish
162 Columbus Ave.
Boston, MA 02116
Phone: 617 292-0082
Fax: 617 292-0083
URL: http://www.finishedit.com

Flying Foto Factory, Inc.

Area(s) of Specialization: Animation, Digital Production

Number of Employees: under 20

The company specializes in producing digital 3D models, visualizations and animation production services, utilizing computer visualization, animation and digital production tools for delivering detailed and accurate digital content for education, medical and legal visualizations, entertainment and marketing applications.

Flying Foto Factory, Inc.
P.O. Box 1166
107 Church Street
Durham, NC 27702
Phone: 919 682-3411
Alt. Phone: 800 682-3411
URL: http://www.flyingfoto.com

4-Front Video Design, Inc.

Area(s) of Specialization: CGI, Multimedia Design

Number of Employees: 8

4-Front Design, Inc. has a staff of artists and designers who interpret concepts, find solutions and execute designs.

4-Front Video Design, Inc.
1500 Broadway 5th Floor
New York, NY 10036
Phone: 212 944-7055
Fax: 212 944-7193
URL: http://www.4-frontdesign.com

Frank Beach and Associates, Inc.

Area(s) of Specialization: Multimedia Production and Consultant

Number of Employees: 8+

Founded in 1979, Beach Associates is a communications and media production and consultation business headquartered in Arlington, Virginia, with an extension office in Lexington, Kentucky, and associates located throughout the United States.

Frank Beach and Associates, Inc.
200 North Glebe Rd.
Suite 720
Arlington, VA 22203-3728
Phone: 703 812-8813

Fax: 703 812-9710
URL: http://www.beachassociates.com

Funny Garbage

Area(s) of Specialization: Print and Interactive Multimedia Design and Production

Number of Employees: 100

Funny Garbage is a full service design and production company that has created web sites, CD-ROMs, title graphics and print campaigns for clients ranging from The Cartoon Network, Compaq Computers, and Nike to Luaka Bop, The American Museum of Moving Image and ID Magazine. Funny Garbage creative directors Peter Girardi and Chris Capuzzo began their artistic life as graffiti writers, before attending the School of Visual Arts. Girardi became the creative director at the Voyager Company, a producer of CD-ROMs and laser discs.

Funny Garbage
73 Spring St.
Suite 605
New York, NY 10012
Phone: 212 343-2534
Fax: 212 343-3645
URL: http://www.funnygarbage.com

Garth Gardner Company, Inc.

Area(s) of Specialization: 2D and 3D Animation Production, Publishing, Video Production, Consulting

Garth Gardner Company develops, publishes, and sells multimedia products in print and electronic media for the educational and professional markets worldwide. In addition, the company also provides services in the form of production and consultation in the areas of computer graphics, animation and multimedia. The company's clients include: Universal Records, Air Jamaica, Florida A&M University, and Fashion Institute of Technology.

Garth Gardner Company, Inc.
4602 John Hancock Ct.
Suite 302
Annandale, VA 22003
Phone: 703 354-8278
Fax: 703 354-8279
URL: http://www.gogardner.com

Gearboxx

Area(s) of Specialization: Web Design with Animation

Number of Employees: 20

Gearboxx provides web and CD-based designs. The company provides services in web site revision, multimedia authoring, script programming, or video and audio production for corporations, nonprofit organizations, government agencies and educational institutions.

Gearboxx
100 Executive Drive, Suite 200-G
Dulles, VA 20166
Phone: 703 904-9880
Fax: 703 783-0071
URL: http://www.gearboxx.com

Giant Studios

Areas of Specialization: Motion Capture Production, Animation

Number of Employees: 25+

Giant Studios is the representative for Biomechanics Inc.'s Motion Reality 3D motion capture production system for the entertainment marketplace. The Motion Reality proprietary tracking and analysis algorithms and suite of software allow 3D professionals to do motion capture production.

Giant Studios, Inc.
2160 Hills Avenue
Suite A
Atlanta, GA 30318
Phone: 404 367-1999
Fax: 404 367-8485
URL: http://www.giantstudios.com

GLC Productions

Area(s) of Specialization: Digital Television, Film, and Music Programming/Production

Number of Employees: 5

Founded in 1988, GLC Productions, Inc. produces film, TV and music programming.

GLC Productions, Inc.
11 Weehawken Street
New York, New York 10014
Phone: 212 691-1038
Fax: 212 242-4911
URL: http://www.glc.com/contact.html

GTV

Area(s) of Specialization: Multimedia Design, Production, Post Production, Marketing

Number of Employees: 7

GTV's office in Midtown Manhattan provides in-house capabilities for clients from conceptual design to a finished campaign. Services and equipment available at GTV include computer animation, D1, Beta SP, and Digital Beta editing, a blue screen insert studio stage with motion control animation stand, paintbox, cameras and lighting, as well as location shooting and art direction.

GTV
1697 Broadway # 404
New York, NY 10019
Phone: 212 246-0154
Fax: 646 473-0257

URL: http://www.gtvnyc.com
E-mail: sales@gtvnyc.com

Henninger video

Area(s) of Specialization: CGI, Film/Video, Sound, Multimedia

Number of Employees: 120

Begun in 1983, Henninger Video now houses Henninger Digital Audio, Henninger Design and Effects, Henninger Digital Captioning, and Henninger Studio Production Services. Henninger Video provides digital on-line editing (D2 and Digital Betacam), random access non-linear editing, digital audio mixing and design, graphic design and animation, Ultimatte 6 studio production capabilities, tape-to-tape color correction, and all digital closed captioning. Henninger Video serves networks, producers, and companies such as The Discovery Channel, Fox Television's America' Most Wanted, CBS News "60 Minutes", Gannett Company, and Guggenheim Productions.

Henninger Video
2601-A Wilson Blvd.
Arlington, Virginia 22201
Phone: 703 243-3444
Fax: 703 243-4023
URL: http://www.henninger.com

Home Run Pictures

Area(s) of Specialization: Film/Video Production, CGI, Animation

Number of Employees: 5+

Home Run Pictures is involved in the production of computer generated imagery, creating animation for television programming, commercials, corporate video, special wide screen presentations, and interactive applications. The company utilizes computer based tools via a network of SGI workstations.

Home Run Pictures
100 First Avenue, Suite 450
Pittsburgh, PA 15222
Phone: 412 391-8200
Fax: 412 391-1772
URL: http://www.hrpictures.com

Image Group Design

Area(s) of Specialization: Post Production

Number of Employees: 500+

The Image Groups' visual effects division Image Design creates visual effects for cable and broadcast television, motion pictures and corporate communications. Image Design utilizes technical tools such as Discreet Logic Flames and Inferno; Quantel Hal, Harry and Paintbox; Alias on Silicon Graphic and Apple work stations.

Image Group Design
401 5th Avenue
New York, NY 10016
Phone: 212 548-7700
Fax: 212 685-4317
URL: http://www.image-group.com

Impact Studios

Area(s) of Specialization: Production, Business Communication, Multimedia

Number of Employees: 3

Impact Studios is a full-service business communications company.

Impact Studios
22 Elizabeth St.
Norwalk, CT 06854
Phone: 203 852-6550
Fax: 203 852-6553
URL: http://www.impactstudiostv.com

Improv Technologies

Area(s) of Specialization: Multimedia Software Development and Distribution

Number of Employees: 40

Improv Technologies makes software to simplify digital content creation and distribution from high-end 3D animation and video game development to Internet production. They produce proprietary and patent-pending technologies to change how disparate forms of digital media and related applications integrate.

Improv Technologies
23 East 31st Street
14th Floor Penthouse
New York, NY 10016
Phone: 212 725-4590
Fax: 212 725-4390
URL: http://www.improv-tech.com

Ingalls

Area(s) of Specialization: Advertising Concept and Design

Number of Employees: 160

Ingalls is an advertising agency in New England. As a full service agency, the company creates Advertising, Interactive Marketing, Design, Direct Response, Public Relations, and Recruitment/Yellow Pages Advertising for clients.

Ingalls
One Design Center Place
Boston, MA 02210
Phone: 617 295-7000
Fax: 617 295-7514
URL: http://www.hmei.com

The Ink Tank

Area(s) of Specialization: Animation, CGI, Film/Video

Number of Employees: 10-12

Founded in 1977, Ink Tank has worked 20 years in studio filmmaking. The company specializes in full service animation, 2D, 3D, character animation, and commercial work. The company's primary markets are commercials, television, and feature films.

The Ink Tank
2W. 47th St., 14th Floor
New York, NY 10036
Phone: 212 869-1630
Fax: 212 764-4169
URL: http://www.inktank.net

Interface Media Group

Area(s) of Specialization: CGI, Animation, Film/Video/Internet Production

Number of Employees: 52

Interface Media Group provides film, video and Internet related production services for professional communicators in the Washington, DC area since 1977. The company services include studio production and teleconferencing, graphic design, production of computer animation and visual effects, resolution, independent digital compositing, non-linear and tape based editing, film to tape transfer and tape to tape color correction, audio production and sound design, satellite and fiber optic transmission, duplication, distribution and world standards conversion, internet related services and the development of specialized software products.

Interface Media Group
1233 20th Street, NW
Washington, DC 20036
Phone: 202 861-0500
Fax: 202 296-4492
URL: http://www.interfacevideo.com

Intoons

Area(s) of Specialization: Performance Animation

Number of Employees: 30

Intoons Performance Animation is a computer generated, interactive character animation system for design of a custom character, mascot or logo. IEG supplies equipment and personnel from a single monitor kiosk to a large video wall presentation. Intoons promotes identity and corporate messages by allowing audiences to talk to and interact with the familiar character or logo at Trade Shows, Concerts, Stadiums or Business Meetings.

Intoons
371 Little Falls Rd.
Cedar Grove, NJ 07009-1250
Phone: 973 857-7242
Alt Phone: 888 446-8666
Fax: 973 857-8867
URL: http://www.intoons.com

The Jim Henson Company

Area(s) of Specialization: Multimedia, Film/Video Production, Publisher

Number of Employees: 600+

The Jim Henson Company is a private, independent multimedia production company, a character licensor in the industry, and home to Jim Henson Television, Jim Henson Pictures and Jim Henson's Creature Shop, and publishers of children's books. The Creature Shop has received two Academy Awards, including one in 1996 for Best Visual Effects for the hit film, "Babe," and the other in 1992 for the Henson Performance Control System.

The Jim Henson Company
117 East 69th Street
New York, NY 10021.
Phone: 212 794-2400 (NY)
Alt. Phone: 323 802-1500 (CA)
Fax: 212 570-1147
URL: http://www.henson.com

John Lemmon Films

Area(s) of Specialization: Clay and Cel Animation

Number of Employees: 2

John Lemmons Films produces clay animation television commercials for clients across the US including Pacific Bell, Dairy Queen, Farmhouse Foods, Cedar Point

Amusement Park, the Coleman Company, IGA Supermarkets and Tandy corporation. The company creates interactive CD-ROM that uses cel animation with clay backgrounds. The studio has produced the package artwork for Interplay's videogame "Clay-Fighter."

John Lemmon Films
4921 Albemarle Rd. Suite 111
Charlotte, NC 28205.
Phone: 704 532-1944
Fax: 704 566-1984.
URL: http://www.jlf.com

Judson Rosebush Company

Area(s) of Specialization: Multimedia Concept-Production, Programming/Design

Number of employees: 5

The Judson Rosebush Company specializes in concept development, project planning and management, content creation, art direction, sound design, precise interactive navigation, software architecture and programming, and testing and mastering. The company's programmers, artists and designers work in multiple programming languages, major multimedia authoring tools, still and video imaging, and desktop publishing. Delivery methods include CD-ROM, World Wide Web and floppy disk.

Judson Rosebush Company
154 West 57th Street, Studio 826

New York, NY 10019
Phone: 212-581-3000
Fax: 212 757-8283
URL: http://www.rosebush.com

Kleiser-Walczak Construction Co.

Area(s) of Specialization: Film/Commercial Animation, Effects, Interactive Media

Number of Employees: 50+

Kleiser-Walczak Construction Co. produces computer generated animation and visual effects for feature films, special venue attractions, commercials and interactive media. The company has production studios in Hollywood, Manhattan, and Massachusetts (at MASS MoCA - the Museum of Contemporary Art).

Kleiser-Walczak Construction Co./Massachusetts
87 Marshall St., Bldng. 1.
North Adams, MA 01247
Phone: 413 664-7441
Fax: 413 664-7442
URL: http://www.kwcc.com

Kleiser-Walczak Construction Co./New York
23 W. 18th. St.
New York, NY 10011
Phone: 212 255-3866
Fax: 212 929-6747
URL: http://www.kwcc.com

L.A. Bruell

Area(s) of Specialization: Video, Animation, Web Design.

Number of Employees: 5

L.A.Bruell is a full service multimedia productions facility offering 3D and 2D computer animation, and world wide web design. L.A. Bruell's animation and musical scores have appeared on television productions, movie trailers, interactive games, on-line services, technical and medical productions, and how-to videos. The company's roster of clients includes: McGraw-Hill, Nynex, PBS, The Cartoon Network, Ex-machina, Inc. Sudler & Hennesey and Intramed (Divisions of Young and Rubicam), The Big Apple Circus and The N.Y.C Police Department L.A.

L.A. Bruell
157 West 57th. St.
Suite 500
New York, NY 10019
Phone: 212 956-0800
Fax: 212 956-3807
URL: http://www.labruell.com

Loop Filmworks

Area(s) of Specialization: Cel Animation, Pixelation, Stop Motion, Live Action, DVD, Web Site Design

Number of Employees: 15+

LOOP Filmworks is involved in cel animation, stop motion, pixelation, live action, DVD and web site design; they have been in existence 10 years.

Loop Filmworks, Inc.
45 Washington Street
Suite 602
Brooklyn, NY 11201
Phone: 718 522-LOOP (5667)
Fax: 718 522-5668
URL: http://www.loopfilmworks.com

Lovett Productions, Inc.

Area(s) of Specialization: Film/Video Production, Editing, CGI, Sound

Number of Employees: 10+

The company was founded in 1989 by Joseph F. Lovett, a 10-year veteran and producer at ABC News' 20/20. Located in New York's SoHo district, Lovett Productions is a fully equipped production and editing facility. The offices consist of an Avid Media Composer 400 and 4000's, 3/4" and Beta dubbing machines, computer graphics equipment, and production office space.

Lovett Productions, Inc.
155 Sixth Avenue 10th Floor
New York, NY 10013-1507
Phone: 212-242-8999
Fax: 212-242-7347
URL: http://www.lovettproductions.com
E-mail: info@lovettproductions.com

Macquarium, Inc.

Area(s) of Specialization: Internal/External Communication Development and Management, Broadcast, Interactive Media, E-Commerce

Number of Employees: 120

Macquarium Intelligent Communications works in communications issues such as development and management of internal and external communications initiatives. The results are expressed through broadcast, interactive media, and web-centric applications such as intranet, extranet, and e-commerce enterprise solutions.

Macquarium, Inc.
1800 Peachtree St. NW
Suite 250 Atlanta, GA 30309-2517
Phone: 404 554-4000
Fax: 404 554-4001
URL: http://www.macquarium.com

Magick Lantern

Area(s) of Specialization: Post Production, Editing, Design, CGI and Animation

Number of Employees: 20

Magick Lantern creates in the areas of post production, editing, design, CGI and animation.

Magick Lantern
750 Ralph McGill Blvd.
Atlanta, GA 30312
Phone: 404 688-3348
Fax: 404 584-5247
URL: http://www.magicklantern.com

Magnetic Image Video

Area(s) of Specialization: Video Post Production, Editing, Internet Television

Number of Employees: 10

Magnetic Image Video is a post production facility, located in lower Manhattan. Established in 1989 to serve the broadcast television community with analog linear, digital linear and non-linear editing, the company also services the international community with internet television.

Magnetic Image Video
119 Fifth Ave.
Fourth Floor
New York, NY 10003
Phone: 212 598-3000
Fax: 212 633-6432
URL: http://www.magneticimage.com

MBC Teleproductions

Area(s) of Specialization: Video, 3D Animation

Number of Employees: 5+

MBC Teleproductions is a full-service production house, capable of creating video and film from the :30 commercial to the live sporting event. Included in the spectrum is industrial, promotional, and educational video, long and short format broadcast production, 2 and 3D graphics, animation, and multimedia design.

MBC Teleproductions
3000 East Rock Rd.
Allentown, PA 18103
Phone: 800 232-3024
Fax: 610 797-6922
URL: http://www.mbctv.com

M&M Creative Services

Area(s) of Specialization: CGI, Web Design, Advertising

Number of Employees: 22

M&M offers services in Graphic Design, Web Design and Advertising.

M&M Creative Services
P.O. Box 2457
Tallahassee, FL 32316
Phone: 888 224-1169
Fax: 850 656-9146
URL: http://www.mmdg.com

Manhattan Transfer

Area(s) of Specialization: Commercial/Television Post Production, Visual Effects and Design

Number of Employees: 150

Manhattan Transfer creates visual effects, design, telecine grading, and editorial work for television commercial clients and episodic series. Additionally Manhattan provides feature film dailies service. The company works on projects ranging from complete channel redesigns to visual effects for high-end commercials. The artists, designers, and animators at Manhattan Transfer work with Discreet's flame, inferno, and fire, Quantel's Henry, HAL and Paintbox, and CG software such as SoftImage | 3D, Alias Maya, 3D Studio Max, Renderman, and a host of proprietary software tools created by in-house programmers.

Manhattan Transfer
545 Fifth Ave.
New York, NY 10017
Phone: 212 687-4000
Fax: 212 818-9252
URL: http://www.mte.com

Marvel Entertainment Group, Inc.

Area(s) of Specialization: Animation, Comic Books

Number of Employees: 100+

Marvel Entertainment Group is a comic book company and the creators of Marvel Comics, creators of "X Men", "Spider Man", and the "Avengers."

Marvel Enterprises, Inc. a character-based entertainment company with operations in five divisions: licensing, toys-via its Toy Biz division, comic book and trade publishing, entertainment and the Internet. Through the ownership of over 3,500 proprietary characters, Marvel licenses its characters in a wide range of consumer products, services and media such as feature films, television, the Internet, apparel, video games, collectibles, snack foods and promotions.

Marvel Entertainment Group, Inc.
387 Park Avenue South
New York, NY 10016
Phone: 212 696-0808
URL: http://www.marvelcomics.com
http://www.marvel.com

Mechanism Digital

Area(s) of Specialization: Film/ Television Digital Effects and Animation, Interactive Media.

Number of Employees: 4+

Mechanism Digital Inc. is a New York City based production studio creating high-end digital effects and animation for film, television, and interactive media. The company's creative team specializes in 3D character animation, morphing, visualization, effects, and blue screen techniques. Actively involved in the 3D computer art industry, Mechanism is a charter member of ECDC (East Coast Digital Consortium) and the company principal Lucien Harriot serves on the Board of Directors for New York City ACM SIGGRAPH.

Mechanism Digital
407 Broome St., 7th Floor
New York, NY 10013
Phone: 212 334-6678
Fax: 212 941-1819
URL: http://www.mechanismdigital.com

Media Education Foundation

Area(s) of Specialization: Film/Video Research and Production for Education

Number of Employees: 8

MEF is involved in media research and production of resources to aid educators and others in fostering analytical media literacy, which is essential to a democracy in a diverse and complex society. MEF has produced some 15 videos on issues of media representation and gender, race, violence, and other concerns. It was founded in 1991 by Professor Sut Jhally producer of the video, "Dreamworlds: Desire, Sex, and Power in Music Video."

Media Education Foundation
26 Center Street
Northampton, MA 01060
Phone: 800-897-0089

Fax: 413 586-8389
URL: http://www.igc.apc.org/mef

Metastream (View Point)

Area(s) of Specialization: Production/
Development 3D Streaming (MTS), 3D
Modeling.

Number of Employees: 800 at Headquater

Metastream is a provider of Internet
visualization technology and 3D rendering
services for on-line retailers. The company
provides a cohesive association of
technology, tools, and partners that enable e-
tailers to create photorealistic 3D product
presentation and sales web sites. Metastream
developed a streaming 3D file format called
MTS, and sells annual licenses to broadcast
in this format to e-commerce sites. In
addition, Metastream provides services for
creating the 3D content and integrating it
into a customer's site. In November 2000
Metastream acquired View Point and
changed its to View Point.

Metastream
498 Seventh Ave., Suite 1810
New York, NY 10018-6718
Phone: 212 201-0800
Fax: 212 201-0801
URL: http://www.metastream.com

Mike's Miniature Movies

Area(s) of Specialization: 2D Digital
Animation for Multimedia/Web

Number of Employees: 1

Mike's Miniature Movies creates animation
that can be used to demonstrate concepts.

Mike's Miniature Movies
Fax: 800 710-7805
URL: http://www.best.com/~mikesand
E-mail: mikesand@best.com

Mindvisions (3D Studios)

Area(s) of Specialization: Web Design,
Electronic Presentations, Interactive CDs,
On-line Marketing

Number of Employees: 6

3D Studios has changed to Mindvisions. The
company develops multimedia projects and
provides in-house design, technical, and
promotion services.

Mindvisions
18859 Emerald City Highway
Destin, FL 32541
Phone: 800 334-9427
Alt Phone: 850 837-6166
Fax: 850 837-0254
URL: http://www.mindvisions.com
http://www.3dstudios.com
E-mail: service@3dstudios.com

MindWorks Multimedia

Area(s) of Specialization: Video/CD-ROM/DVD/Web-Based Production, Post Production

Number of Employees: 60

MindWorks Multimedia's teams produce communications applications for training, marketing, product information, corporate overview, and television commercials. The company covers network sports shows, bilingual training and human resource programs, plus marketing and commercial productions for industries such as textiles, pharmaceuticals, automotive, finance, and many more. The company has video production facilities including non-linear edit suites (Avid and Edit systems), linear BetaSP, graphics design suite, 20x20 studio, and complete BetaSP field camera packages.

MindWorks Multimedia
211 Gregson Drive
Cary, NC 27511-7909
Phone: 919 380-2156
Fax: 919 380-2183
URL: http://www.mwmm.com

Mitch Butler Company, Inc.

Area(s) of Specialization: CGI, Animation, Video Production, Web Design

Number of Employees: 33

Mitch Butler Company, Inc. is a 3D computer animation firm. The services provided include: complete 3D and 2D animation, video production and web design. Clients include corporations such as Viewpoint Datalabs, Hewlett-Packard, Micron Technology, as well as advertising agencies like Elgin Syferd Drake, WRC Advertising and The Johnson Company. The company uses Newtek's Lightwave 3D for Windows NT and a network of Pentium and Pentium II systems, including one Intergraph Pentium II 300Mhz with an Intense 3D Pro 2200 display card, and utilizing Speed Razor for video editing and DPS Perception for video output. Mitch Butler Company and Flimsy Entertainment work together.

Mitch Butler Company, Inc./Flimsy Entertainment
23 East 31st Street, 14th floor
NY, NY 10016
Phone: 212 725-4590
Fax: 212 725-4390
URL: http://www.mitchbutler.com/

Modern Uprising Studios

Area(s) of Specialization: CGI, Animation, Motion Capture

Number of Employees: 8+

Modern Uprising Studios, located in New York, provides motion capture service. Using Motion Analysis' optical-based motion capture system, the company captures movement with realistic motion from Feature Films, Broadcast and Video Games in the Entertainment Industry to the motion of the Performing Arts.

Modern Uprising Studios
Brooklyn Navy Yard
Bldg. 280 Suite 509
Brooklyn, NY 11205
Phone: 718 852-0811
Alt Phone: 718 852-0845
Fax: 718 858-2459
URL: http://www.modernuprising.com

Motion Image

Area(s) of Specialization: Film/Video Production, CGI, Multimedia, Sound, Animation

Number of Employees: 6

Motion Image is a Film and Video Production Company creating visual media for broadcast, corporate, and multimedia. The company's services include production and support for film, video, graphics, 2D/3D animation, and audio design. The company provides production, design and compression services for multimedia projects.

Motion Image
2730 SW Third Ave.
Miami, FL 33129
Phone: 305 859-2000

Fax: 305 859-2412
URL: http://www.motionimage.com

Muffin-Head Productions

Area(s) of Specialization: Advertising, Marketing, Promotions, Web-Design

Number of Employees: 400

The company is involved in sales/marketing, training, brand management, investor relations, targeting consumers, businesses and industry professionals. Utilizing Internet/Intranet, CD-ROM, CD-i, Interactive Kiosks, audio, video and more, Muffin-Head creates strategy and concept development to complete design, programming, engineering and post-production support; all project phases are performed entirely in-house.

Muffin-Head Productions
417 Canal St.
Sixth Fl.
New York, NY 10013
Phone: 212 431-5300
Fax: 212 431-5833
URL: http://www.muffinhead.com

Multimedia Productions

Area(s) of Specialization: web design

Number of Employees: 1+

Multimedia Productions creates web design and links on the internet.

Multimedia Productions
50 West Main Street
Merrimac, MA 01860
Phone: 508 346-0641
URL: http://world.std.com/~ldjackso/
Email: ldjackso@world.std.com

Nick Ericson Studio

Area(s) of Specialization: Special Effects/
Animation Production

Number of Employees: 5+

NES is a full-service animation and post-production studio, located in the Flatiron District of Manhattan, creating high-quality special effects for commercial, broadcast and film productions. The company's styles range from highly stylized 2D-design to photo-realistic 3D-animation.

Nick Ericson Studio
127 West 25th Street
New York, NY 10001
Phone: 212 337-0089
Fax: 212 337-0169
URL: http://www.nickstudio.com

NxView Technologies, Inc.

Area(s) of Specialization: 3D Animation,
Real-time Programming

Number of Employees: 62 (east) 7 (west)

NxView Technologies creates interactive 3D applications for customer service and support, product training, sales demonstrations and e-commerce. The company is based in the Research Triangle Park area of North Carolina.

Nx View Technologies, Inc.
P.O. Box 1429
Cary, NC 27512-1429
Phone: 919 657-3300
Fax: 919 657-3333

NxView Technologies, Inc.
2425 Porter Street, Suite 14
Soquel, CA 95073
Phone: 831 479-8274
Fax: 831 464-8391
URL: http://www.NxView.com

Oculus

Area(s) of Specialization: Film Post
Production, Design and Effects, CGI

Number of Employees: 100+

Oculus services the New York Film community. Oculus offers services from simple scene retouching to complicated visual effects. The Oculus team creates natural and unnatural phenomenon, digital compositing, nonlinear editing, audio sweetening and mixing, title design, rig removal and visual effects supervision.

Oculus
220 East 42nd Street
New York, NY. 10017
Phone: 212 393-2255
Fax: 212 818-0655
URL: http://www.oculusfx.com

Olive Jar Studios, Inc.

Areas of Specialization: Film Stop-motion Animation and Traditional Cell Animation

Number of Employees: 30-60

Founded in 1984, Olive Jar Studios, Inc. is a design and film production studio specializing in animation techniques that include mixed-media, stop-motion, CG, cel, drawn, and live action/special effects.

Olive Jar Studios, Inc.
35 Soldiers Field Place
Boston, MA 02135
Phone: 617 783-9500
Fax: 617 783-9544
URL: http://www.olivejar.com

Olympus Group, Inc.

Area(s) of Specialization: Java Application Development, Multimedia Web Design

Number of Employees: 40

Founded in 1995, Olympus Group, Inc. is based in Alexandria, Virginia specializing in business intelligence technology, Java

application development, XML and multimedia web design. Clients have included Digex, Microsoft, Oracle, UUNET, Applied Theory and Exodus.

Olympus Group, Inc.
2800 Eisenhower Avenue
Floor One
Alexandria, VA 22314-4578
Phone: 703 317-2800
Fax: 703 317-2806
URL: http://www.olympusgroup.com

O'Plenty Animation Studios

Area(s) of Specialization: Traditional Animation, CGI

Number of Employees: 5

O'Plenty Animation is an independent animation studio in Long Branch. The studio's founder and executive producer, Chris Larson has been a part of projects such as "Ren & Stimpy", MTV' S "Liquid Television" and Weird Al Yankovic's Grammy nominated "Jurassic Park" Video. O'Plenty Animation specializes in traditional character animation. The studio was founded in 1995 and produced a Merrill Lynch training film that combined hand drawn cel animation, CGI and live action. The artists that contribute to O'Plenty have worked on Disney's "Aladdin", "The Prince & The Pauper", "Pocahantas", "Fantasia Continued", "Fa Mulan", "Hercules" And "Runaway Brain" as well as Turner's "Cats Don't Dance" and "Iron Giant."

O'Plenty Animation Studios
605 Second Ave.
West End, NJ 07740
Phone: 732 870-6691
Fax: 973 300-1940
URL: http://www.oplenty.com

The Outpost

Area(s) of Specialization: Digital Video Editing, CGI, Sound

Number of Employees: 1+

The Outpost, located in of Brooklyn, NY specializes in video art, documentaries, features, industrial and educational programming, broadcast quality Beta SP mastering, graphics, multi track audio mixing. The company also has an extensive royalty free music collection to offer clients.

The Outpost
118 N. 11th St.
Fourth Floor
Brooklyn, NY 11211
Phone: 718 599-2385
Fax: 718 599-9747
URL: http://www.outpostvideo.com

Palace Production Center

Area(s) of Specialization: Film/Video, Sound, CGI, Animation

Number of Employees: 25-50

PPC houses television, film, and multimedia creative artists. The company works in network specials as well as home video series. The New Media Group creates content for the World Wide Web while the Riverside Stage Company produces readings of new American plays featuring some of the new and established playwrights on the Broadway scene today.

Palace Production Center
29 N. Main St.
South Norwalk, CT 06854
Phone: 203 853-1740
Fax: 203 855-9608
URL: http://www.palacedigital.com

The Pixel Factory, Inc.

Area(s) of Specialization: Computer Graphics, Animation, and Design Development and Production

Number of Employees: 8-20

The Pixel Factory creates computer graphics, animation, and design. The company offers a range of creative services to coordinate productions from start to finish.

The Pixel Factory, Inc.
4081-C L.B. McLeod Rd.
Orlando, FL 32811
Phone: 407 839-1222
Fax: 407 839-1235
URL: http://www.pixfactory.com

Pixel Liberation Front, Inc.

Area(s) of Specialization: Digital Production, Animation, CGI, Visual Effects

Number of Employees: 8

PLF is a visual effects company that offers services in pre-visualization and 3D integration in addition to 3D animation and virtual environments creation. With offices in both New York and Los Angeles, Pixel Liberation Front is a coast to coast full service digital production house.

Pixel Liberation Front, Inc.
New York
150 W. 28 St. #1003
New York, NY 10001
Phone: 212 239-1455
Fax: 212 239-3201

Pixel Liberation Front, Inc.
Los Angeles
1316 Abbot Kinney Blvd.
Venice, CA 90291
Phone: 310 396-9854
Fax: 310 396-9874
URL: http://www.thefront.com
E-mail: plf@thefront.com

Pixel Soup

Area(s) of Specialization: Design for Television/Video/CD-ROM/Internet

Number of Employees: 2

Pixel Soup is a design firm specializing in designing logos and complete identity packages, or creating a complete news, kids or promotion package unique to the company's station. The staff is comprised of designers, producers, photographers, editors, 3D animators and model makers. The staff designs, produces and composites much of the work at Pixel Soup on high-end desktop animation systems.

Pixel Soup
83 Newbury St.
4th floor
Boston, MA 02116
Phone: 617 437-7770
Fax: 617 437-7779
URL: http://www.pixelsoup.com

Planet Three Animation Studio

Area(s) of Specialization: 3D Animation, Visual Effects for Video/Film

Number of Employees: 5

Planet Three Animation Studio, started by Joe F. Jarman, offers animation and visual effects for the film and broadcast industries.

Tools include a network of: Silicon Graphics (SGI) workstations, Alias|Wavefront Maya with Maya F/X, Power Animator with Advanced Animation and Power Modeling modules. Clients include: Lucasfilm, Ltd., Seasonal Films, Renaissance Pictures, Wilmington Regional Film Commission, and DuPont Films. The company creates synthetic characters and integrating them into an environment, to creating photorealistic pyrotechnic and visual effects. The studio works to solves visual problems for directors and producers.

Planet Three Animation Studio
1223 North 23rd Street
Wilmington, NC 28405
Phone: 910 343-3720
Fax: 910 343-3722
URL: http://www.planet3animation.com

Post Modern Editorial, Inc.

Area(s) of Specialization: Film/Video Editing, Post Production, Audio, Motion Control

Number of Employees: 10

Since 1989, Post Modern owner has utilized AVID for non-linear editing. The company provides compression services for video and audio for interactive design or distribution on the web.

Post Modern Editorial, Inc.
684 Antone Street NW
Suite 100

Atlanta, GA 30318
Phone: 404 350-0044
Alt Phone: 404 350-9644
Fax: 404 350-9099
URL: http://www.post-modern.com

Rab-Byte Computer Graphics, Inc.

Area(s) of Specialization: 3D Animation and Computer Graphics

Number of Employees: 3

Rab-Byte Computer Graphics Inc. has a complete paint and animation facility that produces 3D photo-realistic animation. The company has two full service graphic libraries.

Rab-Byte Computer Graphics, Inc.
452 Wilson Ave.
Lindenwold, NJ 08021
Phone: 800 229-0184
Fax: 856 627-6492
URL: http://www.rab-byte.com

Razorfish

Area(s) of Specialization: Web Site Design, Interface Design

Number of Employees: 1,600 (worldwide)

Razorfish plans, designs and builds products and services for web site design and interface design. Its media and entertainment clients includes: America Online, BMG Entertainment, Canal Digital, CBS, Columbia Records, Disney/ABC, E! Online, Elektra Entertainment, Helsinki Media, Jim Henson Productions, Johns + Gorman Films, Lycos, Lyd, Madison Square Garden, Marieberg, Maverick Records, Media One, MTV, National Broadcasting Company, National Public Radio, Nickelodeon, October Films, Polygram Filmed Entertainment, Prodigy Services Co., Road Runner, Screentrade, Sony Theatres, Spray Circus, Stockholm International, and over a hundred others. This public company has over 15 locations worldwide.

Razorfish-New York
32 Mercer Street
New York, NY 10013
Phone: 212 966-5960
Alt. Phone: 800 950-IDEA
Fax: 212 966-6915
URL: http://www.razorfish.com

Razorfish-Boston
101 Main Street
Cambridge, MA 02142
Phone: 617 250-2500
Fax: 617 250-2501

REI Media Group

Area(s) of Specialization: Film Optics/Effects, Print Design, Advertising

Number of Employees: 6

REI Media Group is a film optical house for service to filmmakers. REI Media Group creates title design, optical effects, digital effects, blowups, and design services for posters, press kits and advertising services for new filmmakers and companies such as Paramount, 20th Century Fox, Columbia, Sony, New Line, Miramax and Buena Vista.

REI Media Group
28 West 39th Street
New York, NY 10018
Phone: 212 768-9300
Fax: 212 768-0438
URL: http://www.reimedia.com

Red Car

Area(s) of Specialization: CGI, Commercial Production, sound, and Post Production

Number of Employees: 100 (nationwide)

Red Car edits TV commercials. The staff at Redcar New York consists of graphics artists, sound designers, and type stylists. The company's clientele includes: Wieden & Kennedy, Leo Burnett (leoburnett.com), Young & Rubicam (yandr.com), and Nike. Red Car has offices in Chicago, Dallas, London, Los Angeles, San Francisco, and New York.

Red Car-New York
196 Mercer St.
Penthouse
New York, NY 10012

Phone: 212 982-5555
Fax: 212 982-7179
URL: http://www.redcar.com

Registered Films

Area(s) of Specialization: Film/Video Production, Sound

Number of Employees: 4+

Registered Films is a film and television production company in New York City offering film and video production. The company has a 15,000 sq. ft. studio, equipped with 2 film stages, 2 on-line non-linear video editing suites, full broadcast graphics, a voice-over booth and a Protools audio sweetening and mixing room. Digital is the post production division of (r) Films offering on-line and off-line digital editing, effects, compositing, 2D animation and 3D animation, plus staff and freelance artists, animators, and editors. Registered Films produces television commercials, television programs, documentaries and corporate video projects as well as offering international production services.

Registered Films
121 W. 19th St., Fourth Fl.
New York, NY 10011
Phone: 212 929-4825
Fax: 212 627-1462
URL: http://www.registeredfilms.com

Replica Technology

Area(s) of Specialization: 3D Modeling, CD-ROM Production

Number of Employees: 1

Based in North Collins, New York, Replica Technology is a 3D content developer of high quality 3D Objects and CD-ROM Collections. 3D Collections are used with consumer photo-imaging and business productivity software packages. Collections are also used with commercial 3D modeling, rendering and animation software. Each CD-ROM includes hundreds of models, scenes, textures and pre-rendered Browser images of many models.

Replica Technology
4650 Langford Rd.
North Collins, NY 14111
Phone: 800-714-8184
Alt Phone: 716-337-0621
Fax: 716-337-0642
URL: http://www.replica3d.com

R/GA Digital Studio

Area(s) of Specialization: Interactive Design, Digital Production, E-business development.

Number of Employees: 160

Founded in 1977 R/GA Digital studios consist of two major departments-R/GA Interactive and R/Greenberg Associates. Established in 1993, R/GA Interactive is a strategic design agency that creates web sites, kiosks, CD ROM and games for companies. With over 20 years experience R/Greenberg Associates is an Academy Award-winning digital production company that creates visual effects, 3D graphics, design and motion graphics. Their clients range from Fortune 500 companies to educational institutions and non-profit organizations, including: IBM, Bed, Bath & Beyond, Intel, PBS and several other companies.

R/GA Digital Studio
350 West 39th Street
New York, NY 10018
Phone: 212 946-4060
Fax: 212 946-4010
URL: http://www.rga.com

Rhinoceros Visual Effects

Area(s) of Specialization: 3D Animation

Number of Employees: 60

Rhinoceros Visual Effects and Design is a MultiVideo Group/Gravity company. The MultiVideo Group, Ltd. owned and associated companies include New York-based Rhinoceros Editorial and Post, Cool Beans Digital Audio, Wall to Wall Films and WAX Music and Sound Design. Associated international companies include Gravity Effects in Tel Aviv, and Digital Renaissance in Oberhausen, Germany.

Rhinoceros Visual Effects
Multi Video Group Ltd.
50 E 42nd Street
New York, NY 10017
Phone: 212 697-4466
Fax: 212 972-0702

Rhinodesign

Area(s) of Specialization: Computer graphics and design

Number of Employees: 25

Rhinodesign develops Internet strategies. The company offers media services including new media production, graphic design, web hosting, on-site training, and maintenance, as well as full service integrated marketing.

Rhinodesign
21-B Dowling Rd.
Albany, NY 12205
Phone: 518 438-5100
Fax: 518 438-0055
URL: http://www.rhinodesign.com
E-mail: info@rhinodesign.com

Royal Vision Productions

Area(s) of Specialization: 3D Computer Animation

Number of Employees: 2

Royal Vision Productions, located in South Florida, has been in business since August

1998 and has designed work for different organizations, including churches, schools, educational supply companies, web entrepreneurs and biomedical engineering companies. The company designs graphics for web pages, and specializes in graphic mediums such as logo design, print, photo retouching, and multimedia.

Royal Vision Productions
12850 S.R. 84 #8-25
Davie, FL 33325
Phone: 954 916-1980
URL: http://www.rvproductions.com

Sam and Vick's Café

Area(s) of Specialization: Computer Graphics, Design, and Animation

Number of Employees: 2

Cosmic Bakers is Sam Hadley's computer graphics, design and animation company which uses Kinetix Corporation's 3D Studio Max and a variety of other software packages running on Windows 2000.

Sam and Vick's Café
Box 9901 Connections East
Coral Bay, St. John, USVI 00831
Phone: 340 779-4970
Fax: 340 693-5032
URL: http://www.samnvick.com/cosmic/cosmic.htm

Service Group, Inc.

Area(s) of Specialization: Web Site Design and Implementation, Digital Prints, Animation, CT Legislation

Number of Employees: 6

Service Group, Inc. offers complete design and implementation of web sites from basic home page creation to complete multimedia sites.

Service Group, Inc.
P.O. Box 799
Glastonbury, CT 06033
Phone: 800 432-9706
Fax: 800 432-9706
URL: http://www.servgrp.com

Sonalysts Studios, Inc.

Area(s) of Specialization: Interactive Multimedia, Operations Research, Software Development, Program Management, System Engineering

Number of Employees: 450+

Sonalysts Incorporated, is a multidisciplinary, employee-owned corporation, involved in interactive multimedia, operations research, software development, program management and system engineering.

Sonalysts Studios, Inc.
215 Parkway N.

Waterford, CT 06385
Phone: 800 752-1946
Fax: 860 447-0669
URL: http://www.sonalysts.com

Source W Media

Area(s) of Specialization: CGI, Electronic Media, Production, Printing

Number of Employees: 100

Source W Media has 110-year history as Westinghouse's source for graphic design, electronic media, production and printing. Source W is an integrator of communications technology, content, and design.

Source W Media
New Media Division
11 Stanwix Street
Pittsburgh, PA 15222
Phone: 877 268-9224
Alt Phone: 412 624-3600 or 412 829-6300
Fax: 412 829-6321
URL: http://www.source-w.com

Spicer Productions

Area(s) of Specialization: Film/Video Production and Post Production, Interactive Multimedia, Animation, CGI

Number of Employees: 40

Spicer Productions is a film and video communications company in Baltimore, Maryland, providing creative and production services which include a large studio, digital post-production, graphics, 3D animation, multimedia, digital audio, duplication and Web design.

Spicer Productions
1708 Whitehead Rd.
Baltimore, MD 21093
Phone: 410 560-1212
Fax: 410 252-6316
URL: http://www.spicerpro.com

Spot

Area(s) of Specialization: Film/Video

Number of Employees: 10

Spot works in film and video. Clients include ad agencies Hill Holliday, Arnold, Ingalls, HMME, Clark Goward, and Mullen. Services includes creating Avid cuts through film to tape, on-line and mix.

Spot
334 Newbury St.
Boston, MA 02115
Phone: 617 267-9565
Fax: 617 267-4703
URL: http://www.editatspot.com

Successful Images

Area(s) of Specialization: Educational and Commercial Film/Video/CD Production

Number of Employees: 7+ (freelance)

Successful Images employees include directors, writers, cinematographers, editors and digital artists. The company is involved in developing training videos, educational CD's, marketing presentation, special interest films and commercials.

Successful Images
111 S.W. 6th. Street
Fort Lauderdale, FL 33301
Phone: 954 467-7200
Fax: 954 467-5411
URL: http://www.successfulimages.com

Summer Kitchen Studio

Area(s) of Specialization: Animation

Number of Employees: 2+

Summer Kitchen Studio is an animation production company specializing in hand-rendered techniques including clay-on-glass, a technique that has the quality of molten stained glass, or an animated fingerpainting, stop-motion, cut-outs, xerography, and an array of other styles. The studio's work has been featured in festivals and on television worldwide. The company has been commissioned by ITVS (the Independent Television Service) to create five new animated interstitial spots for kids to be broadcast nationally on PBS children's programming.

Summer Kitchen Studio
44 Bollinger Rd.
Elverson, PA 19520
Phone: 610 286-7818
URL: http://www.netreach.net/~summerkitchen/
E-mail: summerkitchen@netreach.net

Sunbow Entertainment

Area(s) of Specialization: Children's Television Production, Animation

Number of Employees: 25

Sunbow Entertainment is a production company that makes animated children's television. The New York office consists of the management team and Los Angeles office is where the actual animation production is done. Sunbow Entertainment develops an idea, produces for sale, and distributes it all over the world, then markets it and merchandises it. A division of Sony.

Sunbow Entertainment
100 Fifth Avenue, 3rd Floor
New York, NY 10011
Phone: 212 886-4900
Fax: 212 366-4242
URL: http://www.sonymusic.com

Sunburst Technology

Area(s) of Specialization: Digital Educational Software Production and Publication

Number of Employees: 150

Sunburst Technology is a division of Houghton Mifflin Company engaged in creating and publishing teaching materials. About half of the company's products are computer-based programs for grades K-12 that include, among others, problem solving, early learning, tools, language arts, and mathematics. The remaining half of the products are video programs for grades K-12 that include conflict resolution, self esteem, drug education, sex education, and success skills.

Sunburst Technology
101 Castleton Street
Pleasantville, NY 10570
Phone: 914 747-3310
Fax: 914 747-4109
URL: http://www.sunburst.com

Susan Brand Studio, Inc./ Animation

Area(s) of Specialization: CGI, Interactive Media Design, Animation

Number of Employees: 3+

With ten years experience in traditional animation and special effects, Susan Brand formed Susan Brand Studio, Inc. in 1995 to produce design and animation for children's software. In 2000, the studio moved to Maplewood, New Jersey and offers consulting services for web-based projects.

Susan Brand Studio
82 Courter Ave.
Maplewood, NJ 07040
Phone: 973 275-9244
Fax: 973 275-4710
URL: http://www.susanbrand.com

Teleduction, Inc.

Area(s) of Specialization: Broadcast and Educational Film/Video Production and Distribution

Number of Employees: 8+ (freelance)

Teleduction, an independent production company based in Wilmington, Delaware, has produced and distributed programs to broadcast and educational audiences. Teleduction titles range in content from issue-oriented public affairs programs and cultural/historical documentaries to narrative children's programming.

The company is also producing independent programs for national audiences on PBS, Nickelodeon, A&E, The History Channel and BRAVO.

Teleduction, Inc.
305 A Street
Wilmington, DE 19801
Phone: 302 429-0303
Fax: 302 429-7534
URL: http://www.teleduction.com

Terminal Side F/X Studios

Area(s) of Specialization: Animation

Number of Employees: 5

Terminal Side F/X Studios is a freelance Computer Animation provider.

Terminal Side F/X Studios
6507 The Lakes Drive
Raleigh, NC 27609
Phone: 919 676-6959
URL: http://www.tsfx.com

Tribune Broadcasting

Area(s) of Specialization: Multimedia, CGI

Number of Employees: 40,000+

A division of Tribune Media Services, Tribune Broadcasting provides information and entertainment products to newspapers and electronic media. TMS syndicates and licenses comics, features and opinion columns, television listings, Internet, on-line and wire services, and advertising networks.

Tribune Creative Services Group
435 North Michigan Ave.
Chicago, IL 60611
Phone: 312 222-9100
Fax: 312 527-1118
URL: http://www.tribune.com

TZ-NY

Area(s) of Specialization: CGI, Interactive Multimedia, Marketing

Number of Employees: 250

For over 13 years TZ has worked in the development of network, cable and interactive marketing and communications.

TZ-NY
460 West 42nd Street
New York, NY 10036
Phone: 212 564-8888
Fax: 212 967-0691
URL: http://www.telezign.com

Unbound Studios

Area(s) of Specialization: Multimedia, CGI

Number of Employees:

Unbound works with film and television production combined with game and web design, Flash animation and programming capabilities.

Unbound Studios
242 W. 27th Street
3rd Floor
New York, NY 10001
Phone: 212 414-9866
Fax: 212 412-9068
URL: http://www.unboundstudios.com

Universal Studios

Area(s) of Specialization: Multimedia

Number of Employees: 1,000+

Universal Studios is a diversified entertainment company in motion pictures, recreation, television and home-based entertainment. Universal Studios owns Universal Music Group. Core businesses are Universal Pictures, Universal Studios Recreation Group, Universal Television and Networks Group, Universal Studios Consumer Products Group and Spencer Gifts, DAPY, GLOW!.

Universal Studios
P.O. Box 385
Burlington, MA 01803

Universal City Florida
1000 Universal Studios Plaza
Orlando, Florida 32819-7610
Phone: 407 363-8080
Fax: 407 224-7987
URL: http://www.universalstudios.com

Venture Productions

Area(s) of Specialization: Film/Video Production and Post Production

Number of Employees: 45+

Venture Productions is a Florida-based company started in 1979. Since its inception, Venture has expanded from a sole-proprietor field production company to one of the largest full-service production companies in the southeast, with a full-time staff of over 45 employees.

Venture Productions
2095 N. Andrews Ave.
Pompano Beach, FL 33069
Phone: 954 971-4100
Fax: 954 971-4090
URL: http://www.ventureproductions.com

Video Solutions

Area(s) of Specialization: Video/Film Design, Production, Marketing, and Distribution

Number of Employees: 3+

Established in 1991, Video Solutions was created to provide companies, trade associations, non-profit organizations and individuals with video production services. Headquartered in the Washington, DC Area, Video Solutions focuses on three primary communications areas: 1. Promotional & Marketing Programs including Membership, Recruiting, Fund-raisers and Public Relations programs, Direct Mail, Video Brochures, Trade Show Demos, and Broadcast & Cable TV Commercials. 2. Events and Presentations such as public speakers and presentations, video news releases, and private functions. 3. Instructional and Training Videos consisting of On-the-Job Training and Professional Development, Instructional "how to" Programs, and Issue Awareness and Public Relations pieces.

Video Solutions
P.O. Box 25484
Alexandria, VA 22313
Phone: 703 683-5305
Fax: 703 683-5307
URL: http://www.thevideosolution.com

Video Tape Associates

Area(s) of Specialization: CGI, Video Production and Post Production, Multimedia

Number of Employees: 50

Headquartered in Atlanta, VTA serves clients from advertising agencies, production companies, television stations, networks, and corporations. The Atlanta facility is a video post-production center.

Video Tape Associates
1575 Sheridan Rd. NE
Atlanta, GA 30324
Phone: 404 634-6181
Alt Phone: 800 554-8573
Fax: 404 320-9704
URL: http://www.vta.com

ViewPoint Studios

Area(s) of Specialization: Corporate Identity, Promotion, Program Graphics, Visual Effects, Animation

Number of Employees: 23

ViewPoint's team of art directors and compositing artists integrates graphics and animation with live action material to produce seamless visual effects, using technology like Flame, Hal Express, Abekas and Pluto. The animation studio also uses Maya and Alias Power Animator to create imagery.

ViewPoint Studios
140 Gould Street
Needham, MA 02494
Phone: 781 449-5858
Fax: 781 449-7272
URL: http://www.viewpointstudios.com

Vorizon Video Services

Area(s) of Specialization: Film/Video Production, Interactive Television Development

Number of Employees: 100+

Vorizon Video is a wholly owned subsidiary of Bell Atlantic that develops and markets television and communications services. Established in 1992, Bell Atlantic Video/ Vorizon Video is a developer of such interactive television services as video-on-demand and point-and-click home shopping.

Vorizon Video Services
1880 Campus Commons Dr.
Reston, VA 20191
Phone: 703-295-4100
Fax: 703-295-4546
URL: http://www.bellatlantic.com/bvs
http://www.vorizon.com

Wave Works Digital Media

Area(s) of Specialization: Television/Commercial Sound, Video Effects, Animation

Number of Employees: 25

A new media company creating sound tracks for television and radio commercial spots. The company is also equipped to do post production video effects and 3D computer animation.

Wave Works
1100 N. Glebe Rd. 100
Arlington, VA 22201
Phone: 703 527-1100
Fax: 703 527-1308

Wave Works
900 Second St. NE Suite 309
Washington, DC 20002
Phone: 202 842-7678
Fax: 202 842-0019
URL: http://www.waveworks.net

WDDG

Area(s) of Specialization: Web Design and Development

Number of Employees: 15

WDDG is a full service web architecture and design group. The company is focused on designing web sites utilizing technology such as Flash.

WDDG
80 Varick St.
New York, NY 10013
Phone: 212 219-2222
Fax: 212 219-2250
URL: http://www.wddg.com

The Weber Group

Area(s) of Specialization: Communication Multimedia

Number of Employees: 10+

The Weber Group is public relations firm specializing in immediate, interactive and information-driven new media. The Weber Group works in Marketing PR, Brand and Reputation Management, Global Public Relations Management, Public Affairs, Investor Relations, and Media and Presentation Training. The Enterprise Practice provides direct experience in running strategic-level communications programs for technology and consumer technology brands.

The Weber Group
Worldwide Headquarters
101 Main Street
Cambridge, MA 02142
Phone: 617 661-7900
Fax: 617 661-0024

The Weber Group/Greater Washington, DC Area
2300 Clarendon Blvd.
Arlington, VA 22201
Phone: 703 351-5620
Fax: 703 351-5616
URL: http://www.webergroup.com

Women Make Movies, Inc.

Area(s) of Specialization: Film/Video, Film Distribution

Number of Employees: 15

Women Make Movies is a multicultural, multiracial, non-profit media arts organization which facilitates the production, promotion, distribution and exhibition of independent films and videotapes by and about women. Women Make Movies was established in 1972 to address the under representation and misrepresentation of women in the media industry. The organization provides services to both users and makers of film and video programs, with a special emphasis on supporting work by women of color. Women Make Movies facilitates the development of feminist media

through Distribution Services and a Production Assistance Program.

Women Make Movies, Inc.
462 Broadway, 5th Floor
New York, NY 10013
Phone: 212 925-0606
Fax: 212 925-2052
URL: http://www.wmm.com

Wreckless Abandon

Area(s) of Specialization: Commercial and Entertainment Animation

Number of Employees: 20+

Wreckless Abandon Studios is a production company that specializes in clay animation, stop-motion production and 3D computer animation for the commercial and entertainment industries. The company produces non-violent family and children's programming and provides complete services including development, creative, production, effects and post-production.

Wreckless Abandon
17 Connecticut South Dr.
East Granby, CT 06026
Phone: 860 844-7090
Fax: 860 844-7095
URL: http://www.wrecklessabandon.com

XL Translab Animations

Area(s) of Specialization: Computer Animation and Modeling

Number of Employees: 3+

XL Translab Animations produces computer animation and modeling.

XL Translab Animations
1370 Piccard Drive, Suite 120
Rockville, MD 20850
Phone: 301 948-2200
Fax: 301 948-2253
URL: http://www.xltranslab.com

Zander's Animation Parlour

Area(s) of Specialization: Animation, Commercial Campaigns

Number of Employees: 2+

Zander's Animation Parlour is a commercial animation production company producing commercial campaigns. The company's client list includes Kraft, Fisher Price, 7UP, Burger King , Parker Bros., Chase Visa, HBO, Hasbro, Club Med and Cinemax and over fifty animated commercials for AT&T's ongoing " True Voices" 1996 television campaign. ZAP is recognized for 2D classical animation techniques, live action productions and special effects projects. ZAP has produced music videos for EMI Records and Def Jam Records. Zander produced "Gnomes", a 60 minute CBS TV special, as well as an AIDS

Awareness PSA campaign for the AD Council featuring Melissa Etheridge.

Zander's Animation Parlour
118 E. 25th. St.
Tenth Fl.
New York, NY 10010
Phone: 212 477-3900
Fax: 212 674-7171
URL: http://www.zandersanimation.com

Zero Degrees Kelvin

Area(s) of Specialization: Computer Animation, Design

Number of Employees: 2+

ZDK has created logos and commercials for such clients as Arm and Hammer, Johnson and Johnson and several other corporations. The company uses advanced 3D computer graphics software programs to design and create animation.

Zero Degrees Kelvin
304 Hudson St.
New York, NY 10013
Phone: 800 900-1070
Fax: 212 791-2599
URL: http://www.zerodegreeskelvin.com/

ZFx, Inc.

Area(s) of Specialization: 3D Animation for Web Sites

Number of Employees: 13

ZFx is a technology company creating 3D animation for web site. ZFx developed the OZX software, enabling the development and deployment of custom complex interactive websites and Internet-based applications.

ZFx, Inc.
999 Executive Park Blvd.,
Suite 301
Kingsport, TN 37660.
Phone: 423 378-0145
Fax: 423 378-0117
URL: http://www.zfx.com

ZKAD Productions

Area(s) of Specialization: 2D and 3D computer Animation

Number of Employees: 12

ZKAD Productions is a US based company utilizing technology and custom hardware and software to create 3D computer animation and music. The company works with broadcasters such as: the BBC, Channel 4 UK, PBS, ABC, NBC, CBS and the FOX owned BSkyB network.

ZKAD Productions
43 North Court
North East, MD 21901
Phone: 410 287-7483
Fax: 410 287-4391
URL: http://www.zkad.com

Zooma Zooma

Area(s) of Specialization: Commercials, Music Videos, Short Films

Number of Employees: 7+

A bi-coastal production company specializing in commercials, music videos and short films. Established 8 years ago, Zooma Zooma is a production company for young filmmakers to showcase talent.

Zooma Zooma
11 Mercer Street, 3rd floor
New York, NY 10013
Phone: 212 941-7680
Fax: 212 941-8179
URL: http://www.zoomazooma.com

RG/A's new media producer at the studio's recording facilities. Courtesy of Garth Gardner Photography Archive.

Central US

Adtech Animation and Graphic Design

Area(s) of Specialization: Integrated Design for Electronic Media (Web, Video, Film, Multimedia)

Number of Employees: 2

Adtech is a communications electronic media company. Technical capabilities include: particle systems and generation, image morphing, blob metamorphosis, natural phenomenon such as fog & water, lattice deformations, magnets, collisions, ray tracing with reflection, refraction and shadows, rotoscoping, bump mapping, texture mapping, environmental mapping, object metamorphosis, inverse kinematics, programmable painterly effects, glass and chrome effects, non-linear transformations, multiple object deformations, and fractals. Adtech is an SGI based studio working with a variety of 3D and 2D systems including Synergy Custom 3D Software, Houdini 3D Procedural Animation software.

Adtech Animation and Graphic Design
8220 Commonwealth Drive, Suite 201
Eden Prairie, MN 55344.
Phone: 612 944-6347

Advanced Architectural Concepts and TGWB, Inc.

Area(s) of Specialization: Computer Animation and Visualization

Number of Employees: 3

TGWB, INC. creates presentation graphics, photo-realistic animated walkthroughs, multi-media simulations, and other visual aids to visualize the three-dimensional qualities of client's projects.

Advanced Architectural Concepts and TGWB, Inc.
One N. Pennsylvania St. Suite 520
Indianapolis, IN 46204
Phone: 317 630-3110
Fax: 317 630-3112
URL: http://www.tgwb.com

Alec Syme Illustration

Area(s) of Specialization: 3D Illustration, Animation

Number of Employees: 1

Alec Syme illustrations are created digitally. The company's main tools: for 3D, Cinema 4D by Maxon, Photoshop, Illustrator on the Mac. The company is comprised of a trained artist who creates with computer technology.

Alec Syme Illustration
5051 Drew Avenue South
Minneapolis, MN 55410
Phone: 612 925-3996
Fax: 612 925.3996
URL: http://www.alecsyme.com
E-mail: alec@minn.net

Astropolitan Pictures, Inc.

Area(s) of Specialization: Digital Effects, 3D Graphics and Animation, Editing

Number of Employees: 5+

Astropolitan is a Chicago-based film and television production and post-production company that offers a range of services from digital effects and 3D computer animation to on-line editing and original music. Their staff has created visuals for projects with Sony Electronics, Coca-Cola, Motorola, MTV and Paramount Pictures.

Astropolitan Pictures, Inc.
3436 N. Halsted
Chicago, IL 60657
Phone: 773 935-7960
Fax: 773 935-7970
URL: http://www.astropolitan.com

Atomic Imaging

Area(s) of Specialization: Film/Video Production, Digital Imaging, Multimedia, CGI

Number of Employees: 12+

Atomic Imaging started in 1985 as a film and video production house in Chicago. With facilities in Chicago, Las Vegas and Barcelona, Atomic Imaging is international and full-service. The company works on feature films, national television programs and commercials, major live events, interactive multimedia, web pages, computer graphics and animation.

Atomic Imaging World Headquarters
1501 N. Magnolia Avenue
Chicago, IL 60622
Phone: 312 649-1800
Fax: 312 642-7441
URL: http://www.atomicimaging.com

Big Idea Production

Area(s) of Specialization: Children's Multimedia

Number of Employees: 168

Big Idea was founded by computer animator and storyteller Phil Vischer in July of 1993. Phil completed the first half-hour episode of "VeggieTales, Where's God When I'm S-Scared?" before Christmas, 1993. The company has now sold more than 11 million videos. Big Idea works creates home video, music and books with a focus on Christian values..

Big Idea Productions
PO Box 189
Lombard, IL 60148
Phone: 630 652-6000
Fax: 630 652-6001
URL: http://www.bigidea.com

Broadview Media

Area(s) of Specialization: Film/Video, Web Design, Satellite Feeds, Virtual Tours, Television Production

Number of Employees: 50+

With offices in Minneapolis and Chicago, Broadview Media creates content for television, radio, and the Internet. The company serves broadcast and cable networks, ad agencies, corporate clients, web developers and consumers. The company shoots, edits, adds visual effects and provides sound design, original music, and mix. The shows are viewed each week on The Discovery Channel, Home & Garden Television (HGTV), the Learning Channel, and others. The company's commercials can be seen on national TV and often during the Super Bowl.

Broadview Media, Chicago
142 E. Ontario Street
Chicago, IL 60611
Phone: 312 337-6000
Fax: 312 337-0500

Broadview Media, Minneapolis
4455 West 77th Street
Edina, MN 55435
Phone: 952 835-4455
Fax: 952 835-0971

Calabash Animation, Inc.

Area(s) of Specialization: Film and Commercial Animation

Number of Employees: 13+

Calabash Animation is a traditional character animation house specializing in cel, computer, clay, cut-paper, sand animation and more. Calabash produced some of the animation seen in the Warner Bros. feature, "Space Jam." The company has animated TV specials for CBS-owned and operated stations, 10-minute films for Encyclopedia Britannica and many TV commercials. Calabash has the USAnimation/Toon Boom software and Alias/Wavefront on a network of SGI computers.

Calabash Animation, Inc.
657 W. Ohio St.
Chicago, IL 60610-3916
Phone: 312 243-3433
Fax: 312 243-6227
URL: http://www.calabashanimation.com

Capstone Multimedia, Inc.

Area(s) of Specialization: Animated-Interactive Multimedia Presentations

Number of Employees: 2

Capstone Multimedia, Inc. is a small, Minnesota-based corporation focusing on specific digital-presentation needs and requirements. The staff illustrates, animates, films, records, writes, edits, authors, and programs multimedia to create a comprehensive, audience-focused, multimedia-presentation.

Capstone Multimedia, Inc.
1324 Highway 47
Ogilvie, MN 56358-3536
Phone: 320 272-4225
Fax: 320 272-4635
URL: http://www.at-capstone.com

Charlie Uniform Tango

Area(s) of Specialization: Digital Effects, Editing, Post Production

Number of Employees: 15

Charlie Uniform Tango is the creative editorial house owned by president/executive producer Lola Lott and vice president/senior editor Jack Waldrip. The staff includes editor Jon Price, editor Gigi Cone, visual effects artist Dave Laird, graphics editor David Slack, audio engineer Russell Smith, post producer Michele Tongate, assistant editors Keith James and Scott Hanson, editor assistants Marc Pilvinsky and Sarah Baumann, and Missey Dobbs — image & marketing. The company's clients include: PGA Tour, FootAction, Haggar, NationsBank, NCAA, Southwest Airlines, PBS, Reebok, Adidas, GTE and others.

Charlie Uniform Tango
3232 McKinney Ave.
Suite 231
Dallas, TX 75204
Phone: 214 922-9222
Fax: 214 922-9227
URL: http://www.charlietango.com

Character Builders, Inc.

Area(s) of Specialization: Animation for Feature Films (CGI), Television, and

Commercials

Number of Employees: 15-20

Character Builders is a full-service studio specializing in high-quality traditional animation for feature films, television and commercials, providing services such as: animation, storyboarding, sequence direction, design and animation assist, as well as project development and direction. The company's credits include: "Space Jam", "The Swan Princess", "Bebe's Kids", "Betty Boop", "A Goffy Movie", "The Ren and Stimpy Show", "The Quest for Camelot" and others.

Character Builders
1476 Manning Pkwy
Powell, OH 43065
Phone: 614 885-2211
Fax: 614 885-3873
URL: http://www.cbuilders.com

The Creegan Company

Area(s) of Specialization: Animation,
Costume Characters, Audio

Number of Employees: 20

The Creegan Company creates animated
settings for Christmas, Halloween and Easter
as well as other seasonal special events. Some
of the company's clientele has included:
Disney World, Sea World, Hershey's Chocolate
World, shop designs for casinos like
Excalibur and the Venitian in Las Vegas. The
company, whose specialty is animation and
costumes, has a staff that produces
animation not only mechanically powered
and controlled but can also animate displays
and characters that are computer controlled
and pneumatically driven. The staff works in
mechanical, carpentry, costuming and
artistic finishing.

The Creegan Company
508 Washington Street.
Stubenville, OH 43952
Phone: 740 283-3708
Fax: 740 283-4117
URL: http://www.weir.net/-creegans.com
E-mail: creegans@weir.net

Da Vinci Motion Graphics, LLC

Area(s) of Specialization: 3D Stills and
Animation

Number of Employees: 6

Da Vinci Motion Graphics provides
computer-rendered 3D still images and
animation to the advertising, video-
production, engineering, architectural, and
legal communities.

Da Vinci Motion Graphics
7012 NW 63rd Street, Suite 201
Bethany, OK 73008
Phone: 405 972-2262
Fax: 405 971-1723
URL: http://www.dvmg.com

Digital DK Studios

Area(s) of Specialization: Web Site Design
and Development

Number of Employees: 6+

Digital DK provides consultation for many
digital and graphic design projects,
particularly in website design and
development.

Digital DK Studios
9350 South Western St.
Oklahoma City, OK 73159
Phone: 405 413-5588

Fax: 405 703-8069
URL: http://www.digitaldk.com

DNA Productions, Inc.

Area(s) of Specialization: 2D and 3D Characters, Special Effects, Computer Graphics

Number of Employees: 100

DNA Productions, Inc. is a full-service animation company that has operated in Dallas, Texas since 1987, serving the entertainment and commercial markets by providing 2D and 3D character design and animation. In addition, DNA is a creative resource providing script writing, directing and producing for animated series and features. DNA has contributed animation to a range of projects, including Roseanne's "Saturday Night Special" (Fox Television), "The Weird Al Show" (CBS), "steve.oedekerk.com" (NBC) and "Nanna & Lil' Puss Puss" (Showtime, Comedy Central, MTV). DNA utilizes both hand-drawn art and computer graphics. The traditional hand-drawn (2D) animation process is optimized through the use of digital ink & paint and compositing by the USAnimation System software running on SGI computers. LightWave 3D software running on Carrera and Intergraph workstations is used to animate 3D characters.

DNA Productions, Inc.
2201 West Royal Lane, Suite 275
Irving, TX 75063
Phone: 214 352-4694
Fax: 214 496-9333
URL: http://www.dnahelix.com

Dreamscape Design, Inc.

Area(s) of Specialization: Digital Video, Web Services, 3D Graphics and Animation

Number of Employees: 10

Formerly known as Admakers Multimedia, Dreamscape Design Inc. has been providing proactive hi-tech marketing solutions since 1981. In addition to 3D graphics and hi-tech programming, the company consults with clients on a variety of marketing and networking solutions.

Dreamscape Design, Inc.
Corporate Headquarters
1 Henson Place Suite A
Champaign, IL 61821
Phone: 217 359-8484
Fax: 217 239-5858
URL: http://www.dreamscapedesign.com

EDR Media

Area(s) of Specialization: Film and Video Production and Post Production

Number of Employees: 10+

EDR is a group of technology professionals who design and implement integrated hardware and software systems.

EDR Media
23330 Commerce Park Rd.
Cleveland, Ohio 44122
Phone: 216 292-7300
Fax: 216 292-0545
URL: http://www.edr.com

Fearless Eye, Inc.

Area(s) of Specialization: Animation, Visual Effects for Film/Video/Multimedia

Number of Employees: 5

Fearless Eye was founded in 1992 to produce high resolution animation and digital graphics for the commercial, film, entertainment and multimedia industries. Projects range from creating articulated character animation to virtual environments.

Core services include: 2D and 3D animation, visual effects for television and film, simulations & reconstructions, and multimedia CD-ROM's and web page design. Other production capabilities include: character animation, digital compositing, rotoscoping, blue screen, simulations, custom modeling and non-linear film and video production.

Fearless Eye, Inc.
308 W 8th 208
Kansas City, MO 64105

Phone: 816 221-1047
Alt Phone: 800 729-6939
Fax: 816 221-2775
URL: http://www.fearlesseye.com

Fischer Edit

Area(s) of Specialization: Post Production, Advertising

Number of Employees: 15

Fischer Edit is a full service, creative post production facility specializing in film-originated television commercials. Founded in 1991, Fischer Edit works in non-linear off-line editing, special effects work, and finishing.

Fischer Edit
42 South 12th Street
Minneapolis, MN
Phone: 612 332-4914
Fax: 612 332-4910
URL: http://www.fischeredit.com

Gathering of Developers, Inc.

Area(s) of Specialization: Computer and Video Game Publisher

Number of Employees: 20-30

Gathering of Developers, a Texas-based computer and video game publishing company, was founded in January, 1998 to service independent game developers. The

Gathering offers marketing campaigns and a sliding scale royalty rate based on unit sales.

Gathering of Developers, Inc.
2700 Fairmount St.
Dallas, TX 75201
Phone: 214 880-0001
Alt Phone: 887 463-4263
Fax: 214 871-7934
URL: http://www.godgames.com

GenneX Health Technologies

Area(s) of Specialization: Multimedia and Web Development in the Medical Field

Number of Employees: 10

GenneX Healthcare Technologies offers the full range of internet services to health and medical organizations. Incorporated in 1994, GenneX is involved in internet and health information.

GenneX Health Technologies
2201 W. Campbell Park Dr. #226
Chicago, IL 60612.
Phone: 312 226-6750
Fax: 312 226-6755.
URL: http://www.gennexhealth.com
E-mail: gennex@gennexhealth.com.

Ghost Productions, Inc.

Area(s) of Specialization: Animation, Post Production, Effects Design

Number of Employees: 10+

Commercial Production: Artists at Ghost Productions Inc. create storyboards and animatics then shoot, edit, animate and create all the necessary effects to complete their client's commercials. Litigation: with animation the company explains the insides and workings of an unsafe product and replay an accident multiple times with unlimited camera angles. Tissue, bone and instruments: animation can be used to explain surgical procedures, implants and educate patients. Web Casting: Add Flash, Shockwave, Fireworks, Quicktime movies and animation to clients' web sites for added appeal. The company can optimize and compress video and animation to playback efficiently on virtually any server. Interactive DVD, CD-ROM, and HTML can be scripted with completely interactive interfaces.

Ghost Productions, Inc.
7616 Currell Blvd. Suite 150
Woodbury, MN 55125
Phone: 651 702-4088
URL: http://www.ghostproductions.com

Gourmet Images

Area(s) of Specialization: Media Production

Number of Employees: 3

Gourmet Images is a high-end visual media shop to handle projects from inception to duplication, or handle any of the elements in between such as corporate informational or motivational videos, music videos, broadcast television programs and commercials, CD-ROM authoring or web page design. The staff consists of writers, producers, directors, DP's, sound recordists, editors, graphic designers and animators.

Gourmet Images
144 N. 38th Ave.
Omaha, NE 68131-2302
Phone: 402 558-4985
Fax: 402 556-3646
URL: http://www.gourmet-images.com

Grace & Wild Digital Studios

Area(s) of Specialization: Teleproduction for Commercial, Broadcast, and Communication Markets

Number of Employees: 215

Grace & Wild Digital Studios specializes in teleproduction services for the commercial, broadcast and corporate communications markets. Located in Studio Center, Grace & Wild Digital Studios offer clients a range of services, including: Video Camera Packages, Three Sound Stages, Teleconferencing and Two-Way Fiber Optic Feeds, Satellite Uplinks and Downlinks, Advanced Film Transfer and Color Enhancement Capabilities, Graphics and Animation Capabilities, including Computer, Cel and Clay Animation, Component Digital On-line Editing, Multi-

format On-line Editing, Avid Off-line and On-line Non-linear Editing, and Video Duplication and Standards Conversion.

Grace & Wild Digital Studios
23689 Industrial Park Drive
Framington Hills, MI 48335
Phone: 800 451-6010
Fax: 248 471-2312
URL: http://www.gwstudio.com

Green Rabbit Design Studio, Inc.

Area(s) of Specialization: 2D and 3D Animation, Traditional Animation, Digital Effects

Number of Employees: 6

Green Rabbit has been producing animation for the past 5 years. Green Rabbit produces 2D and 3D animation, traditional (character) cel animation and special effects for video. Production equipment includes Quantel's Hal express (with transform fx) as well as Silicon graphics, Alias Power Animator, Softimage, Liberty and Elastic Reality. Additionally, the company utilizes several Macintosh workstations with Photoshop, Adobe Illustrator, QuarkXpress and Animation Stand. Clients include Small But Mighty Films, Riester Corporation and Regional Public Transit Authority's Clean Air Campaign.

Green Rabbit Design Studio, Inc.
7229 E. First. Ave. Ste. C
Scottsdale, AZ 85251
Phone: 602 425-9003
Alt Phone: 800 804-2005
URL: http://www.greenrabbit.com

HDMG Digital Post & Effects

Area(s) of Specialization: Post Production,
Digital Effects

Number of Employees: 12+

HDMG offers direct operator contact in post
production and digital effects.

HDMG Digital Post & Effects
6573 City West Parkway
Minneapolis, MN
Phone: 612 943-1711
Fax: 612 943-1957
URL: http://www.hdmg.com

HD Vision, Inc.

Area(s) of Specialization: CGI, Multimedia,
Film/Video, High Definition Television

Number of Employees: 6+ (freelance)

Since March of 1993 HD Vision has been
working with producers, directors and
corporations in the broadcast, entertainment,
advertising and product marketing
industries. Equipment and staff includes
single-camera and multi-camera mobiles on

the road to create high quality pictures for
clients while including choices such as:
analog or digital technology, CCD or tube
cameras, pre-production planning; multi-
camera location work, post-production,
electronic graphics, HDTV engineering and
production seminars, custom interface
equipment and network origination.

HD Vision, Inc.
6305 N. O'Connor Rd., Suite 126
Irving, TX 75039-3507
Phone: 972 432-9630
Fax: 972 869-2516
URL: http://www.hdvision.com

Hellman Associates, Inc.

Area(s) of Specialization: Design, Illustration,
Animation, Marketing

Number of Employees: 30

Hellman Associates, Inc., was founded in
1967 as a design house and expanded to
incorporate illustration and animation. The
organization is a full-service marketing and
advertising agency serving national and
international clients. Locations include:
Waterloo, Des Moines, Dubuque, and
Newton, Iowa; and Minneapolis, Minnesota.
Hellman Associates, Inc., employs individuals
in the areas of marketing, creative, and
support services.

Hellman Associates, Inc.
1225 W. Fourth St.

Waterloo, Iowa 50702
Phone: 319 234-7055
Fax: 319 234-2089
URL: http://www.hellman.com

Human Code, Inc.

Area(s) of Specialization: Digital Content, Animation, Audio, Film/Video

Number of Employees: 300+

Human Codes Inc. have been providing custom e-commerce, smart toys, learning systems and on-line marketing communications for the entertainment industry, educators, and entrepreneurs since 1993. The company works in the internet, computer, broadband, iTV and wireless media.

Human Code (Austin Studios)
319 Congress Ave.
Suite 100
Austin, Texas 78701
Phone: 512 477-5455
Fax: 512 477-5456
URL: http://www.humancode.com

Imageworks Computer Graphics Imaging, Inc.

Area(s) of Specialization: Graphics, Computer Animation, Interactive Multimedia, Web Site Design

Number of Employees: 50

Imageworks Computer Graphics Imaging Inc. was established in 1995 in Austin, Texas, and specializes in web site design and technology solutions. Imageworks offers clients complete project development capability in web site design and development, interactive multimedia authoring, and graphic art design.

Imageworks Computer Graphics Imaging, Inc.
PO Box 80083
Austin, Texas 78708-0083
Phone: 512 832-8664
URL: http://www.imageworkscgi.com

Innervision Productions, Inc.

Area(s) of Specialization: 2D and 3D Graphics, Video and Audio, Web Design and Interactive CD-ROM Design

Number of Employees: 32

Innervision Productions, Inc. creates 2D and 3D graphics in addition to traditional video, audio and Multimedia.

Innervision Productions, Inc.
11783 Borman Dr.
St. Louis, MO 63146
Phone: 314 569-2500
Fax: 314 569-3534
URL: http://www.innervis.com

Intelecon

Area(s) of Specialization: Digital Editing, 2D and 3D Animation, Specializing in presentations for trade shows and other events

Number of Employees: 85

Intelecon Services Inc., headquartered in Dallas, provides business communications technology and producer services, audio-visual rentals, sales, installations and staging services. The company offers turnkey solutions for productions, concerts, corporate events, tradeshows and multimedia. Services include Stereoscopic 3D, 2D and 3D animation, on-line and off-line nonlinear uncompressed digital editing, special effects, 3D visualizations, audio, lighting, rigging, video walls, large screen and panoramic projection.

Intelecon
8818 John W. Carpenter Fwy.
Dallas, TX 75247
Phone: 214 571-0622
Alt Phone: 800 466-9125
Fax: 214 571-0100
URL: http://www.intelecon.com

Janimation, Inc.

Area(s) of Specialization: 3D Animation, Design, Visual Effects

Number of Employees: 9

Janimation offers full production services and effects supervision from pre-production through finishing. Janimation's network of Silicon Graphics, Intergraph NT workstations, and Power Macs connects the animators, designers and compositors. Graphics cards provide animators with instant feedback, which enable further experimentation, softer shadows and motion blur.

Janimation, Inc.
840 Exposition Avenue.
Dallas, TX 75226
Phone: 214 823-7760
Fax: 214 823-7761
URL: http://www.janimation.com

Juntunen Media Group

Area(s) of Specialization: Post Production, DVD Authoring, Graphics, Special Effects

Number of Employees: 45

Juntunen Media Group is an integrated media development firm located in Minneapolis, working in media, internet, video and print.

Juntunen Media Group
708 N. First St.
Minneapolis, MN 55401
Phone: 612 341-3348
Alt Phone: 800 535-4366
Fax: 612 341-0242
URL: http://www.juntunen.com

Kaleidoscope Animation, Inc.

Area(s) of Specialization: 3D Modeling and Animation, Training, Professional Support

Number of Employees: 35

Kaleidoscope Animations works in high-end 3D animation applications and modeling tools. The company provides storyboards to the final render.

Kaleidoscope Animation, Inc.
23625 Commerce Park Rd.
Suite 130
Beachwood, OH 44122
Phone: 216 360-0630
Fax: 216 360-9109
URL: http://www.kascope.com
http://www.dinerinc.com

Lamb and Company

Area(s) of Specialization: 2D and 3D Computer Animation, CGI, Traditional Cel Animation

Number of Employees: 10

Based in Minneapolis, Minnesota, Lamb & Company has created imagery for television, film, video, games, rides, and forensic presentations. Lamb & Company combines techniques such as 2D and 3D computer animation with cel animation and live action.

Lamb and Company
2429 Nicollet Avenue
Minneapolis, MN 55404

Phone: 612 872-1000
Fax: 612 879-5776
URL: http://www.lamb.com

Laredo Productions, Inc.

Area(s) of Specialization: Film/Video, Multimedia

Number of Employees: 25+

Laredo can post for digital broadcast television, as well as the 4:3 digital and analog formats and 16:9 widescreen DTV. In addition to high-end video post, the company accommodates complete off-line post production for film projects, providing frame-accurate EDLs for negative cutters and optical houses.

Laredo Productions, Inc.
3080 N. Civic Center Plaza
Suite 45
Scottsdale, AZ 85251-7932
Phone: 480 947-5255
Fax: 480 947-5285
URL: http://www.laredoproductions.com

Leaping Lizards, Ltd.

Area(s) of Specialization: Digital Film and Video, Interactive CD-ROM and DVD authoring, Web Design

Number of Employees: 2 (plus freelancing)

Leaping Lizards, Ltd. is a Design, Effects and Animation Studio, located in Southfield, Michigan, working with advertising, marketing and corporate communications companies. Leaping Lizards' staff creates graphics, animation, & interactive content for Digital Video & Film, Interactive CD/DVD, Internet and Print. Leaping Lizards offers a proprietary Digital Graphics System which features networking of Quantel Paintbox, Accom DDR, Power PC Macintoshes, NT and Silicon Graphic work stations. The company specializes in cross-platform motion graphics for high-end video, interactive and web design.

Leaping Lizards, Ltd.
29829 Greenfield Rd., Ste. 103
Southfield, MI 48076
Phone: 248 423-9311
Fax: 248 423-7945
URL: http://www.leapinglizards.com

Level 5

Area(s) of Specialization: Corporate ID/ Logos, Design Visualization, Virtual Reality, Character Animation

Number of Employees: 1+

Level 5 produces and processes digital content that can be delivered via analog and digital video (television, videocassette, VR theme ride, VRML, Internet/Intranet, CD-ROM, DVD, DV), analog and digital stills and presentations (charts, graphs, prints, Internet/Intranet, Powerpoint), and analog or digital music (cassette, Internet/Intranet, MIDI).

Level 5
PO Box 388
Fargo, ND 58107-0388
Phone: 701 232-1295
URL: http://www.level5.com
E-mail: mail@level5.com

LiveWire Marketing, Inc.

Area(s) of Specialization: CGI, Multimedia

Number of Employees: 18

Livewire Marketing Inc. offers comprehensive marketing services for helping clients develop, implement, and manage Web marketing strategies.

LiveWire Marketing, Inc.
4814 Washington Blvd, Suite 300
St Louis, MO 63108
Phone: 314 361-8500
Fax: 314 361-0500
URL: http://www.lwm.com
E-mail: info@lwm.com

Match Frame Post Production

Area(s) of Specialization: Graphics, Telecine, Post Production, Interactive DVD Authoring

Number of Employees: 35 (plus freelance)

Match Frame is a digital production company. The company has capabilities in Telecine, Graphics, Post Production and Interactive DVD Authoring.

Match Frame Post Production
8531 Fairhaven
San Antonio, TX 78229
Phone: 210 614-5678
Alt Phone: 800 929-2790
Fax: 210 616-0299
URL: http://www.matchframe.com

Maximillion Zillion Animation

Area(s) of Specialization: Long Form Cel Animation, Concept/Scripting and Video Production

Number of Employees: 3

Maximillion Zillion Animation has been providing cel animation since 1990. Hand drawn frames and custom character creations along with concept, scripting, and production are all available as a turnkey package. Storyboards are supplied to establish a concrete visual preview, or animation can be drawn from storyboards and characters.

Maximillion Zillion Animation
502 State St.
St. Louis, MO 39520

Phone: 228 463-0612
Fax: 228 463-0616
URL: http://www.mzanimation.com

Mere Productions, Inc.

Area(s) of Specialization: Virtual Environments, 3D Visualization and Animation, Interactive Media Design

Number of Employees: 5-10

Mere Productions designs and creates virtual environments for motion pictures, television and interactive games, 3D models, animation and real-time interaction.

Mere Productions, Inc.
P.O. Box 8682
Austin, Texas 78713
Phone: 512 303-5036
Fax: 512 303-7098
URL: http://www.mere3d.com

Midway Games Inc.

Area(s) of Specialization: Video Game Design and Development

Number of Employees: 300+

Midway Games Inc. develops and manufactures coin-operated arcade and home video game entertainment products. Midway publishes video games for Nintendo, Sega, Sony and personal computer platforms. The Midway and Atari brands have generated games such as Pong, Defender, Missile Command, Pac-Man, Centipede, NBA Jam, Cruis'n USA, and Mortal Kombat. Midway is based in Chicago, Illinois. Midway Home Entertainment has offices in Corsicana, Texas and San Diego, California. Atari Games is based in Milpitas, California.

Midway Games Inc.
3401 N. California Avenue
Chicago, IL 60618
Fax: 773 961-2376
URL: http://www.midway.com

Mirage Digital

Area(s) of Specialization: Virtual Modeling, 3D Design, Sound

Number of Employees: 4

Mirage Digital is a creative/technical design and implementation service company for broadcast, entertainment, corporate and live shows. Housed in the Great Scott Studio center, a commercial post production facility in Phoenix, AZ, the company provides the video and show market with virtual set, 3D high resolution video and surround sound technology.

Mirage Digital
Great Scott Studio Center
834 North 7th. Ave.
Phoenix, AZ 85007
Phone: 602 254-1600

Fax: 602 495-9949
URL: http://www.miragedigital.com

Network Century / Cinema Video

Area(s) of Specialization: Network Services, Programming, Web Development, Production, Post Production, Duplication

Number of Employees: 45

Network Century has acquired Cinema Video, a film and video production house. The company works in multimedia and video broadcast.

Network Century
211 E. Grand Ave.
Chicago, IL 60611
Phone: 312 644-1650
Fax: 312 644-2096
URL: http://www.networkcentury.com

Nvision, Inc.

Area(s) of Specialization: E-Commerce Solutions

Number of Employees: 300+

Nvision, Inc. provides 3D products and services for animation, visual effects, game development, reverse engineering, rapid prototyping, and inspection/gaging. Nvision has proprietary and patented tools and works with clients such as Digital Domain, Dream Quest, Disney, Interplay, Hughes Christensen, and Northrop-Grumman.

Nvision, Inc.
1400 Turtle Creek Blvd
Suite 209
Dallas, TX 75207
Phone: 214 752-0007
Fax: 214 752-0018
URL: http://www.nvision.com

Omni Studio, Inc.

Area(s) of Specialization: Graphic Design, Illustration, Animation, Multimedia

Number of Employees: 7

Omni Studio, Inc. offers graphic design, illustration, animation, and production art. The company's clients include industries in the areas of sports and leisure, electronics, computer technology, wood products, health care, food products and travel.

Omni Studio, Inc.
603 West Franklin Street
Boise, Idaho 83702
Phone: 208 344-1332
Fax: 208 344-1878
URL: http://www.gotoomni.com

Oops Animation, Inc.

Area(s) of Specialization: 2D and 3D Graphics and Animation

Number of Employees: 8

Oops Animation Inc. located in Minnesota and has a 3D animation, graphics and special effects facility. Software programs include: Maya, PowerAnimator, Alias, Softimage, 3D Studio Max, Flint, Composer and Adobe After Effects. For visual marketing objectives comprehension, Oops Animation offers 3D animation and special effects for television commercials, sales messages or the improvement of technical training.

Oops Animation, Inc.
600 Washington Ave. North, Suite B103
Minneapolis, MN 55401
Phone: 612 340-9598
Fax: 612 340-9601
URL: http://www.oopsanimation.com

Paradigm Productions

Area(s) of Specialization: 3D Computer Graphics, Animation, Multimedia

Number of Employees: 2

Paradigm Productions, LLC of Memphis, Tennessee, was founded in March of 1992 to provide 3D computer graphics and animation services. The company also produces medical visualization, exhibit design, television, video production, legal reenactments, and interactive multimedia.

Paradigm Productions
5124 Poplar Avenue, Suite 106
Memphis, Tennessee 38117
Phone: 901 685-7703
URL: http://www.2dimes.com

Picturestart

Area(s) of Specialization: 3D Design and Animation for Video/Film

Number of Employees: 1+

Picturestart works in the areas of animation, compositing, design and editorial projects.

Picturestart
5060 Addison Circle, Suite 2836
Addison, TX 75001
Phone: 972 490-6351
Fax: 972 490-6352
URL: http://www.picturestart.com

Pixel Farm

Area(s) of Specialization: Graphic Design/Special Effects, Advertising

Number of Employees: 15

Pixel Farm specializes in special effects, compositing, graphic design, and film transfer, for broadcast and corporate projects: Clients include Harley Davidson,

ABC, Best Buy, Kmart, Target, VH-1, Ocean Spray, and Hostess.

Pixel Farm
251 First Avenue North
Minneapolis, MN 55401
Phone: 612 339-7644
Fax: 612 339-7551
URL: http://www.pixelfarm.com

PopTop Software, Inc.

Area(s) of Specialization: Computer Strategy Game Development and Production

Number of Employees: 20+

PopTop Software Inc. is a developer of computer strategy games. In 1998, PopTop released Railroad Tycoon II, and several follow-ups and ports have followed in the last 2 years. PopTop is currently primarily focused on the game Tropico.

PopTop Software Inc.
1714 Gilsinn
Fenton, MO 63026
Phone: 214 303-1202
URL: http://www.poptop.com

Red Car

Area(s) of Specialization: Film/Video

Number of Employees: 24+

Red Car Dallas consists of graphics artists, sound designers, type stylists, & special effects personnel, working in film and video. Clients include: Wieden & Kennedy, Leo Burnett (leoburnett.com), and Young & Rubicam (yandr.com).

Red Car-Dallas
2600 Hibernia St.
Dallas, TX 75204
Phone: 214 954-1996
Fax: 214 954-4499
URL: http://www.redcar.com

Red Car-Chicago
455 e. Illinois
Suite 370
Chicago, IL 60611
Phone: 312 645-1888
Fax: 312 645-1866
URL: http://www.redcar.com

Reel FX Creative Solutions

Area(s) of Specialization: Animation, CGI, Multimedia, Film/Video

Number of Employees: 20+

Reel FX Creative Studios produces, concepts, creates, animates, composites, edits, sound designs and mixes for TV, HDTV, and Film.

Reel FX Creative Solutions
2211 N. Lamar
Suite 100
Dallas, TX 75202
Phone: 214 979-0961

Alt Phone: 214 632-2188
Fax: 214 979-0963
URL: http://www.reelfx.com

Reelworks Animation Studio

Area(s) of Specialization: 2D Animation

Number of Employees: 10+

Reelworks Animation Studio, Inc. is a full service traditional animation studio specializing in the commercial production of character animation, moving illustration and animation combined with live action. Reelworks Animation studio has been creating character-driven animated spots since 1979, using a painterly hand-done style. The studio has created spots for clients like Coca Cola, Time Magazine, and Hersheys.

Reelworks Animation Studio
318 Cedar Avenue South
Suite 300
Minneapolis, MN 55454
Phone: 612 333-5063
Fax: 612 333-7970
URL: http://www.reelworks.com

Spyglass, Inc.

Area(s) of Specialization: Providing Web Software and Services

Number of Employees: 200+

Spyglass is a provider of strategic Internet consulting, software and professional services for content providers, service operators and device manufacturers. Spyglass Professional Services provides consulting for defining, developing and delivering complete, end-to-end projects.

Spyglass, Inc.
1240 E. Diehl Rd.
Naperville, IL 60563
Phone: 630 505-1010
Fax: 630 505-4944
URL: http://www.spyglass.com

Strictly FX

Area(s) of Specialization: Laser Production, Special Effects.

Number of Employees: 15+

Strictly FX is a company that designs, implements, and produces live special effects. Its commitment is to transparently design and perform shows for an event, completely in-house.

Strictly FX
213 W. Institute Place
Suite 505
Chicago, IL 60610
Phone: 312 255-0305
Fax: 312 255-0306
URL: http://www.strictlyfx.com

Technisonic Studios

Area(s) of Specialization: Film/Video, CGI, Multimedia, Animation, Sound

Number of Employees: 25

Technisonic Studios develops high-concept audio and visual media for television, radio, the Internet, film, corporate videos, DVD, CD-ROM and kiosks for clients across the United States and in Europe. The company's staff includes sound designers, graphic artists, editors, cinematographers, animators, producers, computer programmers, engineers and support staff.

Technisonic Studios
500 S. Ewing
Suite G
St. Louis, MO 63103
Phone: 314 533-1777
Fax: 314 533-6527
URL: http://www.technisonic.com

There TV

Area(s) of Specialization: Film/video

Number of Employees: 10

There TV consists of broadcast designers, animation directors and digital artists working in film and video.

There TV
1351 West Grand Avenue
Chicago, IL 60622
Phone: 312 421-0400

Fax: 312 421-1915
URL: http://www.theretv.com

Tribune Media Services

Area(s) of Specialization: Syndicated Comic Strips and Web Concepts

Number of Employees: 100+

TMS is a provider of information and entertainment products to newspapers and electronic media. TMS syndicates and licenses comics, features and opinion columns, television listings, Internet, on-line and wire services, and advertising networks.

Tribune Media Services
435 N. Michigan Ave.
Suite 510
Chicago, IL 60611
Phone: 312 222-9100
URL: http://www.tribune.com

Tricky Pictures

Area(s) of Specialization: CGI and Animation for Television Commercials

Number of Employees: 26

Tricky Pictures is a production studio specializing in stop motion animation and live action special effects. The company designs and produces television commercials, television broadcast design, music videos, and short films.

Tricky Pictures
720 N. Franklin, Ste. 400
Chicago, IL 60610
Phone: 312 944-7400
URL: http://www.trickytricky.com

Trinity Animation & Visual Effects

Area(s) of Specialization: Animation and Visual Effects

Number of Employees: 3

Trinity offers services relating to modifying captured images, creating new 3D environments and characters, and combining live action with computer-generated imagery. Trinity has created animation and visual effects for national audiences, including broadcast television and major motion pictures. The company has experience with motion morphs, painterly effects, wire-removal and combining separately filmed pyrotechnics with live action. It can put live action into a 3D rendered scene, or mix 3D animated characters with live action.

Trinity Animation & Visual Effects
676 SE Bayberry Lane, Suite 103B
Lee's Summit, MO 64063-4389
Phone: 800 548-1578
Fax: 816 525-1594
URL: http://www.trinity3d.com

TUV Productions RRR by ABC of Film

Area(s) of Specialization: Animation, Film/Video, Multimedia, CGI

Number of Employees: 5+

A motion-picture-making-company working in the world of cinematography, animation and movie-making, computer-graphics web design and media.

TUV Productions RRR by ABC of Film
4410 Clayburn Dr.
Indianapolis, IN 46268
Phone: 317 872-FILM
Fax: 317 872 -3456

Vidox Image and Data

Area(s) of Specialization: Commercial Films/Videos, Interactive Multimedia

Number of Employees: 10

Vidox Image & Data has been creating commercials, documentaries and industrial videos since 1982. The company specializes in communicating through on-screen presentation and the computer and video skills converge when producing for interactive formats such as live presentation, electronic product kiosks, and World Wide Web pages.

Vidox Image and Data
1223 St. John Street

Lafayette, LA 70506
Phone: 337 237-1700
Fax: 337 237-1712
URL: http://www.vidox.com
E-mail: chris@vidox.com

Virtual Pictures Company

Area(s) of Specialization: Graphic Design, 3D Design

Number of Employees: 5+

VPC designs and authors CD-ROM titles, websites, 3D animation and motion graphics for the corporate, broadcast, and motion picture industries. The company also composes musical compositions for client's projects.

Virtual Pictures Company
1438 W. Broadway Rd.
Ste. B-210
Tempe, AZ 85282
Phone: 480 894-0607
URL: http://www.virtualpictures.com
E-mail: vpc@virtualpicture.com

Visuality LLC

Area(s) of Specialization: Web design, Storyboards, Scripts, Interactive Media Production

Number of Employees: 5

Visuality functions as a full service preproduction, post production, and interactive design (web sites CD-ROM). Visuality provides preproduction services such as script writing, storyboards, concept development, casting, and production services such as location shooting, lighting, green screen and audio, and post production services such as off-line non-linear editing, on-line editing, 3D computer graphics and media design. In addition it provides interactive services such as web design and CD ROM development.

Visuality LLC
5980 Executive Dr., Suite A
Madison, WI 53719
Phone: 608 271-3305
Fax: 608 271-3328
URL: http://www.visuality.com

VT/TV Graphics and Post

Area(s) of Specialization: Post Production

Number of Employees: 16

VT/TV provides visual effects, editing, 3D animation, turnkey production and/or complete project management.

VT/TV Graphics and Post
5120 Woodway, Suite 9011
Houston, TX 77056
Phone: 713 877-1877
Fax: 713 877-8002
URL: http://www.vt-tv.com

Webpromotions, Inc.

Area(s) of Specialization: Web Site Design and Development, Corporate Identity, Logos, Illustration, Animation for Broadcast

Number of Employees: 6

Webpromotion conveys a client's image through the design of websites, logos, ad banners, graphics and animations. Webpromotion's animation projects for video have been used in broadcast television, at national conventions and in corporate video productions.

Webpromotions, Inc.
7740 29th Avenue
Kenosha, Wisconsin 53143
Phone: 262 605-1201
URL: http://www.webpromotion.com
E-mail: video@webpromotion.com

Winner Communications, Inc.

Area(s) of Specialization: Television Broadcast

Number of Employees: 100

Founded in 1981, Winner Communications originally produced syndicated Quarter horse racing telecasts. Winner now produces a variety of programming for ESPN, ESPN2, and numerous local and regional television outlets. Winner production personnel have contributed to telecasts of major events such as the Olympic Games, the Breeders' Cup, Major League Soccer's championship game (MLS Cup), and Thoroughbred racing's Triple Crown. Winner Communications is a full-service television production and multimedia company.

Winner Communications Inc.
6120 South Yale
Tulsa, OK 74136
Phone: 918 496-1900
Fax: 918 494-3786
URL: http://www.winnercomm.com

Cel animator at Curious Pictures in New York on the production of HBO's "A Little Curious." Courtesy of Garth Gardner Photography Archive.

Inking a scene at Curious Pictures for HBO's "A Little Curious." Courtesy of Garth Gardner Photography Archive.

West Coast

525 Studios

Area(s) of Specialization: Digital Effects Design and Post Production Services

Number of Employees: 40

525 Studios provides high-end Digital Effects Design and Post Production Services. Clients include agencies and directors involved in advertising, music, television, feature films, and new media. The company's services include: pre-production planning/ visual effects design, on-location supervision / shoot consultation, telecine transfers in NTSC/PAL, HD and 2K, 2D & 3D effects and compositing, and editing. 525's equipment includes: 5 Infernos, 2 Henrys running Infinity, an Avid Editing bay, 2 Spirit HD Telecines, and a CGI lab.

525 Studios
1632 5th St.
Santa Monica, CA 90401
Phone: 310 525-1234
Fax: 310 525-2501
URL: http://www.525studios.com

Academy of Television Arts & Sciences

Area(s) of Specialization: Film/Video, Multimedia

Number of Employees: 50+

The Academy of Television Arts & Sciences, founded in 1946, is a non-profit corporation devoted to the advancement of telecommunications arts and sciences and to fostering creative leadership in the telecommunications industry. In addition the Academy is involved in recognizing outstanding programming and individual, engineering achievements for Primetime and Los Angeles Area programming, ATAS sponsors meetings, conferences and activities for collaboration on a variety of topics involving traditional broadcast interests, new media and emerging digital technology. The Academy publishes Emmy magazine, produces the ATAS Hall of Fame and through the ATAS Foundation, is responsible for the ATAS Archive of American Television (AAT), ATAS/UCLA Television Archives, ATAS Foundation Library at USC, College Television Awards, the Internship Program, S.T.A.R.T. Communications, the Visiting Artists Program and the Faculty Seminar.

Academy of Television Arts & Sciences
5220 Lankershim Blvd.
North Hollywood, CA 91601-3109
Phone: 818 754-2830

Fax: 818 761-2827
URL: http://www.emmys.org

Aces Research, Inc.

Area(s) of Specialization: Multimedia, CGI, Software Development

Number of Employees: 5

Aces Research, Inc. (Aces), founded in 1993, designs, develops, and markets Windows and Macintosh multimedia software for consumers, educators, librarians, and distributors worldwide. Aces has in-house development staff of product managers, programmers, graphic designers, interface specialists, curriculum design specialists, and authoring experts.

Aces Research, Inc.
46750 Fremont Blvd. 107
Fremont, CA 94538
Phone: 510 683-8855
Fax: 510 683-8875
URL: http://www.acesxprt.com

Acme Filmworks Animation

Area(s) of Specialization: Animation, CGI, Multimedia

Number of Employees: 25

Acme Filmworks is an animation production house located in Hollywood, California. Acme offers animation styles and techniques including Stop Motion, Typography, Photo Collage, Design, Traditional Character Animation and Computer Graphics. Acme has produced commercials, identifiers, title sequences and short subjects for a host of corporations and organizations such as AT&T, Nabisco, Starbucks, NBC, Levi's, Weight Watchers, Nike, Coca-Cola, Toyota, Reebok, Amnesty International, Walt Disney, and Universal Pictures.

Acme Filmworks Animation
6525 Sunset Blvd. #10
Hollywood, CA 90028
Phone: 323 464-7805
Fax: 323 464-6614
URL: http://www.acmefilmworks.com
E-mail: acmeinfo@acmefilmworks.com

A.D.2, Inc.

Area(s) of Specialization: CGI, Multimedia

Number of Employees: 12

A.D.2, Inc. has been developing and producing marketing materials since 1980 and digital products for more than fourteen years. Clients include: Amblin Entertainment, Columbia/TriStar Pictures and Hilton Hotels, among others.

A.D.2, Inc.
2118 Wilshire Blvd.
Suite 205
Santa Monica, CA 90403

Phone: 310 394-8379
Fax: 310 451-0966
URL: http://www.ad2.com

Adobe Systems, Inc.

Area(s) of Specialization: CGI, Multimedia

Number of Employees: 1400

Adobe Systems Incorporated helped launch the desktop publishing revolution in 1982 and continues to work in graphics, publishing, and electronic document delivery. Many of the images on the Web today were created or modified with one or more of Adobe's products, such as Adobe Photoshop, Adobe Illustrator, Adobe Acrobat, Adobe GoLive, Adobe InDesign, Adobe FrameMaker, Adobe PageMaker, Adobe Premiere, and Adobe After Effects.

Adobe Systems Inc./ San Jose
345 Park Ave.
San Jose, CA 95110-2704
Phone: 408 536-6000
Fax: 408 537-6000
URL: http://www.adobe.com

Adobe Systems Inc./ Seattle
Number of Employees: 500+
801 N. 34th. St.
Seattle, WA 98103
Phone: 206 675-7000
Fax: 206 675-6809
URL: http://www.adobe.com

Advantage Audio

Area(s) of Specialization: Audio for Animation and Film Effects

Number of Employees: 15

Advantage Audio is a full service audio production and post production, featuring animation sound and effects creation. In a typical year the studio completes the audio post production work for more than 200 half-hour episodes of animation for broadcast television, as well as longer format projects for home video release.

Advantage Audio
1026 Hollywood Wy.
Burbank, CA 91505
Phone: 818 566-8555
Fax: 818 566-8963
URL: http://www.advantageaudio.com

Advox

Area(s) of Specialization: 3D Animation, Post Production, Telecine

Number of Employees: 3

Founded in 1989, ViewPoint Mexico used Silicon Graphics computers equipped with Softimage. The company creates 3D animations for the commercial market. In 1993 Viewpoint Mexico became Advox, continuing to work in animation for the Television market.

Advox
77 Mark Drive Suite 4
San Rafael, CA 94903
Phone: 415 479-6970
Alt Phone: 800 563-5070
Fax: 415 479-6945
URL: http://www.advox-us.com

Aftershock Digital

Area(s) of Specialization: Video Editing

Number of Employees: 1+

Founded in 1994 by editor Fritz Feick, Aftershock provides post-production, editorial, visual effects, sound design, and graphic design to the advertising, film and television industries.

Aftershock Digital
8222 Melrose Ave. Ste. 304
Los Angeles, CA 90046
Phone: 800 230-2290
Alt Phone: 323 658-5700
Fax: 323 658-5200
URL: http://www.aftershockdigital.com

A.I. Effects, Inc.

Area(s) of Specialization: Motion Picture Visual Effects

Number of Employees: 4

A.I. Effects Inc. creates visual effects for film, television, commercials, special projects, and computer graphics and interactively. The company's projects include works on such projects as HBO's "From the Earth to the Moon", "True Lies", "Terminator II", "Near Dark", "Fright Night II", "Super Mario Bros"., "The Abyss", "Coneheads", "Star Trek-The Next Generation", "Dracula", and" The Last Action Hero." AI is also involved in stereoscopic imaging.

A.I. Effects, Inc.
7114 Laurel Canyon Blvd., Ste. A
North Hollywood, CA 91605
Phone: 818 764-2063
Fax: 818 764-2065
URL: http://www.aifx.com

Alias-Wavefront

Number of Employees: 500+

Area(s) of Specialization: 2D And 3D Graphics Software Development

Alias|Wavefront develops software for the film and video, games and interactive media, industrial design and visualization markets. Based in Toronto, Alias|Wavefront is a wholly owned, independent software subsidiary of Silicon Graphics, Inc.

Alias-Wavefront
Santa Barbara
614 Chapala Street
Santa Barbara, CA 93101
Phone: 416 362-9181
Alt. Phone: 800 447-2542

Fax: 416 369-6140
URL: http://www.aw.sgi.com

Phone: 303 939-8515
Fax: 303 939-8516
URL: http://www.allvideoproduction.com

All Video Production

Area(s) of Specialization: 3D Animation, Digital Video Editing, Post Production, Audio, CD-ROM and DVD Authoring

Number of Employees: 2+

All Video Production, Inc. provides concept to completion video production including marketing, tradeshow, public relations, advertising, cinematic, video news releases, product information, training, and project documentation. The company uses digital video field gathering equipment; on-line non-linear post-production equipment and offers broadcast quality, high definition 3D animation. The post-production facilities offer on-line editing with digital special effect compositing, audio sweetening, narration, and a CD production music library. Other services include: script and storyboard generation, talent search, location scouting, high end "rush" and "dailies" editing, world standards conversion, studio production, aerial videography, digital cinematic production, digital still photography and 3D animated cinematic compositing.

All Video Production
5311 Western Ave.
Suite C
Boulder, CO 80301

American Production Services

Area(s) of Specialization: CGI, Multimedia, Animation, Film/Video, Sound

Number of Employees: 80-90

In existence for 20 years, American Production Services offers digital video and audio editing and distribution services, including HDTV production. The company operates the APS High Definition Center, offering complete HDTV production services. American Production Services also help publish a magazine focused on the high definition HDTV production.

American Production Services
2247 15th. Ave. West
Seattle, WA 98119
Phone: 206 282-1776
Alt Phone: 888 282-1776
Fax: 206 282-3535
URL: http://www.apsnw.com

An-Amaze-Tion

Area(s) of Specialization: Computer Animation, Digital Audio/Video Editing,

Forensic Courtroom Animation, Architectural

Number of Employees: 4+

An-Amaze-Tion is a computer animation and digital audio/video production house specializing in broadcast quality animation. The company works in all facets of the field including, but not limited to: Architectural/ Environmental, Broadcast/Special Effects, CBT-Computer Based Training, Engineering, Forensic, Multimedia, and Marketing/ Advertising.

An-Amaze-Tion
5775 E. Los Angeles Ave.
Suite 230
Simi Valley, CA 93063
Phone: 805 578-9560
Fax: 805-578-9553
URL: http://www.an-amaze-tion.com

Angel Studios

Area(s) of Specialization: CGI, Multimedia

Number of Employees: 90+

Angel Studios creates 3D real-time interactive entertainment that mixes high-end technology, creativity, and gameplay. The company's software technology includes physics, adaptive AI, and organic animations. Angel Studios develops a wide variety of immersive interactive entertainment for consoles, PCs, arcades, OEM demos, and location-based entertainment.

Angel Studios
5966 La Place Court, Suite 170
Carlsbad, CA 92008
Phone: 760 929-0700
Fax: 760 929-0719
URL: http://www.angelstudios.com

Animalu Productions

Area(s) of Specialization: 3D Imaging and Animation for Film/Video/CD-ROM/Gaming Industry

Number of Employees: 2

Animalu Productions creates Animation and 3D Imaging for the CD-ROM, video, film and game industries.

Animalu Productions
633 San Leon
Irvine, CA 92606
Phone: 949 261-1179
URL: http://www.animalu.com
E-mail: animalu@animalu.com

Animation and Effects

Area(s) of Specialization: Design, Production of Effects, Cel and Claymation Animation for Film, Television, Interactive Media

Number of Employees: 2

Animation and Effects creates visuals using cel and claymation techniques among others. Animation and Effects works on a fixed bid basis covering all design services from storyboards to final production.

Animation and Effects
235 Rockaway Beach
Pacificia, CA 94044
Phone: 650 355-7635
URL: http://www.animationandeffects.com
E-mail: webresponse@animationandeffects.com

ARG Cartoon Animation Studio

Area(s) of Specialization: Animated GIFS

Number of Employees: 1

ARG Cartoon Animation has animated GIFs, all original, including a dancing cartoon alphabet, on-line greeting cards, dancing words, an art gallery called Click Media, and the Abnormal Toons. The company produced a CD titled "The RAG! Kartoon Klips" which contains cartoons and animated alphabets.

ARG Cartoon Animation Studio
3645 Jeannine Dr., Suite 211-A
Colorado Springs, CO 80917
Phone: 719 955-5955
URL: http://www.artie.com

Arkiteck, Inc.

Area(s) of Specialization: CGI, 3D Modeling, Animation, Sound

Number of Employees: 2+

Arkitek Studios creates sound, 3D animation, and multimedia for clients including Microsoft, AT&T, Sierra On-line, MCI, RealNerworks, Intel, Hewlett Packard, Raster Ranch Ltd. and MagiGroup. The company conceives and produces visual elements, and also enhances the impact with music composition and sound design.

Arkiteck, Inc.
3213 W. Wheeler St., Ste. 196
Seattle, WA 98199
Phone: 206 286-0337
Fax: 206 282-3548
URL: http://www.arkitek.com/drh

Artbeats Software Inc.

Area(s) of Specialization: Royalty Free Digital Film Archive

Number of Employees: 18+

The Artbeats Digital Film Library (ADFL) is an approach to stock footage. The company provides high quality royalty-free, hassle-free digitized stock footage on CD-ROM.

Artbeats Software Inc.
Box 709
Myrtle Creek, OR 97457

Phone: 800 444-9392
Alt Phone: 541 863-4429
Fax: 541 863-4547
URL: http://www.artbeats.com

Artichoke Productions

Area(s) of Specialization: Film and Video Production, Audio Production

Number of Employees: 10+

Artichoke Productions was founded in 1981 by Paul Kalbach. Artichoke Productions creates film and video production packages, computer graphics and animation, and has a multimedia studio for film/video/audio.

Artichoke Productions
4114 Linden St.
Oakland, CA 94608
Phone: 510 655-1283
Fax: 510 655-0117
URL: http://www.artichokepro.com

Atom Films

Area(s) of Specialization: Short Film Distribution

Number of Employees: 140+

Atom acquires licenses to short films, animations, and digital media, and secures distribution via television networks, airlines, theaters, home video and DVD, the Internet, broadband services, and more. The company works with filmmakers, producers, and media companies. Since its inception in late 1998, Atom has signed a number of shorts, including the 1999 Academy Award nominee Holiday Romance.

Atom Films
815 Western Avenue, Suite 300
Seattle, WA 98104
Phone: 206 264-2735
Fax: 206 264-2742
URL: http://www.atomfilms.com

ATV-All Things Video

Area(s) of Specialization: Broadcast graphics

Number of Employees: 12+

After 14 years of service to the video production industry in Sacramento, All Things Video offers Closed Circuit System design and sales in addition to Professional and Broadcast services.

All Things Video
2424 Glendale Lane
Sacramento, CA 95825
Phone: 916 973-9100
Alt Phone: 888 973-9149
Fax: 916 480-2722
URL: http://www.allthingsvideo.net

Available Light, Ltd.

Area(s) of Specialization: Visual Effects, Animation

Number of Employees: 7+

Available Light LTD. creates animation, digital visual effects, rotoscoping, including camera and optical service. The company uses software programs such as Lightwave, some 3D Studio Max, After Effects, Digital Fusion, Photoshop and Elastic Reality.

Available Light Ltd.
1125 South Flower Street
Burbank, CA 91502
Phone: 818 842-2109
URL: http://www.availablelightltd.com

Ayres Group

Area(s) of Specialization: Animation

Number of Employees: 14

The company creates animation.

Ayres Group
750 B Street, Suite 42
San Diego, CA 92101
Phone: 619 696-6800
Fax: 619 696-6868
URL: http://www.ayres42.com

Baer Animation Company, Inc.

Area(s) of Specialization: Animation

Number of Employees: 6+

The Baer Animation Company, incorporated in 1984, has created and produces animation for features, including the Benny the Cab and Toontown sequences for "Who Framed Roger Rabbit" and "The Prince and The Pauper," as well as national and international commercials. The company has expanded into the production of CD Rom games, theme entertainment shows, and features made for video and television series and specials. The staff has experience in production from concept through script, story board, design, animation, special effects, and digital paint and composite. They also integrate animation with live action.

Baer Animation Company, Inc.
7743 Woodrow Wilson Dr.
Los Angeles, CA 90046-1211
Phone: 323 874-9122
Fax: 323 874-7690
URL: http://www.baeranimation.com

Bandelier, EFX

Area(s) of Specialization: Commercial Film and Video, Cel Animation, Rotoscoping, 2D and 3D Computer Animation

Number of Employees: 6

The company's animators have produced spots for AT&T, Vlasic Pickles, Kellogg's Cereals, Budweiser, and Kodak. Bandelier uses traditional cels and computer programs to produce 2D, 3D, Rotoscope, stop motion, and CGI animation.

Bandelier, EFX
6808 Academy PKWY East NE
Suite B-1
Albuquerque, New Mexico 87109
Phone: 505 345-8021
Fax: 505 345-8023
URL: http://www.bandelier.com

Banned from the Ranch

Area(s) of Specialization: Film and Video Production

Number of Employees: 10+

Banned from the Ranch Entertainment ("BFTR") is a production company connecting digital technology and the entertainment industry for over 18 years.

Banned From the Ranch
2048 Broadway
Santa Monica, CA 90404
Phone: 310 821-8518
Fax: 310 821-8938
URL: http://www.bftr.com
E-mail: info@bftr.com

Base2 Studios

Area(s) of Specialization: CGI, Film/Video, Multimedia

Number of Employees: 15

Base2 Studios' creates using CGI, film/video and multimedia.

Base2 Studios
2800 North Spear Blvd.
Denver, CO, 80211
Phone: 303 455-5200
Fax: 303 455-1110
URL: http://www.base2studios.com

BearByte Animation

Area(s) of Specialization: Modeling, Animation, Effects

Number of Employees: 2+

BearByte Animation provides custom 3D modeling, animation, and digital effects to the advertising, entertainment and computer gaming industries. BearByte Animation can provide custom 3D models, simple flying logos and photo realistic animated epics.

BearByte Animation
15637 Calle El Capitan
Green Valley, CA 91350
Phone: 805 270-0138
URL: http://www.bearbyte.com
E-mail: bear@bearbyte.com

Bill Melendez Production

Area(s) of Specialization: Cel Animation

Number of Employees: 10+

Since it's founding in 1964, Bill Melendez Productions has animated cartoon characters, including the "Peanuts" characters created by Charles M. Schulz. The first of 75 "Peanuts" specials was "A Charlie Brown Christmas." The company has nine Emmys, and a Peabody Award for Broadcasting Excellence.

Bill Melendez Production
13400 Riverside Dr # 201
Sherman Oaks, CA 91423
Phone: 818 382-7382
Fax: 818 382-7377
URL: http://www.billmelendez.net

Blizzard Entertainment

Area(s) of Specialization: Research and Development & Design of Computer Entertainment Products

Number of Employees: 130+

Headquartered in Irvine, Calif., Blizzard Entertainment was founded in 1990 under the name Silicon & Synapse. Blizzard Entertainment is a publisher of entertainment software games, including the "Warcraft series", "Diablo", and "Starcraft."

Blizzard Entertainment
P.O. Box 18979
Irvine, CA 92623
Phone: 949 955-1382
Fax: 949 955-0157
URL: http://www.blizzard.com

BLADE Simulation

Area(s) of Specialization: 3D and 2D Animation

Number of Employees: 1

BLADE Simulation creates access to computer generated modeling and animation. Computer photo-realistic images and animation are used to clarify ideas.

BLADE Simulation
P.O. Box 55656
Seattle, WA 98155
Phone: 206 992-2191
URL: http://www.bladesim.com

Bluelight Animation

Area(s) of Specialization: 2D and 3D Animation

Number of Employees: 2

Bluelight Animations offers: 3D motion graphics, Titles, Logos, Special Effects - Fog, Explosions, Fire, Rays and More, Character Animation, 2D and 3D Morphing, Virtual Environments, 2D Graphics, Concept Design, Design and Trouble-shooting for toy and game construction, Illustration and Storyboards, Internet - Web Page Design (incl. HTML Programming), Full Raytrace and Raycast, Final Output To Any Format Including Video, Film, and QuickTime.

Bluelight Animation
PO Box 5643
Berkeley, CA 94705
Phone: 510 338-1212
URL: http://www.bluelightanim.com

Blur Studio, Inc.

Area(s) of Specialization: Visual Effects, Animation, Film and Video

Number of Employees: 11+

Blur specializes in character development and animation, photorealistic effects, digital compositing, and intergalactic battle sequences.

Blur Studio, Inc.
1130 Abbot Kinney Blvd.
Venice, CA 90291
Phone: 310 581-8848
Fax: 310 581-8850
URL: http://www.blur.com

Brilliant Digital Entertainment

Area(s) of Specialization: 3D Animations for the Internet

Number of Employees: 10

Brilliant Digital Entertainment is an entertainment content provider and technology developer for the Internet and television markets. The Company is focused on two principal market segments: (1) The development and distribution of 3D, digitally animated interactive content for the Internet, in small file sizes/shorter download times and full-screen images, developed using Brilliant's proprietary software. (2) Technology and tools for the development of Internet ready content. Tools are designed to enable the production of content for distribution via the Internet. These include technologies for lay-up of animation files, automated lip synchronization, data compression and interactive scriptwriting.

Brilliant Digital Entertainment
6355 Topanga Canyon Blvd.
Suite 120
Woodland Hills, CA 91367
Phone: 818 615-1500
Fax: 818 615-0995
URL: http://www.bde3d.com

Calico Creations, Ltd.

Area(s) of Specialization: CGI, Visual Effects

Number of Employees: 6

For over 23 years, Calico World Entertainment has created traditional and digital animation, visual effects, and design for television, feature films and electronic entertainment. Aligned with World Events Productions, the company is a source for broadcast entertainment, from concept through international distribution. Utilizing VEIL Technology, the studio provides interactive programming and promotions for television, the Web and site-based entertainment.

Calico Creations LTD
10200 Riverside Dr.
N. Hollywood, CA 91602-2539
Phone: 818 755-3800
Fax: 818 755-4643
URL: http://www.calicoworld.com

California Image Associates

Area(s) of Specialization: Production and Post Production

Number of Employees: 22+

Cal Image works in Production and Post Production.

California Image Associates
11333 Sunrise Park Drive
Rancho Cordova, CA 95742
Phone: 916 638-8383
Fax: 916 638-4442
URL: http://www.calimage.com

Camera Control, Inc.

Area(s) of Specialization: Motion Camera Control

Number of Employees: 7

Camera Control Inc., makes live action motion control available to the commercials and visual effects industry in Los Angeles. The facility 'Camera Control' (Santa Monica, CA) operates two MRMC Milo rigs and has serviced commercials, music videos and feature film projects for over two years. The Milo/Flair system received one of "Academy of Motion Picture Arts & Sciences" technical awards.

Camera Control, Inc.
3317 Ocean Park Boulevard
Santa Monica, CA 90405
Phone: 310 581-8343
Fax: 310 581-8340
URL: http://www.cameracontrol.com

Catalyst Productions

Area(s) of Specialization: Production and Post Production, 3D Animation

Number of Employees: 40+

Catalyst Productions is a full-service graphics, 3D animation, video production and post production facility, specializes in creating hi-tech, scientific, and industrial tutorials for a wide range of clients.

Catalyst Productions
1431 Center St.
Oakland, CA 94607
Phone: 510 836-1111
URL: http://www.catalystproductions.com

Celluloid Studios

Area(s) of specialization: computer animation

Number of Employees: 25+

Celluloid Studios produced the pilot for "South Park" entitled "Spirit of Christmas" (a.k.a.. Jesus vs. Santa Claus) at the Denver facility. "Spirit of Christmas" established the cut paper animation and irreverent humor which evolved into Comedy Central's series "South Park."

Celluloid Studios
2128 15th Street
Denver, CO 80202
Phone: 303 595-3152
Fax: 303 595-4908
URL: http://www.celluloidstudios.com
e-mail: animate@celluloidstudios.com

Centropolis Effects

Area(s) of Specialization: Production and Post Production, Visual Effects

Number of Employees: 12+

Based on SGI and Intel hardware, CFX has departments for character animation, 3D camera tracking, 3D computer graphics effects, 2D digital compositing, 35mm scanning and recording, and roto/paint. The company is equipped with Discreet Logic Infernos along with Cineon Tornadoes and Cineon Storms. The CG are created with Softimage, Houdini, and Alias software as well as a set of proprietary tools. CFX has produced computer-generated graphics and digital compositing for television shows and feature films-including "Flubber", "Contact", "The Faculty", "Providence", and "Storm of the Century." CFX was the lead digital effects house on "Godzilla", contributing over 240 character animation shots to the film and over 160 digital composites.

Centropolis Interactive
10202 West Washington Blvd.
Astaire Building, Suite 2610
Culver City, CA 90232
Phone: 310 204-7300
Fax: 310 204-7301
URL: http://www.centropolis.com

The Chandler Group

Area(s) of Specialization: Production and Post Production, Film and Video Visual Effects

Number of Employees: 10

The Chandler Group is a film-based company to handle visual effects projects from advanced planning to post production. The company is involved in visual effects projects from classics like Star Wars, Blade Runner, and Close Encounters of the Third Kind to the stylistic ventures of Tim Burton's Batman franchise. Blockbusters include: "Godzilla" and "Armageddon." The company creates music videos with artists like Madonna, Elton John, Puff Daddy, Will Smith, TLC, Garth Brooks and Michael Jackson. The company has been involved with commercials for products like Coca-Cola, Kodak, Fed Ex, Skittles, Budweiser and McDonald's.

The Chandler Group
4121 Redwood Ave.
Los Angeles CA 90066.
Phone: 310 305-7431
Fax: 310 306-2532
URL: http://www.cgvfx.com

Chiodo Brothers Productions, Inc.

Area(s) of Specialization: Visual Effects for Film and Video

Number of Employees: 5

Chiodo Brothers Prod., Inc. is an independent production company working in special effects such as stop-motion animation, live action puppetry, make-up effects, miniatures, mechanical props and computer animation. The brothers created "The Teenage Mutant Ninja Turtles", "Ninja Turtles: The Next Mutation" television show. The staff fabricated the new turtles and all the villains for The Teenage Mutant Ninja Turtles television show using computer controlled animatronics. The company has worked on a variety of projects, including the Power Rangers feature film and the ground-breaking nine screen, 360 degree film "Dinosaur Adventure", a centerpiece of Iwerks Entertainment's Cinetropolis theme park.

Chiodo Brothers Productions, Inc.
110 W. Providencia Ave.
Burbank, CA 91502
Phone: 818 842-5656
Fax: 818 848-0891
URL: http://www.chiodobros.com

CHOPS & Associates Live Animation

Area(s) of Specialization: Live Animation, Digital Puppeteering

Number of Employees: 8+

CHOPS & Associates Live Animation is the home of Pentium-based Performance Animation, a virtual reality experience that brings 3D characters to life, using real-time animation and video displays. These company's characters are used to attract people to trade show booths, to entertain attendees at sales meetings and to get attention at special events. CHOPS & Associates books performances for 1-5 day events and creates custom 3D characters for animation on the system.

CHOPS & Associates Live Animation
P.O Box 6290
Incline Village, NV 89450
Phone: 800 449-2421
Alt Phone: 559 855-4960
Fax: 775 832-4468
URL: http://www.chops.com

Cinema Now

Area(s) of Specialization: On-line Distributor of Independent Films

Number of Employees: 10+

Cinema Now was established to be an on-line community for independent film watchers and film makers.

Cinema Now
4553 Glencoe Ave.
Suite 200
Marina Del Rey, CA 90292
Phone: 310 314-9506
Fax: 310 773-0071
URL: http://www.cinemanow.com

Cinema Production Service

Area(s) of Specialization: Visual Effects for Film and Video

Number of Employees: 15

Cinema Production Services, Inc. (CPS) was created to produce miniatures and models. CPS is designed as a free standing resource to commercial filmmakers and all other visual designers working throughout the entertainment industry. The company offers a range of services, from basic stage rental to complete commercial art development and photography. CPS' staff includes model makers, welders, painters and designers.

Cinema Production Service
7631 Haskell Avenue
Van Nuys, CA 91406-2006
Phone: 818 989-2164
Fax: 818 989-2174
URL: http://www.cpsfx.com

Cinema Research

Area(s) of Specialization: Title Design, Special Visual Effects and Digital Composition

Number of Employees: 35

Cinema Research creates Title Design, and Digital & Special Effects.

Cinema Research
6860 Lexington Ave.

Los Angeles, CA 90038
Phone: 323 460-4111
Fax: 323 962-9429

CinePartners Entertainment

Area(s) of Specialization: Production and
Post Production

Number of Employees: 4

In 1996, CinePartners Entertainment, Inc.
was founded to manage feature films and
television programs from inception to final
product. CinePartners operates in three main
areas: creative/production, sales/marketing,
and finance.

CinePartners Entertainment
10801 National Blvd. #103
Los Angeles, CA 90064
Phone: 310 475-8870
Fax: 310 475-0890
E-mail: cinepartners@jps.net
URL: http://www.cinepartners.net

Cinesite Film Scanning and Recording

Area(s) of Specialization: Visual Effects for
Film and Video

Number of Employees: 175

Cinesite opened in 1992, as a wholly owned
subsidiary of Eastman Kodak Company.

Cinesite is a full service digital effects
company providing a range of services,
including digital compositing, 2D & 3D
effects, wire and object removal, film stock
repair and restoration, and digital film
scanning and recording. Cinesite serves the
motion picture, commercial, and special
venue markets. Using both traditional film
techniques and computer-generated imagery
to build characters, environments and
backgrounds, the team employs a range of
digital processes to assemble the imagery
into a shot. Cinesite has completed visual
effects work on such films as "Armageddon",
"Dr. Dolittle", "Primary Colors", "The Truman
Show", "Lost In Space", "Sphere", "Air Force
One", "Event Horizon", "Tomorrow Never
Dies", "Jerry Maguire", "Space Jam", and
"Smilla's Sense Of Snow."

Cinesite, Inc.
1017 N. Las Palmas Ave. Suite 300
Los Angeles, CA 90038
Phone: 323 468-4400
Fax: 323 468-4404
URL: http://www.cinesite.com

Click 3x

Area(s) of Specialization: Visual Effects and
Animation for Film and Video

Number of Employees: 25

Click 3X design studios offers digital effects,
animation, and broadcast design for the

commercial, film, and television markets. The digitally linked operations are located in New York, Los Angeles, and Atlanta. Click 3X specializes in visual effects design and supervision, computer animation, character design and compositing. The studios are linked via T-1 lines and operate multiple Silicon Graphics 3D workstations, Windows NT, Macintosh platforms and an AVID nonlinear off-line suite, as well as a Henry suite and Inferno/Flame compositing suites running on Silicon Graphics Onyx II supercomputers.

Click 3x
2415 Michigan Avenue
Santa Monica, CA 90404
Phone: 310 264-5511
Fax: 310 264-5512
URL: http://www.click3x.com

COBI Digital

Area(s) of Specialization: All Digital Production Facility

Number of Employees: 4

COBI Digital is owned by California Oregon Broadcasting, Inc., a company that was founded in 1933. COBI, an Oregon corporation, owns five television stations: KOBI-TV in Medford, KOTI-TV in Klamath Falls, KOBI-TV in Coos Bay, KLSR-TV in Eugene, and KEVU-TV in Eugene, as well as Crestview Cable Television in Prineville.

COBI Digital became an all-component digital production facility in the Northwest in 1993, and uses Digital Betacam from Sony.

COBI Digital
125 S. Fir Street
Medford, OR 97501
Phone: 888 262-4937
Alt Phone: 541-776-5802
Fax: 541 779-5564
URL: http://www.cobidigital.com

Colorado Studios

Area(s) of Specialization: Post Production-Film and Television

Number of Employees: 36

Colorado Studios is a production and post-production facility, with studios at the former site of Stapleton Airport and in downtown Denver. In 1995-96, the TV mini-series "The Shining" was filmed at the Stapleton studio, followed by several independent features. Since 1983, Colorado Studios has held the contract for shooting and editing worldwide for PBS' Newshour. Mountain Mobile Television, a part of Colorado Studios, provides the mobile units for all Rockies, Nuggets, and Avalanche games, plus other events for all the major networks.

Colorado Studios
2400 N. Syracuse St.
Denver, CO 802
Phone: 800 882-6561

Fax: 303 388-9600
URL: http://www.coloradostudios.com

Communication Bridges

Area(s) of Specialization: Custom web design, and E-commerce.

Number of Employees: 2+

Communication Bridges produces videos and designs web sites.

Communication Bridges
1330 Lincoln Ave # 306
San Rafael, CA 94901
Phone: 415 454-5505
Alt Phone: 888 530-5505
URL: http://www.combridges.com
E-mail: info@combridges.com

Composite Image Systems/CIS

Area(s) of Specialization: Digital Visual Effects for Film and Video

Number of Employees: 30

CIS is a digital effects company whose credits include "Titanic", "Contact", and "Terminator" along with the many movies the company has worked on, CIS also contributed effects for "Star Trek Voyager", and the "X-Files."

Composite Image Systems/CIS
1144 N. Las Palmas Ave.
Los Angeles, CA 90038
Phone: 323 463-8811
Fax: 323 962-1859
URL: http://www.cishollywood.com

Component Post

Area(s) of Specialization: Post Production for Film and Video

Number of Employees: 3

Component Post is a post production house in Silicon Valley with a client base ranging from Apple Computer to Ziff-Davis.

Component Post
3350 Scott Blvd., Bldg. 63
Santa Clara, CA 95054
Phone: 408 980-5166
Fax: 408 980-9697
URL: http://www.cpost.com

Computer Café

Area(s) of Specialization: 3D Animation and Digital Visual Effects for Film and Video

Number of Employees: 17

Computer Café is a 3D Animation/Digital Effects company specializing in photo realism and character animation. Clientele range from national ad agencies and production companies to major Hollywood studios and television networks. Some clients include: Walt Disney Pictures, Touchstone Pictures, Paramount Pictures, Trimark

Pictures, NBC, DDB Needham Chicago, Chiat Day Los Angeles, Pittard Sullivan and Will Vinton Studios. The staff includes storyboard artists, designers, writers, editors, animators, effects producers and on-set supervisors.

Computer Café
3130 Skyway Dr., Ste. 603
Santa Maria, CA 93455
Phone: 805 922-9479
Fax: 805 922-3225
URL: http://www.computercafe.com

Computer Graphics Systems Development

Area(s) of Specialization: Digital Simulation and Virtual Reality

Number of Employees: 15

Computer Graphics Systems Development Corporation was founded by Roy Latham in 1990. The company provides products and services related to visual simulation and virtual reality. Services include consulting on product design, product evaluation, custom system development, sponsored research, and intellectual property work (including patent preparation, expert witness, and infringement analysis). Products include a newsletter, Real Time Graphics; software for 3D data base construction, selling Sony head mounted displays, and, in the future, complete simulator products.

Computer Graphics Systems Development
2483 Old Middlefield Way, Suite 140
Mountain View, CA 94043
Phone: 650 903-4920
Fax: 650 967-5252
URL: http://www.cgsd.net

Continuity Studios

Area(s) of Specialization: 3D animation, computer assisted animation

Number of Employees: 20+

Continuity has developed various properties, of its own and others including "Buckly o' Hare", "Skeleton Warrios", "CyberRad", "Ms. Mystic", "Nighthawk", etc. for TV and Comics. Neal Adams: the Sketch Book was compiled by Arlen Schumer. It spans Adams' comics career, revealing unpublished works, his thought process, and storytelling techniques.

Continuity Studios
4710 W. Magnolia Blvd.
Burbank, CA 91505
Phone: 818 980-8852
Fax: 818 980-8974

Continuity Studios
62 W. 45th Street, 10th Floor
New York, NY 10036
Phone: 212 869-4170
Fax: 212 764-6814
URL: http://www.nealadams.com

URL: http://www.nealadamsentertainment.com
e-mail: nadams@earthlink.net

Crazy Horse Editorial, Inc.

Area(s) of Specialization: CGI, Film/Video, Multimedia, Animation

Number of Employees: 15

Crazy Horse Editorial is a post-production company offering creative and technical services for the advertising and promotional communities. Crazy Horse has four Avid Editing Systems, Jaleo compositing, Softimage CGI, and Macintosh graphics. The Avids, Jaleo and graphics suites are networked together to provide the transfer of files without unnecessary outputs. Crazy Horse is also wired for composite, RGB and serial D-1 formats for current and future high quality broadcast operations.

Crazy Horse Editorial, Inc.
912 Colorado Ave.
Santa Monica, CA 90401
Phone: 310 451-7311
Fax: 310 458-0118
URL: http://www.crazyhorse.com

Creative Industries and Technology

Area(s) of Specialization: Computer Animation, Graphic Design, Interactive Design

Number of Employees: 4

Creative Industries and Technology is a multi-faceted computer animation company that offers services including: computer animation, graphic design, and web design.

Creative Industries and Technology
P.O. Box 7400
Tempe, AZ 85281-7400
Phone/ Fax: 480 317-0480
URL: http://www.citanimation.com

Cruse & Company

Area(s) of Specialization: Optical Special Effects

Number of Employees: 2

Cruse & Company creates optical special effects.

Cruse & Company
7000 Romaine St.
Los Angeles CA 90038
Phone: 323 851-8814
Fax: 323 851-8788

Curious Pictures

Area(s) of Specialization: CGI, Design, Animation, Television Production, Effects

Number of Employees: 50+

Curious Pictures is an international design and television production company producing comedy, graphically inspired live-action, special effects, graphics and animation of all types. The staff of directors, designers, artists and animators produces TV commercials, on-air graphics/titles and television programming. The company was founded in early 1993 as a division of Harmony Holdings, Inc.

Curious Pictures
440 Lafayette Street
New York, NY 10003
Phone: 212 674-1400
Alt Phone: 212 674-7600
Fax: 212 674-0081
URL: http://www.curiouspix.com

Curious Pictures San Francisco
1360 Mission Street Suite 201
San Francisco, CA 94103
Phone: 415 437-1400
Fax: 415 437-1408

Cyber F/X, Inc.

Area(s) of Specialization: Digital Imaging Hardware and Software

Number of Employees: 20

Cyber F/X, Inc. located in Southern California, provides imaging technology. The company uses Cyberware digitizing process to service a wide variety of clients in the entertainment and design industries, such as: Animators, Prop Makers, Designers, Sculptors, Film Producers, Special Effects Houses, Interactive CD-ROM Creators, Theme Park Designers, Music Video Producers, and Video Game Developers. The company also uses CNC-Sculpting machines.

Cyber F/X, Inc.
615 Ruberta Ave.
Glendale, CA 91201
Phone: 818 246-2911
Fax: 818 246-3610
URL: http://www.cyberfx3d.com

David Allen Productions

Area(s) of Specialization: Stop Animation, Visual Effects, Puppet Animation

Number of Employees: 2

David Allen Productions
918 W. Oak St.
Burbank, CA 91506
Phone: 818 845-9270

Debut Entertainment, Inc.

Area(s) of Specialization: Production and Post Production for Film and Video

Number of Employees: 5+

Debut Entertainment produces a range of educational and entertainment programs, corporate and organizational promotions and television commercials for telecommunications, advertising and entertainment industries. It is also the post-production center for Asian-American commercials like AT&T, California State Lottery, Bank of America, Sears, Southern California Edison and many others. In addition, its computer graphics department produce DVD titles for feature films in Asian languages. Debut Entertainment's in-house recording studio is another convenience to post-production. Voice-over recording, adding sound effects and music, making revisions, and final mix are all services offered.

Debut Entertainment, Inc.
923 E. 3rd St. Suite 112
Los Angeles, CA 90013
Phone: 213 626-7636
Fax: 213 626-0395
URL: http://www.debutinc.com

Design Visualization Partners

Area(s) of Specialization: Computer Graphics

Number of Employees: 15+

Design Visualization Partners creates immersive environments for computer graphics. The company uses design skills with computer graphics technology. Studio DVP's work is based in the technology of real-time simulation.

Design Visualization Partners (DVP)
1040 N. Las Palmas Ave.
Building 30
Hollywood, CA 90038
Phone: 213 860-3506
Fax: 213 860-3507
URL: http://www.desviz.com

Digiscope

Area(s) of Specialization: 2D and 3D Animation

Number of Employees: 5

Digiscope
2308 Broadway
Santa Monica, CA 90404
Phone: 310 315-6060
Fax: 310 828-5856
URL: http://www.digiscope.com

Digital Capture

Area(s) of Specialization: Animation for Web

Number of Employees: 2

Digital Capture is a provider of 3D GIF Animations for web page design. Based in

San Francisco, the company's products were created from original work using various CAD applications, broadcast-quality design/ animation products, and image editing packages.

Digital Capture
1140 Hampshire
San Francisco, CA 94110
Phone: 415 824-8680
URL: http://www.dcapture.com

Digital Domain

Area(s) of Specialization: Production and Post Production, Visual Effects, CGI, 3D Animation

Number of Employees: 450+

Digital Domain is a technological studio to create content and visual imagery for feature films, and music videos. Digital Domain was conceived by ex-Industrial Light + Magic Vice President Scott Ross, four time Academy Award winning creature-creator Stan Winston, and Academy Award winning writer, producer, director James Cameron. This business team partnered with IBM and Cox Enterprises with the goal of being the finest digital studio in the world.

Digital Domain
300 Rose Avenue
Venice, CA 90291
Phone: 310 314-2800

Fax: 310 314-2888
URL: http://www.d2.com

Digital Factory

Area(s) of Specialization: Motion Picture Sets Building

Number of Employees: 148

Digital Factory is a company that caters to the mechanical needs of the entertainment industry. The company designs and manufactures movie sets in a large scale manufacturing facility.

Digital Factory
P.O. Box 598
Ceres, CA 95307
Los Angles Office
Phone: 323 660-2223
Fax: 425 944 6834
URL: http://www.digitalfactory.com

Digital Farm

Area(s) of Specialization: Post Production, Interactive DVD and CD-ROM Authoring, Web Site Design

Number of Employees: 3

Digital Farm is a video, DVD, and multimedia production and post-production company. Employees work on projects ranging from corporate promotional videos to broadcast commercials, as well as interactive kiosks, DVD's, CD-ROMs, and web page support.

Digital Farm
3800 Aurora Ave. N., Ste. 280
Seattle, WA 98103
Phone: 206 634-2677
Fax: 206 634-2676
URL: http://www.digitalfarm.com

Digital Firepower

Area(s) of Specialization: Digital Environment Creation

Number of Employees: 10

Digital Firepower is a team of artists specializing in the creation of virtual environments through the medium of digital matter paintings. The company remains small to concentrate on one area of visual effects. With studios in Hollywood and a second in London, the company offers matte work to major studio productions and smaller independent films on both sides of the Atlantic.

Digital Firepower
P.O. Box 2937
Los Angeles, CA 90078
Phone: 323 467-9438
Fax: 323 467-9099
URL: http://www.digitalfirepower.com

Digital Imagination

Area(s) of Specialization: Audio and Video Production, Animation, and Interactive Design

Number of Employees: 15

A multimedia based company involved in various aspects of producing multimedia environments, including presentation, hosting sites, audio-video production, animation, e-commerce, and web design.

Digital Imagination
2801 Townsgate Rd., Ste. 101
Westlake Village, CA 91361
Phone: 805 497-7303
Fax: 805 230-9208
URL: http://www.digitalimagination.com

Digital Muse

Area(s) of Specialization: Visual Effects for Film and Video

Number of Employees: 8+

Digital Muse was founded in early 1996 by John F. Gross. Digital Muse creates digital effect shots for film, television, commercials, rides, and other venues. The Digital Muse Commercial Division does compositing with Quantel's Henry's V- Infinity, Eyeon's Digital Fusion and Discreet Logic's Flint.

Digital Muse
1337 Third St. Third Floor

Santa Monica, CA 90401
Phone: 310 656-8050
Fax: 310 656-8055
URL: http://www.dmuse.com

Digital Visionaries 1

Area(s) of Specialization: Video Production and Post Production, Interactive CD-ROM Authoring, 3D Animation

Number of Employees: 1

An authorized Macromedia Developer, Digital Visionaries is a development firm in the use of Macromedia Director to create interactive multimedia authoring for computer, kiosks, CD, and internet/intranets. Digital Visionaries works in video production, from pre-production to post, and specializes in digital post-production with 3D compositing and special effects in both Lightwave 3D and 3D Studio Max.

Digital Visionaries 1
14009 Barner St.
Sylmar, CA 91342
Phone: 818 364-0397
Alt Phone: 888 899-9164
Fax: 818 364-0397
URL: http://www.dvhome.com

Digital Wave Productions

Area(s) of Specialization: Visual Effects for Film and Video, CD-ROM and DVD Authoring

Number of Employees: 1

Digital Wave is a video post production boutique, specializing in non-linear AVID editing and 2D/3D motion graphics. Employees work on a variety of projects, including films, commercials, documentaries, CD-ROMs, and DVD's. Other services include video compression, voice over narration and writing.

Digital Wave Productions
2580 NW Upshur St.
Portland, OR 97210
Phone: 503 227-9283
Alt Phone: 800 858-9283
Fax: 503 227-2636
URL: http://www.dwavep.com

Dimensions 3

Area(s) of Specialization: Stereoscopic Television/Film/Print Media

Number of Employees: 2

DIMENSION 3 works in 3D glasses, 3D TV (3D video), 3D film (3D motion picture), and 3D art and 3D print media. The company has experience in 3D art conversion and 3D print media, which have been used for Web sites, in books, magazines, and posters.

Dimensions 3
5240 Medina Rd.
Woodland Hills, CA 91364
Phone: 818 592-0999
Fax: 818 592-0987
URL: http://www.3dcompany.com
e-mail: info@go3d.cc

DJN Studios Inc.

Area(s) of Specialization: Animatics

Number of Employees: 1+

DJN Studios Inc.
16313 Clark Ave.
Bellflower, CA 90706
Phone: 562 920-7004
E-mail: golathst@earth.com

DMK Productions, Inc.

Area(s) of Specialization: 3D architectural rendering and Modeling

Number of Employees: 10

DMK Productions provides 3D visualization and presentation graphics, models and scenes suited to the Architecture, Building, Engineering, Land Planning, Product Design, Film and Game Development industries. Using Pentium PC workstations, the company specializes in 3D Studio MAX modeling and rendering, Set Design, and in Perspective Sketching and Storyboarding.

Employees can work directly from the client's AutoCAD drawing files, traditional Plans and Elevations, a variety of meshes or from "scratch".

DMK Productions
2395 N. Elmdale Ave.
Simi Valley, CA 93065
Phone: 805 583-3901
Fax: 805 583-3911
URL: http://www.dmkproductions.com
e-mail: info@dmkproductions.com

Downstream

Area(s) of Specialization: Post Production for Film and Video

Number of Employees: 50

DownStream does post production for video and film, merging traditional post-production with new media.

Downstream
1650 NW Naito Pkwy., Suite 301
Portland, OR 97209
Phone: 503 226-1944
Fax: 503 226-1283
URL: http://www.downstream.com

Dreadnought Pictures

Area(s) of Specialization: Animation

Number of Employees: 10

Dreadnought Pictures is an animation studio. The company focuses on one or two projects at a time. Dreadnought is developing a series of short, computer generated films, for an animated television series or feature film.

Dreadnought Pictures
7010 20th Ave. NE
Seattle, WA 98115
Phone: 206 985-0259
Fax: 206 985-0266
URL: http://www.dreadnought.com
E-mail: ericf@dreadnought.com

Dream Theater

Area(s) of Specialization: Visual Effects for Film and Video, Interactive DVD and CD-ROM Authoring

Number of Employees: 45

Dream Theater is a fully integrated, digital media production studio operating two major divisions, Dream Theater Studios and Dream Theater Interactive. Dream Theater Studios is the visual effects unit, developing and producing high end computer graphic visual effects and animation for location based entertainment, feature film, television, video and game products. Dream Theater Interactive develops and produces interactive media for various delivery pathways including world wide web, CD-ROM, DVD, Corporate presentations and kiosk.

Dream Theater
16134 Hart St., Ste. 200
Studio City, CA 91604
Phone: 818 376-8480
Fax: 818 376-8484
URL: http://www.dreamtheater.com

DreamWorks SKG

Area(s) of Specialization: Special Effects, 3D Computer Animation.

Number of Employees: 1200

Steven Spielberg, Jeffrey Katzenberg and David Geffen founded DreamWorks SKG in October 1994. The company creates, develops, produces and distributes film and music entertainment. DreamWorks SKG produces live-action motion pictures, animated feature films, network, syndicated and cable television programming, home video and DVD entertainment and consumer products.

DreamWorks SKG
100 Universal City Plz.
Universal City, CA 91608
Phone: 818 733-7000
Fax: 818 733-6155
URL: http://www.dreamworks.com

Duck Soup Produckions

Area(s) of Specialization: Traditional and Experimental Animation for Film and Video

Number of Employees: 30

Duck Soup Studios is a Los Angeles based animation studio doing traditional and experimental animation with computer special effects and compositing. With SGI and Mac workstations, the company composites live-action with animation of all forms. As a traditional animation studio the company character animates, in 2D and 3D using all of the available tools. Duck Soup uses the USAnimation digital ink and paint system, Alias/Wavefront's Power Animator and Maya, and Softimage. On the Mac side the company creates visual effects, compositing, and interactive animation using Adobe After Effects, Photoshop, Illustrator, Macromedia Director.

Duck Soup Produckions
2205 Stoner Ave.
Los Angeles, CA 90064
Phone: 310 478-0771
Fax: 310 478-0773
URL: http://www.ducksoupla.com

EdgeX Studio

Area(s) of Specialization: Media Production, Film, Video

Number of Employees: 2+

EdgeX Studios has experience in film, video, and architecture. The studio is a media design firm specializing in motion graphics and website design and development. The company produces promos, interstitial and opens, graphically intensive websites, and strategically targeted identity systems across media.

EdgeX Studio
P.O Box 29314
Los Angeles, CA 90029
Phone: 213 368-8925
URL: http://www.edgexstudio.com
E-mail: edgex@anet.net

Edmark Corporation

Area(s) of Specialization: New Media development for Educational Purposes

Number of Employees: 200

Using the computer as a learning tool, Edmark combines new multimedia technologies with educational strategies to create educational software products. Their software's combination of guided learning and open-ended exploration allows students to conduct "hands-on" experiments and develop higher-level thinking and problem-solving skills.

Edmark Corporation
P.O. Box 97021
Redmond, WA 98073-9721
Phone: 800 691-2986
Alt Phone: 425 556-8400
Fax: 425 556-8987
URL: http://www.edmark.com

Effects/Gene Young

Area(s) of Specialization: Special Visual Effects

Number of Employees: 1

Effects/Gene Young creates special visual effects.

Effects/Gene Young
517 W. Windsor Rd.
Glendale, CA 91204
Phone: 818 848-7471
Alt Phone: 818 243-8593
Fax: 818 243-8593

Elektrashock, Inc.

Area(s) of Specialization: Animation, Interactive Design, Visual Effects

Number of Employees: 17

Founded in 1997 by Darnell Williams and Rosa Farre and located in Venice Ca, ElektraShock is a full service digital boutique. The staff works in character animation as well as corporate presentation.

Elektrashock, Inc.
1320 Main St.
Venice, CA 90291
Phone: 310 477-9337
Fax: 310 399-4972
URL: http://www.elektrashock.com

Encore Productions

Area(s) of Specialization: Film and Video Production, Interactive Design

Number of Employees: 2

Encore Productions, a division of Encore Motion Pictures, is a Seattle-based communications and technology firm specializing in film and video production and interactive multimedia. The company offers comprehensive creative and technical services, including design, production, and implementation of presentations, kiosks, training and other marketing communications applications, including broadcast, video and print media.

Encore Productions
611 Market Street
Suite 4
Kirkland, WA 98033
Phone: 425 828-3621
Fax: 425 828-6587
URL: http://www.encore611.com

Encore Visual Effects

Area(s) of Specialization: Visual Effects

Number of Employees: 100+

Encore creates visual effects for television, music videos, commercials and for feature films. Clients include: Miramax, DreamWorks, David E. Kelley, 20 Century Fox, Paramount, and others.

Encore Visual Effects
6344 Fountain Ave.
Hollywood, CA 90028
Phone: 323 466-7663
Fax: 323 467-5539
URL: http://www.encorevideo.com

Epoch Ink Corp.

Area(s) of Specialization: Animation

Number of Employees: 2+

Epoch Ink Animation is a full-service animation studio located in Santa Monica. The company crafts all forms of animation production from TV series, specials, shorts and commercials to theatrical shorts and features. Epoch Ink is producing 25 episodes of "Captain Simian and the Space Monkeys" and "Dot and Spot's Amazing Christmas Adventure." Epoch Ink is an independent studio in Los Angeles, with ties to animations studios in Japan and Korea.

Epoch Ink Corp.
1517 20th St.
Santa Monica, CA 90404-3407
Phone: 310 829-9955
Fax: 310 829-9907
URL: epochink@primenet.com

Europa Films

Area(s) of Specialization: Visual Effects, Interactive Design, title design

Number of Employees: 5

Europa is a collective of filmmakers, designers, animators and producers, integrating motion graphics and live action direction with design for feature film main titles, advertising and commercials. The company's clients include: Tristar Pictures, NBC Television, Virgin Interactive, MGM, Aspect Ratio, Dreamworks SKG, Paramount Pictures, and RCA Records.

Europa Films
2057 N. Las Palmas Ave.
Los Angeles, CA 90068
Phone: 323 969-8831
Fax: 323 969-8830
URL: http://www.europafilms.com

Excite@Home

Area(s) of Specialization: Digital Communications

Number of Employees: 2500

Now Excite joined with @Home Network, to form Excite@Home, a new media company providing home and business customers with 24-hour access to services at different speeds over numerous communications devices, including PCs, pagers, cellular Phones, and television sets.

Excite@Home
450 Broadway Street
Redwood City, CA 94063
Phone: 650 556-5000

Fax: 650 556-5100
URL: http://www.excitehome.net

Eye Candy Post

Area(s) of Specialization: Film and Video
Post Production

Number of Employees: 10

Eye Candy Post is a film and television Post
Production Facility in Los Angeles for on-line
and off-line clients to use D2, Digital
Betacam, Betacam and 3/4" videotape. Eye
Candy Post's facility features four Avid off-
line bays, a Softimage|DS bay plus three Avid
on-line bays.

Eye Candy Post
3575 Cahuenga Blvd. West
Suite 595
Universal City, CA 90068
Phone: 323 850-5567
Fax: 323 850-7467
URL: http://www.eyecandypost.com

Fat Box, Inc.

Area(s) of Specialization: Post Production,
Animation

Number of Employees: 20

Located in San Francisco, the company
provides 3D CG animation, graphics, and
multiple post edit and special effects suites;

Fat Box is an on-staff collaboration of visual
marketing and advertising professionals. Fat
Box specializes in broadcast television and
filmmaking.

Fat Box, Inc.
499 Seaport Court, 2nd floor
Redwood City, CA 94063
Phone: 650 363-8700
Fax: 650 363-8860
URL: http://www.fatbox.com
E-mail: infor@fatbox.com

Film Roman

Area(s) of Specialization: Animation

Number of Employees: 400

Film Roman is an animation studio that
produces animated television series, specials
and feature films. The studio also maintains
licensing and merchandising and
international distribution arms. Film Roman
is working on "The Simpsons", "King of the
Hill" and "Bobby's World."

Film Roman, Inc.
12020 Chandler Blvd
Suite 300
N. Hollywood, CA 91607
Phone: 818 761-2544
URL: http://www.filmroman.com

Flamdoodle Animation, Inc.

Area(s) of Specialization: Animation Studio

Number of Employees: 24

Flamdoodle Animation, Inc. is a full service traditional animation studio providing services from conception to completion for productions in all media, and outputting to all video and film formats at feature film quality. Utilizing the aimo digital system and CD quality, digidesign based audio editing on high-end workstations, the company offers automated lip-synching, in-betweening and digital ink-and-paint.

Flamdoodle Animation Inc.
6 Cuesta LN
Santa Fe, NM 87505-8782
Phone: 505 982-3132
Fax: 505 466-3525
URL: http://www.flamdoodle.com

Flash Film Works

Area(s) of Specialization: Modeling, 3D Animation, Digital Matte Paintings

Number of Employees: 10

Flash Film Works is a beta site for four of the CGI software manufacturers; the company participates in the on-going development of products. Flash Film Works staff includes programmers, animators, 3D matte artists and compositors. The company also conducts a training program, teaching all aspects of the visual effects craft.

Flash Film Works
3349 Cahuenga Blvd, Suite 2B
Los Angles CA 90068
Phone: 323 851-1440
Fax: 323 851-4586
URL: http://www.flashfilmworks.com

Flint & Steel Productions, Inc.

Area(s) of Specialization: Web Design

Number of Employees: 1+

Flint & Steel creates interactive web presentations.

Flint & Steel Productions, Inc.
PMB#12 353-E East 10th St.
Gilroy, CA 95020
Phone: 408 848-8839
URL: http://www.flintandsteel.net
E-mail: webmaster@flintandsteel.net

Flip Your Lid Animation Studios

Area(s) of Specialization: Animation for Film and Web

Number of Employees: 10

Co-founders, Jay Jacoby and Steve Soffer established Flip Your Lid, Animation in 1998 to create and produce original animation for television and commercials. In June of 1999, the company launched a new division focusing exclusively on character animation and web design for the internet. Flip Your Lid creates advertising and promo campaigns for the entertainment industry including Disney, Fox, Universal, 20th Century Fox, NBC, CBS, Turner Broadcasting, Encore, Paramount, Sony and A&E.

Flip Your Lid Animation Studios
650 N. Bronson Ave., Ste. 223
Los Angeles, CA 90004
Phone: 818 222-0700
Fax: 818 996-6391
URL: http://www.flipyourlid.com

Flying Rhino Productions

Area(s) of Specialization: Film and Video Production, CGI

Number of Employees: 20+

Flying Rhino Productions generates content in the form of Video and Film Production, 2D and 3D Animation, Digital Video and Computer Media for over 8 years. The staff includes producers, directors, writers, designers, art directors, animators, artists and editors. Flying Rhino is equipped with high-end multi-processor NT and Mac workstations, both NT 4.0 and Novell servers, a full digital video and internet development department, 3 post-production edit suites and a full audio department. The company's edit suites are equipped with a Turbo Cube real time non-linear edit system, a CMX A/B roll Beta SP edit system, and a Stratasphere suite.

Flying Rhino Productions
400 Tamal Plaza, Suite 406
Corte Madera, CA 94925
Phone: 415 927-4466
Fax: 415 927-1197
URL: http://www.flying-rhino.com

Flying Spot, Inc.

Area(s) of Specialization: Post Production

Number of Employees: 25

Flying Spot was founded as a post-production design boutique in Seattle, Washington in 1992. The Flying Spot creates graphic design and editorials, and series editing, title sequence, and design. Flying Spot offers seven digital editing suites, nine design and animation suites, super high-resolution 8:8:8 telecine, and post-production.

Flying Spot, Inc.
1008 Western Ave.
Seattle, WA 98104
Phone: 206 464-0744
Alt Phone: 800 963-7678
Fax: 206 464-0416
URL: http://www.flyingspot.com

Foundation Imaging

Area(s) of Specialization: Visual Effects for Film and Video

Number of Employees: 155+

Foundation Imaging, a computer animation/special effects company based in Valencia, California, was founded in 1992 by Ron Thornton and Paul Bryant to create computer visual effects, miniatures and motion control for the entertainment industry. The company has created effects for theme park attractions such as, "Star Trek: The Experience" for the Las Vegas Hilton Hotel and "Journey to Atlantis" for Sea World/Florida. FI has also created visual effects for Star Trek: Voyager and "Star Trek: Deep Space Nine." Foundation Imaging contributed to the making of Tristar Pictures' "Contact." The company creates, designs and produces digital special effects for network and syndicated television projects, feature films, multimedia projects and theme parks around the world.

Foundation Imaging
24933 West Avenue Stanford
Valencia, CA 91355
Phone: 805 257-0292
Fax: 805 257-7966
URL: http://www.foundation-i.com

Four Media Company

Area(s) of Specialization: 2D and 3D animation, computer graphics and compositing

Number of Employees: 100+

Four Media Company is a provider of technical and creative services to the entertainment industry. 4MC outsourcing solutions are used in the United States and worldwide by producers, distributors and other owners of television programming, feature films and similar entertainment content. The name Four Media Company is derived from the Company's core services in film, video, sound and data.

Four Media Company
2813 West Alameda Ave.
Burbank, CA 91505-4455
Phone: 818 840-7000
Outside California: 800 423-2277
URL: http://www.4mc.com

Fox Animation Studios

Area(s) of Specialization: Animation for Film

Number of Employees: 400+

Fox Animation Studios employs artists, technicians and craftsmen. The company produces classically-animated feature films. As a feature animation facility, the studio houses 83 Silicon Graphics Indy and Indigo computers, plus two Challenge servers and one Onyx server.

Fox Animation Studios
2747 E. Camelback Rd.
Phoenix, AZ 85016
Phone: 602 808-4600
Fax: 602 808-4699
URL: http://www.foxanimation.com

Fred Wolf Films

Area(s) of Specialization: Animation for Films

Number of Employees: 5

The core of Fred Wolf Films' business is in the conceptual development and production of animated films. Red Wolf Films is comprised of two studio locations, one in Burbank, California and the other in Dublin, Ireland. All creative work, concepts, design, script writing, dialogue recording, color, locating and design, storyboards and direction of animation action are executed at the Fred Wolf Films studios. Following these steps, the body of production using all of the above-mentioned pre-production elements is completed in contracted studio facilities in the Far East and Europe.

Fred Wolf Films
4222 W. Burbank Blvd.
Burbank, CA 91505
Phone: 818 846-0611
Fax: 818 846-0979
URL: http://www.fredwolffilms.com

Fusionworks, Inc.

Area(s) of Specialization: Speech Recognition Development

Number of Employees: 10

Greg Fisch and Susan Kennedy founded Fusionworks, Inc. in 1998 to design and create products that use speech recognition and technology to create interactive products. From toys and CD-ROMs, to aviation training software, the Fusionworks' team develops products that incorporate interactive technologies. The company specializes in natural language speech recognition integration, robotics and animatronics, infrared and radio frequency communications, and developing the software that integrates them all.

Fusionworks, Inc.
10100 Pioneer Blvd. Suite 103
Santa Fe Springs, CA 90670
Phone: 562 941-0397
Fax: 562 941-8236
URL: http://www.fusionworksinc.com

Gentle Giant Studios

Area(s) of Specialization: Digital Modeling and Scanning, Toy Design, Maquette

Sculpture, Product Animation, Quicktime VR Studio, Stereo lithography, Complete Mobile Digital Services.

Number of Employees: 20+

Gentle Giant combines computer-based 3D digital scanning, modeling and prototyping technologies with traditional sculpting, molding, casting and painting skills to create models and data for films, games and toys. The company's clients include: Digital Domain, DreamWorks, SKG, Lightstorm Entertainment, LucasFilm Ltd., Marvel Comics, Mattel, Inc., Nickelodeon, Universal Studios, Walt Disney Company, Warner Bros. and Twentieth Century Fox.

Gentle Giant Studios
1115 Chestnut St.
Burbank, CA 91506
Phone: 818 557-8681
Fax: 818 557-8684
E-mail: cr.gentlegiant@usa.net

Giant Killer Robots

Area(s) of Specialization: Animation, CGI, Multimedia

Number of Employees: 5

Giant Killer Robots is a digital effects company formed by animators Mike Schmitt, Peter Oberdorfer and John Vegher to create high-quality computer animation for film and television. The company deals with all aspects of the entertainment industry, creating effects for movies, commercials and video games.

Giant Killer Robots
576 Natoma Street
San Francisco, CA 94103
Phone: 415-863-9119
Fax: 415 863-9108
URL: http://www.killerobot.com
E-mail: giant@killerobot.com

Gigawatt Studios

Area(s) of Specialization: Interactive Design for Games, Web, and CD-ROM

Number of Employees: 27

Gigawatt Studios is a digital production studio located in Hollywood, CA. Gigawatt uses technical, creative, and production facilities to create interactive game entertainment, multimedia and web site development. Gigawatt is represented by International Creative Management, and has established relationships with publisher's and distributors in the interactive multimedia and game industry. Gigawatt has been contracted to develop high-end 3D graphic adventures for the PC platform as well as location based interactive entertainment.

Gigawatt Studios
6255 Sunset Boulevard
Hollywood, CA 90028
Phone: 323 856-5245

Fax: 323 856-5240
URL: http://www.gwatt.com

Gosch Productions

Area(s) of Specialization: Film and Video Production, Audio Production

Number of Employees: 20

Gosch Productions provides a full service film/video production house and sound stage to initiate and complete production seamlessly under one roof. The company has fifteen years of experience.

Gosch Productions
5144 Vineland Ave.
North Hollywood, CA 91601
Phone: 818 509-3530
Fax: 818 509-3534
URL: http://www.gosch.net

Grafx

Area(s) of Specialization: Web Design, Video, Training

Number of Employees: 10

Grafx was founded in 1982 and incorporated in 1984. Its first products were early interactive presentation production and delivery tools such as PC Paint and GRASP. Grafx has served technology companies by providing marketing, sales and training materials.

Grafx
1046A Calle Recodo
San Clemente, CA 92673
Phone: 949 361-3475
Fax: 949 248-0139
URL: http://www.gfx.com

H-gun Labs-Unplugged

Area(s) of Specialization: Animation

Number of Employees: 10+

The company creates 2D and 3D computer animation in Chicago and San Francisco. H-Gun West (the San Francisco location) produces much of the work in-house. H-Gun West is a MAC/SGI-based facility, utilizing 2D and 3D programming.

H-Gun Labs
587 Shotwell
San Francisco, CA 94110
Phone: 415 648-4386
Fax: 415 920-3911
URL: http://www.hgun.com
E-mail: info@hgun.com

Hammerhead Productions

Area(s) of Specialization: Film and Video Production, Visual Effects

Number of Employees: 11

Hammerhead Productions, founded in February, 1995, is a digital film production company. The company is involved in creating digital visual effects used in making the company's own films and producing films for other studios. The company writes scripts, and software. Film credits include: "X Men", "Woman on Top", "Deep Blue Sea", "For the love of the Game", "Paulie", "For Richer or Poorer", "My favorite Martian", "Showgirls", and several other features.

Hammerhead Productions
Studio City, CA
Phone: 818 762-8643
Fax: 818 762-7311
URL: http://www.hammerhead.com

Hansard Vision Productions-FX

Area(s) of Specialization: Blue Screen, Front and Rear Projection

Number of Employees: 10+

Hansard Vision works in the field of Projection-Fx. In 1948 Robert L. Hansard, Sr. founded the original Hansard company. The first feature using the Hansard System was the 1948 version of "Joan Of Arc" starring Ingrid Bergman filmed at the Hal Roach Studios. The company is now involved in blue screen and front and rear projection.

Hansard Vision Productions-FX
6056 W Jefferson Blvd

Los Angeles, CA 90016
Phone: 310 840-5660
Fax: 310 840-5662
URL: http://www.hansardvision.com
E-mail: hansard@hansardvision.com

Happy Trails Animation llc

Area(s) of Specialization: Animation All Types

Number of Employees: 5

Situated in Portland, Oregon, animators Andy and Amy Collen create, produce and direct traditional, digital, and mixed media. The company offers cel animation, DV photo manipulation, character and background design, pastels, inks and watercolors, sand and other materials, paper cutout animation, flat clay animation, and various forms of computer technology. Full production from storyboard to finished master. Soundtracks are often composed by musician and soundman Greg Ives, who has played with Miles Davis, Dizzy Gillespie, and Quincy Jones.

Happy Trails Animation LLC
3916 SW Huber St.
Portland, OR 97219
Phone: 503 245-1154
Fax: 503 244-2533
URL: http://www.sns-access.com/~anima

Helium Productions, Inc.

Area(s) of Specialization: 3D Computer Animation, CGI

Number of Employees: 11

Helium's infrastructure is built around Silicon Graphics hardware and several software platforms. With a capacity of seven animation seats, each staff member works on SGI Octane workstation. Including the loaded SGI Challenge render farm, the company's facility contains a total of 30 CPUs available. The company utilizes several 3D production software tools including Side Effects' Houdini and Prisms, Alias/Wavefront's Maya and Pixar's Photo-realistic Renderman as well as proprietary composite and resource management tools. Also available is a compliment of Mac-based machines for 2D image manipulations. Digital disk recorders are used for viewing and testing purposes. The company develops custom code for building, animating, image processing, motion control, and renderers.

Helium Productions, Inc.
2690 N. Beachwood Drive
Hollywood, CA 90068
Phone: 323 467-9323
Fax: 323 467-9396
URL: http://www.heliumproductions.com

Hornet Animation

Area(s) of Specialization: 3D Animation, Digital Effects, Motion Graphics

Number of Employees: 1+

Hornet Animation develops, produces and creates computer animation, visual effects and motion graphics, for use in feature films, title sequences, logo treatments, music videos, editing and broadcast sports events. The design team composed of 2D and 3D animators, creates 3D models and designs realistic textures, life-like animations, and complex compositing.

Hornet Animation
5777 West Century Blvd. Suite 1640
Los Angeles, CA 90045
Phone: 310-641-1964
URL: http://www.hornetinc.com

House Film Design

Area(s) of Specialization: Animation and Title Design

Number of Employees: 2+

House Film Design
16735 Yucca St.
Los Angeles, CA 90028
Phone: 323 462-0128

House of Moves Motion Capture Studios

Area(s) of Specialization: CGI

Number of Employees: 20-25

House of Moves, in it's fifth year of operation, provides motion capture services, stock 3D data, and custom 3D animation tools for the entertainment industry. The company has completed hundreds of animation projects including: electronic games, TV commercials, feature films, broadcast television series and on-line character animation/content for the Web. Motion capture technology, originally designed as a way for orthopedic surgeons to pinpoint irregularities in the human gait, has evolved into a technology whereby a human performance can be digitized and utilized to drive the motion of 3D characters. While motion capture is usually limited to humanoid characters, House of Moves has captured other types of characters as well.

House of Moves Motion Capture Studios
5318 McConnell Ave.
Los Angeles, CA 90066
Phone: 310 306-6131
Fax: 310 306-1351
URL: http://www.moves.com

Howard A. Anderson Company

Area(s) of Specialization: Tiles, Optical, Digital Film Effects, Second Unit Photography

Number of Employees: 22+

Howard Anderson Company provides the following capabilities for clients' projects: motion picture post-production, special photographic effects, title and logo design/animation, computerized motion control animation camera, composites from blue screen photography, complete insert stage, and 2nd Unit/location photography crews, storyboards, matte paintings/composites, miniatures, effects supervision, and supervision for blue screen photography, silicon graphics- MAC/IBM, 3D graphic design, computer animation, wire and rig removal, digital compositing, image warping and morphing, digital effects capabilities, multi-layer composites, blue/green/non-screen, roto-scoping, motion tracking (single and multiple point), image retouching, matte painting and image manipulation, and scratch/dirt removal/restoration, warping and morphing of images, and 3D title or logo design and animation.

Howard A. Anderson Company
5161 Lankershim Blvd. Suite 120
North Hollywood, CA 91601
Phone: 818 623-1111

Fax: 818 623-7761
URL: http://www.haopticals.com

Human Code, Inc.

Area(s) of Specialization: Interactive Design

Number of Employees: 40

Human Code Inc. provides custom e-commerce, smart toys, learning systems and on-line marketing communications for the entertainment industry, educators, and entrepreneurs. Since 1993 the company has worked in design, production and implementation of experiences for the internet, computer, broadband, iTV and wireless media.

Human Code (Presage Studios)
901 E. Street
Suite 300
San Rafael, CA 94901
Phone: 415 454-7007
Fax: 415 454-6992
URL: http://www.humancode.com

Image G/Ikongraphics

Area(s) of Specialization: Motion Control Cinematography

Number of Employees: 30

Image G is a provider of motion control cinematography and related special effects services to the entertainment, advertising,

and multimedia industries. Founded by Tom Barron in 1984, the company has worked in computer-controlled camera technology and developed new techniques to create ever more sensational visual effects.

Image G/Ikongraphics
10900 Ventura Blvd.
Studio City, CA 91604
Phone: 818 761-6644
Fax: 818 761-8397
URL: http://www.imageg.com

Imaginary Forces

Area(s) of Specialization: Film and Video Production, Interactive Design

Number of Employees: 80+

Imaginary Forces (IF) is the fusion of thought, images, movement and sound. As storytellers, the company's purpose is to experiment and create for the media in which it works: film, broadcast, print, site and interactive design.

Imaginary Forces
6526 Sunset Boulevard
Hollywood, CA 90028
Phone: 323 957-6868
Fax: 323 957-9577
URL: http://www.imaginaryforces.com

Imagination Workshop

Area(s) of Specialization: Computer Generated Animations

Number of Employees: 1

Jack Walsh's Computer Generated Animations is a web gallery that offers projects ranging from commercial broadcast animations/visual effects to computer generated three-dimensional worlds.

Imagination Workshop
19822 Collins Rd.
Santa Clarita, CA. 91351
Phone: 661 298-9615
URL: http://www.smartlink.net/~jwalsh

Industrial Light And Magic

Area(s) of Specialization: Visual Effects, Animation, Film and Video Production, CGI

Number of Employees: 1,000+

Founded in 1975 by George Lucas, Industrial Light and Magic created a new kind of filmmaking coupling extraordinary innovative visual effects with meticulous realism. Just north of San Francisco, Industrial Light and Magic has created visual effects for hundreds of feature films including "The Star Wars Prequals."

Industrial Light and Magic
Lucas Digital, Ltd. LLC
P.O. Box 2459

San Rafael, CA 94912
Phone: 415 448-2000
Fax: 415 456-0833
URL: http://www.ilm.com

Inertia Pictures, Inc.

Area(s) of Specialization: Interactive Design, Visual Effects

Number of Employees: 6

Inertia Pictures is a full service digital entertainment, design, and production company located in Santa Monica, California. Inertia offers design using technology for on-line animation, 3D computer graphics, concept design for television, games, feature films, and theme park films and toys.

Inertia Pictures, Inc.
1503 Franklin St.
Santa Monica, CA 90404
Phone: 310 829-5491
Fax: 310 829-7291
URL: http://www.inertia.com

Infinite Dimensions Studios

Area(s) of Specialization: Web Development, Animation, Video, Game Characters

Number of Employees: 25

Infinite Dimensions Studios help customers create websites, films, television programs or live Internet shows. The staff has experience in traditional television and film, and expertise in computer generated content.

Infinite Dimensions Studios
33 Sorrento Way
San Rafael CA, 94901
Phone: 415 454-6806
Fax: 415 456-2623
URL: http://www.idscorp.com

International Cartoons and Animation Center, Inc.

Area(s) of Specialization: Cartoon Development

Number of Employees: 100

International Cartoons & Animation Center, Inc. (ICAC, Inc) is an animation studio specializing in producing direct-to-video, lip-synched, multilingual children's animated cartoons. The company's productions are generated in six different languages (English, Arabic, French, Malay, Urdu and Turkish). The staff redraws the characters to lip-synch to each language. The company's original stories promote positive and universal family values. The videos feature classical 2D animation style. ICAC, Inc. continues to expand in production capabilities and international marketing and sales.

International Cartoons and Animation Center, Inc.
1823 E 17th St. Suite 203
Santa Ana, CA 92705

Phone: 714 953-5778
Fax: 714 560-0744
URL: http://www.familytoons.com

Intrepidus Worldwide

Area(s) of Specialization: Interactive Design

Number of Employees: 2

Intrepidus is a privately owned company with offices in Santa Monica, California operating through two separate groups: broad based media production and entertainment management.

Intrepidus Worldwide
3000 West Olympic Blvd.
Santa Monica, CA 90404
Phone: 310 315-4805
Fax: 310 315-4806
URL: http://www.intrepidus.com

Introvision International

Area(s) of Specialization: Special Effects and Visual Effects

Number of Employees: 1

Introvision International creates visual effects and special effects.

Introvision International
1011 N. Fuller Ave.
West Hollywood, CA 90046
Phone: 323 969-1930

Island Fever Productions, Inc.

Area(s) of Specialization: Character Animation, Visual Effects, Production

Number of Employees: 2

Established in 1997, Island Fever Productions is a computer graphics production facility located in Santa Monica, CA that provides computer generated character animation and visual effects for films and commercials using SGI computer equipment and software.

Island Fever Productions, Inc.
824 11th. Street Suite #8
Santa Monica, CA 9040
Phone: 310 656-3011
Fax: 310 656-3021
URL: http://www.island-fever.com

Jamaica Bay

Area(s) of Specialization: Post Production, Interactive Design, Animation

Number of Employees: 3

The company works with JBay's D1 suite, Avid, and Illusion to create animation, interactive design, and post production work.

Jamaica Bay
3111 N. Central Ave., Ste. 105
Phoenix, AZ 85012
Phone: 602 274-3348
Alt. Phone: 800 274-5229
Fax: 602 274-5878
URL: http://www.jbay.com

The Jim Henson Company

Area(s) of Specialization: Puppetry

Number of Employees: 100+

The Jim Henson Company has been in family entertainment for more than 40 years. The Company's productions and characters began in 1955 with Muppet creator Jim Henson's first local telecast, "Sam & Friends", have continued to entertain children of all ages around the world. Today, The Jim Henson Company is a multimedia production company, a character licensor, a publisher of children's books and home to Jim Henson Television, Jim Henson Pictures, Jim Henson Interactive and Jim Henson's Creature Shop. The Jim Henson Company has been acquired by EM. TV & Merchandising AG, based in Munich, Germany. Jim Henson Interactive is responsible for the worldwide digital expression, development and creative production of the Company's intellectual properties owned by the organization which include, "The Muppets", "Farscape", "Bear in the Big Blue House", "Mopatop's Shop", "Construction Site!" and "Dark Crystal". Formed in 1998, the division has worked with a variety of partners including, Sony,

Microsoft, Intel, Havas, Psygnosis, IBM, Activision, and the Sun/Netscape Alliance.

The Jim Henson Company
1416 North LaBraea Avenue
Hollywood, CA 90028.
Phone: 323 802-1500
Fax: 323 802-1825
URL: http://www.henson.com

Jim Keeshen Productions

Area(s) of Specialization: Animation for Film and Video, 3D Animation for the Internet

Number of Employees: 2

Keeshen has produced TV commercials and test spots for major companies including Disney, Proctor & Gamble, Levi Strauss, Raid, Lexus, Mazda and Mattel. The company has produced animation for the Internet such as fully animated segments with sound for America on Line, and created animated characters for the new 3D Vchat rooms for Microsoft. JKP is developing several animated interactive games and CD-ROM programs for children and teens. The Peppered Leopard Cookbook is a learning tool for cooking and nutrition. Fashion Fun explores the world of fashion and cosmetology. In 1982 Keeshen incorporated into Jim Keeshen Productions and specialized in producing animation and animatics / photomatics for ad agencies in L.A., S.F., N.Y., St. Louis and Chicago.

Jim Keeshen Productions
1950 Sawtelle Blvd. Suite 220
Los Angeles, CA 90025
Phone: 310 478-7230
Fax: 310 478-5142

Joseph Abbati

Area(s) of Specialization: Film/Video, Multimedia, CGI

Number of Employees: 1

Joseph Abbati is an art director and designer. The company creates advertisements, packaging, logos, sales brochures, and web page designs. Clients have included: Colossal Films: Time-Warner, Organic On-line, WorldCom, Intel, Hewlett Packard, Mac Home Journal, Parenting Magazine, Visages, Generra, Code Bleu Jeans, Delta Burke Design, The North Face, and Marjorie Baer.

Joseph Abbati
1931 Mason Street
San Francisco, CA 94133-2725
Phone: 415 673-2341
E-mail: jlabbati@creative.net

K & J Design

Area(s) of Specialization: Computer Animation, Illustration, Film, Web

Number of Employees: 2

K&J Design creates 3D and 2D computer animations, models, illustrations and graphics for a variety of venues including: feature films, TV, commercials, architects, display firms, industrial design firms, company informational films and brochures, court forensics, and individuals.

K & J Design
4322 Ensenada Pl.
Woodland Hills, CA 91364
Phone: 818 710-6672
Fax: 818 710-6673
URL: http://www.kjdesign.net

Kenimatlon Animation Services

Area(s) of Specialization: Film Animation Service

Number of Employees: 1+

Kenimation Animation Services creates titles, aerial images, montages, and animation.

Kenimation Animation Services
1424 N. Wilcox Ave.
Hollywood, CA 90028
Phone: 323 462-2679
E-mail: kenru@media1.net

Klasky Csupo, Inc.

Area(s) of Specialization: Animation

Number of Employees: 400+

Klasky Csupo, Inc. created television shows such as "Rugrats", "Duckman", "Aaahh!!! Real Monsters" and "The Simpsons." With an Eastern European flare, the animators of Klasky Csupo produce television shows, commercials, music videos and title designs. The company is owned and operated by founders Arlene Klasky and Gabor Csupo.

Klasky Csupo Inc.
1258 N. Highland Ave.
Hollywood, CA 90038
Phone: 323 468-5978
Fax: 323 468-3021
URL: http://www.klaskycsupo.com

Kleiser-Walczak Construction Co.

Area(s) of Specialization: CGI, Visual Effects for Film and Video

Number of Employees: 40

Kleiser-Walczak Construction Co. produces computer generated animation and visual effects for feature films, special venue attractions, commercials and interactive media. The staff works out of production studios in Hollywood, Manhattan, and Massachusetts.

Kleiser-Walczak Construction Co.
6105 Mulholland Hwy.
Hollywood, CA 90068

Phone: 323 467-3563
Fax: 323 467-3583
URL: http://www.kwcc.com

Krakatoa Digital Post, Inc.

Area(s) of Specialization: Post Production
Editing

Number of Employees: 2+

Krakatoa Digital Post serves the needs of
independent producers in their post-
production facility. The staff assists clients
with show open, promo or trailer cut, digital
effects, entire series, documentary or feature.

Krakatoa Digital Post, Inc.
419 S. Flower St.
Burbank, CA 91502
Phone: 818 562-1206
Fax: 818 848-7637
URL: http://www.krakatoapost.com

Krell Wonders

Area(s) of Specialization: Creature effects,
Props, Stop-motion Animation

Number of Employees: 2+

Krell Wonders, located in Burbank,
California, specializes in animatronic special
effects for film and TV, as well as the design
and creation of custom-made stop-motion
animation armatures. Since 1985, the

company has been making full and partial
armatures for many characters in both films
and TV commercials—including the
Pillsbury Doughboy before he went digital!
The company engineers armatures from
stainless steel and aircraft aluminum, for
strength and durability. The armatures are
reusable and practically maintenance-free.

Krell Wonders
7746 Clybourn Ave.
Burbank, CA 91352
Phone: 818 768-7260
Fax: 818 768-7520
URL: http://www.krellwonders.com

Kurtz & Friends Films

Area(s) of Specialization: Cel Animation and
Special Effects for commercials, Film Titles.

Number of Employees: 15+

Kurtz & Friends Films works in special
effects, cel animation and film titles.

Kurtz & Friends Films
2312 W. Olive Ave.
Burbank, CA 91506
Phone: 818 841-8188
Fax: 818 841-6263
URL: http://www.kurtzandfriends.com
E-mail: kurtz99@ix.netcom.com
bobkurtz@aol.com

L@it2D

Area(s) of Specialization: Film and Television Production, Interactive Design

Number of Employees: 4

L@it2'd is a digital entertainment design company, working from concept to delivery of content for Broadcast Television, Film, and Interactive media. The company combines organic design with technology.

L@it2D
6815 W. Willoughby Ave., Ste. 102
Los Angeles, CA 90038
Phone: 323 856-0700
Fax: 323 856-0704
URL: http://www.lati2d.com

Landmark Entertainment Group

Area(s) of Specialization: TV and Themepark Design

Number Of Employees: 30+

Since its inception in 1980, Landmark Entertainment Group has been creating forms of entertainment for the global audience. Landmark Entertainment Group is a diversified entertainment company that has worked internationally since 1980. Founded by Gary Goddard and Tony Christopher, Landmark creates, develops, and produces live entertainment, film and television productions, licensing and merchandising properties, interactive development, as well as theme parks and attractions for the theme park and leisure industry.

Landmark Entertainment Group
5200 Lamkershin Blvd.
North Hollywood, CA 91601
Phone: 818 753-6700
Fax: 818 753-6767
URL: http://www.landmarkusa.com

Landor Associates

Area(s) of Specialization: Web Design, Graphic Design

Number of Employees: 1500+

Landor Associates is an international image management consultancy with 49 years in the design business and offices in 14 countries with over 500 employees worldwide, specializing in corporate identity, environmental and packaging design. Project teams are interdisciplinary, made up of designers, architects, production specialists, marketing professionals, naming experts and market research professionals. The company creates visual identity systems.

Landor Associates
1001 Front Street
San Francisco, CA 94111
Phone: 888 252-6367

Fax: 415 365-3190
URL: http://www.landor.com

Laser Media, Inc.

Area(s) of Specialization: Digital graphics, Laser Productions

Number Of Employees: 15

LaserMedia is a laser effects firm established in 1974, now producing laser effects for entertainment, promotion and theme park installations. Laser Media works in laser display technology, animation and special effect lighting.

Laser Media, Inc.
6383 Arizona Circle
Los Angeles, CA 90045
Phone: 310 338-9200
Fax: 310 338-9221
URL: http://www.lasermedia.com

LaserPacific Media Corporation

Area(s) of Specialization: Post Production for Film and Video, Interactive Design

Number of Employees: 100+

LaserPacific implements technology and services to the television, motion picture and digital media industries. LaserPacific's facilities offer services necessary to assist the creators of motion picture film and digitally captured content prepare creative assets for distribution via analog or digital broadcast, file servers, DVD, Laser Disc, DVD-Rom, CD-ROM, by satellite or the Internet.

LaserPacific Media Corporation
Phone: 323 462-6266
Fax: 323 464-6005
URL: http://www.laserpacific.com
E-mail: info@laserpacific.com

Launch Media, Inc.

Area(s) of Specialization: Interactive Design

Number of Employees: 200+

Launch Media, Inc. creates interactive design. The company is a resource for music and entertainment through multimedia.

Launch Media, Inc.
2700 Pennsylvania Avenue
Santa Monica, CA 90404
Phone: 310 526-4300
Fax: 310 526-4400
URL: http://www.launch.com

The Leprevost Corp.

Area(s) of Specialization: Graphic Design

Number of Employees: 5+

The Leprevost Corp. works in graphic design.

The Leprevost Corp.
6781 Wildlife Rd.
Malibu, CA 90265
Phone: 310 457-3742
URL: http://www.levprevost.com

Lighthouse Graphics, Inc.

Area(s) of Specialization: Computer Animation and Modeling

Number of Employees: 3

Founded in 1993, LGI is a computer animation studio based in Reno, Nevada. The company produces animation for commercial broadcasts, industrial videos, films, CD-ROM, print media and the web. Specializing in computer animation and modeling, LGI offers two and three-dimensional treatments of logos and text, particle effects, lighting effects, morphing, hand sculpting and 3D scanning, computer modeling and lip synch. The company uses blueprints and schematic references to create virtual constructs for fly-through presentations, technical instructions, and architectural applications.

Lighthouse Graphics, Inc.
1280 Terminal Way #5
Reno, Nevada, 89502
Phone/Fax: 775 324-5588
URL: http://www.lgireno.com

Little Fluffy Clouds, Inc.

Area(s) of Specialization: 3D Computer Animation and Design

Number of Employees: 2+

Little Fluffy Clouds was founded in May 1996 by English designer/producer, Betsy De Fries and Dutch director Jerry van de Beek. The company specializes in all forms of digital animation and design, offering story boarding, character development and creative design, special effects, editing, compositing and New Media. LFC presents a complete design and production facility for broadcast and web-based graphics. The company uses traditional animation techniques and incorporates computer animation. The company's New York location is represented by Curious Pictures.

Little Fluffy Clouds, Inc.
Pier 29 Annex
San Francisco, CA 94111
Phone: 415 621-1300
URL: http://www.littlefluffyclouds.com

Liquid Light Studios

Area(s) of Specialization: Animation for Film and Video, Animated Shorts

Number of Employees: 6

Liquid Light Studios is a 3D Design and Animation studio located in West Los Angeles. Established in January, 1996, Liquid

Light Studios worked within the broadcast arena which has led to such credits as "Ally McBeal's Dancing Baby", promos for "E! Entertainment Television", and character animation for "The Rosie O'Donnell Show." Liquid Light also applied its discipline of 3D to film and architecture.

Liquid Light Studios
1093 Broxton Ave., Ste. 220
Los Angeles, CA 90024
Phone: 310 443-5551
Fax: 310 443-5542
URL: http://www.liquidlightstudios.com

Loko Pictures

Area(s) of Specialization: Paper Manipulation, Painting on Glass, Cel Animation, Sand Animation

Number of Employees: 4

Loko Pictures is an animation studio based in Los Angeles formed by a collaboration of animators/artists. Loko Pictures has produced intro. ID jobs, title sequences, and animation for CD-ROMs & interactive web based documents. Loko offers traditional cell, cut out, sand, and 3D computer animation. Most of the artists at Loko Pictures are graduates of the CalArts film and animation program, with a background in art and animation. The company has an editing system, Deck Alpha Workstation, Lightwave 3D, and Video-action Pro, using After Effects,

Photoshop, Illustrator, and Painter. An Amiga workstation is used for traditional paper animation production for pencil testing.

Loko Pictures
548 South spring St.
Suit 921
Los Angeles, 90013
Phone: 213 622-4398
Fax: 213 622-2177
URL: http://www.lokopic.com

LOOK! Effects, Inc.

Area(s) of Specialization: Visual Effects for Film and Video

Number of Employees: 25

LOOK! has 2D and 3D artists with experience as visual effects supervisors and artists of both feature film and commercial projects, including the opening sequence of *Armageddon* and *Volcano*.

LOOK! Effects, Inc.
1611A El Centro Ave.
Los Angeles, CA 90028
Phone: 323 469-4230
Fax: 323 469-4931
URL: http://www.lookfx.com

LucasArts Entertainment Co.

Area(s) of Specialization: Interactive Entertainment Software

Number of Employees: 500 +

LucasArts was founded in 1982 by filmmaker George Lucas to provide an interactive element in his vision of a multi-faceted game company. The work produced combines storytelling, character development and settings. LucasArts Entertainment Company LLC is one of five Lucas companies. Lucas Digital Ltd. LLC, comprised of Industrial Light & Magic and Skywalker Sound, provides visual effects and audio post-production services to the entertainment industry. Lucasfilm Ltd. includes George Lucas' feature film and television activities, as well as THX, Lucas Licensing Ltd. is responsible for the merchandising of all Lucasfilm's film and television properties. Lucas Learning Ltd. offers interactive software products that provide learning opportunities through exploration and discovery.

LucasArts Entertainment Co.
P.O Box 10307
San Rafael, CA 94912
Phone: 415 472-3400
Alt. Phone: 888 532-4263
Fax: 415 444-8240
URL: http://www.lucasarts.com

Lucasfilm Ltd. and Lucas Licensing Ltd.

Area(s) of Specialization: Digital Effects

Number of Employees: 1,100

Based in Marin County, California, Lucasfilm Ltd. is an independent production company. The company includes all of the George Lucas' feature film and television activities, and houses the business affairs, finance, information technology and services, research library/archives, Internet, Skywalker Ranch operations, marketing, and human resources divisions.

Lucasfilm Ltd.
P.O. Box 2009
San Rafael, CA 94912
Phone: 415 662-1800
Fax: 415 662-2460
URL: http://www.lucasfilm.com

Lucas-THX

Area(s) of Specialization: Sound Effects

Number of Employees: 500+

Lucas-THX provides film presentation in the exhibition and consumer electronics industry. The Professional THX Sound System is currently in over 1,400 theaters worldwide. There are more than 80 THX disc titles on the market.

THX Division
P.O. Box 10327
San Rafael, CA 94912
Phone: 415 492-3900
Fax: 415 492-3999
URL: http://www.thx.com

Lumeni Productions, Inc.

Area(s) of Specialization: Title Graphics, Special Effects and Computer Animation.

Number of Employees: 12+

The company produces computer animation, main and end titles, motion graphics and special effects

Lumeni Productions, Inc.
1632 Flower St.
Glendale, CA 91201
Phone: 818 956-2200

Lumens

Area(s) of Specialization: DVD Production, Computer Animation, Software Development

Number of Employees: 4

Lumens Studios' DVD production staff works on DVD titles, and has clients that include: Buena Vista Home Video, Warner Bros., TriMark, Anchor Bay, Fox, and Image Entertainment. The company's software, Afterburn, delivers 3D photorealistic volumetric effects to the 3D Studio MAX community. Afterburn can turn MAX 2 particle system to realistic clouds, fire, smoke, explosions, and nebula. Results are fully 3D and Volumetric. Afterburn's volumetrics are self-shadowing and interact with volumetric lights. The system provides five different types of noise.

Lumens
820 Grant Ave.
Novato, CA 94945
Phone: 415 897-1801
Fax: 707 546-8912
URL: http://www.lumens.com

Lunarfish

Area(s) of Specialization: Interactive Design and Animation

Number of Employees: 2

Lunarfish creates animation and interactive design.

Lunarfish
San Francisco & Los Angeles
Phone: 888 445-0246
Fax: 888 445-0247
URL: http://www.lunarfish.com
e-mail: info@lunarfish.com

Lyric Media

Area(s) of Specialization: Production, Animation, Multimedia Development, Software

Number of Employees: 2

Lyric Media provides video production, computer animation & multimedia development services. Lyric also provides custom 3D animation software development services, particularly in support of 3D Studio MAX. The company is located in Silicon Valley.

Lyric Media
215 Alexander Ave.
Los Gatos, California 95030
Phone/Fax: 408 395-8444
URL: http://www.lyric.com

M80 Interactive Marketing

Area(s) of Specialization: Interactive Design and New Media

Number of Employees: 20+

M80 is an Internet marketing company specializing in music, films, and other new media. M80 Interactive Marketing was launched in the summer of 1998 by former Maverick Recording Company Head of New Media Dave Neupert. M80 uses the street team model that is currently used by most major labels and translates it to the Internet. A grassroots strategy, direct contact of music fans by music fans on-line, was a strategy that Dave used while working on various projects at Maverick.

M80 Interactive Marketing
2301 Hyperion Avenue
Los Angeles, CA 90027
Phone: 310 253-7097

Fax: 310 253-7010
URL: http://www.m80im.com

MacLeod Productions

Area(s) of Specialization: Visual Effects

Number of Employees: 2

MacLeod Productions creates visual effects.

MacLeod Productions
2617 5th St.
Santa Monica, CA 90405
Phone: 310 395-4739

Macromedia, Inc.

Area(s) of Specialization: Interactive Design

Number of Employees: 1000+

Macromedia is focused on Web designers, consumers, and the enterprise, delivering Internet products and technologies designed for the Web. Macromedia's Web Publishing products are showcased on the company's Web sites. To address the training and education needs of the enterprise, Macromedia is building upon its Web Publishing to create new Web Learning solutions.

Macromedia, Incorporated
600 Townsend Street
San Francisco, CA 94103
Phone: 415 252-2000

Fax: 415 626-0554
URL: http://www.macromedia.com

Magic Box Productions, Inc.

Area(s) of Specialization: Virtual Reality & Interactive Media

Number of Employees: 50

Magic Box Productions, Inc. provides consulting services, focusing on computer graphics, animation, multimedia, virtual reality and the Internet. Magic Box and Magic Bow productions include design services in the fields of digital media and multimedia entertainment and display systems.

Magic Box Productions, Inc.
345 N. Maple Dr., #222
Beverly Hills, CA 90210
Phone: 310 550-0243
URL: http://www.mbp.com
E-mail: webmaster@mbp.com

Magico

Area(s) of Specialization: 3D Animations and Images

Number of Employees: 1

Magico's clients include: Disney, LucasArt, Time Warner, CAPCOM, Sega, 3DO, San Francisco Production Group (General Motors television ads), and Midland Production. Work is done in Alias Power Animator with Studio Paint for texturing. The animator also uses Amazon Paint, Composer and Mac.

Magico
Phone: 510 339-2554
URL: http://www.magico.net
E-mail: alon@magico.net

Manex Entertainment

Area(s) of Specialization: 3D Animation, Visual Effects

Number of Employees: 80

Manex Interactive is the special effects of Manex Entertainment combined with digital multimedia design and production. Manex Interactive draws from its visual effects heritage to work on the Internet and other interactive projects. Manex has created effects for feature films and commercials such as: "Mission Impossible 2", "Bless the Child", "Romeo Must Die", "Jordan to the Max", "Crouching Tiger", "Deep Blue Sea", "American Beauty", "The Matrix", "What Dreams May Come", and "Muppets From Space."

Manex Entertainment
1040 West Midway Avenue
Alameda, CA 94501-5012
Phone: 510 864-0600
Fax: 510 864-9669

Manex Entertainment
8522 National Boulevard, Suite 103
Culver City, CA 90232
Phone: 310 838-3456
Fax: 310 838-1713
URL: http://www.mvfx.com

Master Designs Computer Graphics

Area(s) of Specialization: Model Building and Visual Effects

Number of Employees: 2

Master Designs Computer Graphics was formed to provide computer work (CAD) and computer-aided machining (CAM) for in-house model shops and small companies. Master Designs has added digital graphics to its line of services, such as photo manipulation, 3D modeling, rendering, animation, and special effects. The company builds many types of models which include: architectural, study, detailed (museum), topographical, or even accident reconstruction models, models that may be used for presentation, movie special effects, display, or legal purposes.

Master Designs Computer Graphics
P.O. Box 26172
Tempe, Arizona 85285-6172
Phone: 480 966-7983
Fax: 480 966-7984
URL: http://www.goodnet.com/~ej61095

Matte World Digital

Area(s) of Specialization: Visual Effects

Number of Employees: 100

Specializing in the creation of realistic digital and traditional special visual effects, Matte World Digital offers digital 2D and 3D computer graphics and compositing, a full model shop for miniature creation, complete motion control facilities and blue and green screen stages.

Matte World Digital
24 Digital Drive #6
Novato, CA 94949.
Phone: 415 382-1929
Fax: 415 382-1999
URL: http://www.matteworld.com

The Media Staff

Area(s) of Specialization: Recording for Audio

Number of Employees: 4+

The Media Staff helps clients with communications such as: audiobook and voice-over recording, scoring and sweetening, foreign language conversions, video production and non-linear editing. The company records, edits, scores, mixes and sweetens commercials, corporate videos, and radio drama.

The Media Staff
8425 West 3rd Street
Los Angeles, CA 90048
Phone: 323 658-8996
Fax: 323 658-8994
URL: http://www.themediastaff.com
E-mail: jerry@themediastaff.com

Media X

Area(s) of Specialization: Interactive Design

Number of Employees: 30

MediaX Corporation is a multimedia development and publishing company with expertise in real-time, 3D multimedia/interactive and on-line technology. MediaX has grown from a two-person studio to a turnkey multimedia house with more than 15 employees. In 1996, MediaX became a publicly held company when it merged with ZeitgeistWerks in Los Angeles. The client list, past and present, includes: EMI/Capital Records, MCA, Dow Jones/Wall Street Journal, New Line Cinema, Toshiba, Apple Computer, Inc. and Iwerks.

Media X/ Los Angeles
8522 National Boulevard
Suite 110
Culver City, CA 90232
Phone: 310 815-8002
Fax: 310 815-8096

Media X/ Santa Cruz
303 Potrero Street, 42-302

Santa Cruz, CA 95060
URL: http://www.mediax.com

Merwin Creative

Area(s) of Specialization: Creative Design for Film, Interactive Design

Number of Employees: 27

For the past 18 years, Merwin Created has worked on major corporate product launches and full image campaigns as well as neighborhood public affairs.

Merwin Creative
419 Occidental Ave. South
Suite 208
Seattle, WA 98104
Phone: 206 621-7552
Fax: 206 343-0271
URL: http://www.merwincreative.com

Mesmer Animation Labs

Area(s) of Specialization: Training for Computer Animation

Number of Employees: 11

Mesmer Animation Labs offers professional training for digital artists, is an authorized training center for softimage, Alias|Wavefront, and NewTek graphics tools. Clients include Microsoft, Electronic Arts, LucasArts, Psygnosis, Boeing, and others.

Mesmer Design-Seattle
1116 NW 54th St.
Seattle, WA 98107
Phone: 206-782-8004

Mesmer Animation Labs
562 Mission
San Francisco, CA 94105
Phone: 415-495-1636
Fax: 206-782-8101
URL: http://www.mesmer.com

Method

Area(s) of Specialization: Visual Effects for
Film and Video

Number of Employees: 4

Method specializes in visual effects for
commercials and music videos. The
company's services range from pre-
production planning, pre-visualization and
set supervision to compositing, matte
painting and 2D and 3D animation and
modeling. Method operates on SGI,
Macintosh and NT workstations.

Method
1546 Seventh St., Second Fl.
Santa Monica, CA 90401
Phone: 310 899-6500
Fax: 310 899-6501
URL: http://www.methodstudios.com

Metrolight Studios

Area(s) of Specialization: Visual Effects for
Film and Video, 3D Animation

Number of Employees: 30+

Metrolight Studios Inc. uses computer
animation tools to tell a story a filmmaker
can imagine, or visualize a message a
broadcaster requires, using the capabilities of
CGI studios.

Metrolight Studios, Inc.
5724 W. 3rd St., #400
Los Angeles, CA 90036
Phone: 323 932-0400
Fax: 323 932-8440
URL: http://www.metrolight.com

Metropolis Digital, Inc.

Area(s) of Specialization: Video Games

Number of Employees: 20+

Working in console and PC games, Metro3D
has expertise in game development, digital
effects, content creation, and entertainment
software publishing. The company has in-
house proprietary development tools coupled
with the management experience of its key
executives who have brought to market
arcade and console games among them, the
legendary "Street Fighter IITM" series.
Metro3D is developing and publishing
original titles for next generation systems,
including Sega's "Dreamcast", as well as

future game hardware from Sony and Nintendo, such as the Playstation 2.

Metropolis Digital, Inc.
12 S. First St., Ste. 1000
San Jose, CA 95113
Phone: 408 286-2900
Fax: 408 286-2970
URL: http://www.metro3d.com

Metropolis Editorial

Area(s) of Specialization: Post Production

Number of Employees: 6

The suites at Metropolis Editorial have access to PC's, Mac, printers, modems and faxes. The company has editors, artists and producers for post production work.

Metropolis Editorial
950 Battery Street
Third Floor
San Francisco, CA 94111
Phone: 415 434-0160
Fax: 415 434-0162
URL: http://www.metropoliseditorial.com

MDFX

Area(s) of Specialization: Print, Web, Video

Number of Employees: 10+

MDFX is a Tempe, AZ based advertising and direct marketing agency providing services including print/directmail production, comprehensive video production and post-production, website development, multimedia authoring, animation and media planning/placement.

MDFX
3228 S. Fair Ln.
Tempe, AZ 85282
Phone: 602 426-8000
Fax: 602 426-8005
URL: http://www.market-direct.com

Midway Games, Inc.

Area(s) of Specialization: Video Games

Number of Employees: 250

Midway Games Inc. is a developer and manufacturer of coin-operated arcade and home video game entertainment products. Arcade games are manufactured under both the Midway and Atari Games brands. Midway Home Entertainment, a subsidiary of Midway Games, designs, markets and distributes video games under the Midway trademark for home game platforms. Midway publishes video games for Nintendo, Sega, Sony and personal computer platforms. The Midway and Atari brands have generated games such as "Pong", "Defender", "Missile Command", "Pac-Man", "Centipede", "NBA Jam", "Cruis'n USA", and "Mortal Komba."

Midway Games, Inc.
10110 Mesa Rim Rd.

San Diego, CA 92121
Phone: 858 658-0348
Fax: 858 658-9574
URL: http://www.midway.com

Midway Games West, Inc.
675 Sycamore Drive
Milpitas, CA 95035
Fax: 408 434-5888
URL: http://www.midway.com

Mirage Media

Area(s) of Specialization: Film and Video Production and Post Production

Number of Employees: 2

Established in 1983, Mirage Media is a full service video production company offering services from the initial concept through the completed video production. The company assists in production from field shooting to professional pre & post production.

Mirage Media
1301 Post St.
San Francisco, CA 94109
Phone: 415 495-3477
Fax: 415 447-1996
URL: http://www.videomirage.com

Mixin Pixls

Area(s) of Specialization: Animation

Number of Employees: 5

Digital design and animation studio Mixin Pixls opened its doors in January 1998. The company was launched by Co-Founder/Henry Artist Mark Dennison and Co-Founder/Animation Director Harri Paakkonen. The Mixin Pixls team creates animation and effects for numerous clients including Intel, Budweiser, Dirt Devil, Frito Lay, Pontiac, Spirit, Honda, United Airlines, Kraft and Pacific Life. Mixin Pixls is located in Santa Monica. The Santa Monica studio features a Henry bay, two CGI suites, a Mac Graphics station, a central conference room, and other client service amenities in a 4,000 square-foot environment.

Mixin Pixls
1335 4th Street Suite 200
Santa Monica, CA 90401
Phone: 310 917-9141
Fax: 310 917-9142
URL: http://www.mixinpixls.com
E-mail: mpixls@mixinpixls.com

Mobility, Inc.

Area(s) of Specialization: Digital Animation for Film and Video

Number of Employees: 5

Mobility is a digital animation studio providing full service 3D and 2D animation for the feature film, HDTV and commercials. Mobility contributed to "What Dreams May Come." The company staff can structure and re-configure software and hardware needs appropriate to particular productions. Mobility combines digital effects with small teams and flexible software and hardware infrastructure.

Mobility Inc.
555 Rose Avenue, #8
Venice, CA 90291
Phone: 310 664-9664
Fax: 310 664-9554
URL: http://www.mobus.com

Modern Digital

Area(s) of Specialization: Editorial, Graphics, Visual Effects, Film Transfer

Number of Employees: 20+

The company is uses computer software programs such as Flame, Avid, Maya and Telecine. Clients include: Disney, Dentsu, FCB Worldwide, Nike, Publicis, Microsoft, Intel, and The Bon Marche.

Modern Digital
1921 Minor Avenue
Seattle, Washington 98101
Phone: 206 623-3444
Fax: 206 340-1548
URL: http://www.moderndigital.com

Modern VideoFilm

Area(s) of Specialization: Computer Animation, Visual Effects and Motion Control

Number of Employees: 700

Modern VideoFilm works in visual effects, computer animation and motion control.

Modern VideoFilm
4411 W. Olive Ave.
Burbank, CA 91505
Phone: 818 840-1700
Fax: 323 850-6151

Mondo Media

Area(s) of Specialization: Animation for Video/Film/Web

Number of Employees: 120

Founded in 1988 and based in San Francisco, Mondo Media is a new media company that creates, develops, and syndicates animated entertainment for the Web, television and the interactive television markets. The production facility is staffed by more than 100 artists, animators, writers, producers and business staff.

Mondo Media
135 Mississippi Street
San Francisco, CA 94107
Phone: 415 865-2700
Fax: 415 865-2645
URL: http://www.mondominishows.com

Montana Edit, Inc.

Area(s) of Specialization: Post Production for Film and Video, Interactive Design

Number of Employees: 2

Montana Edit is a film and video edit studio began in 1992. The company serves the entertainment and advertising communities with Avid edit systems and training and with personal service and support.

Montana Edit, Inc.
1131 Montana Avenue
Santa Monica, CA 90403
Phone: 310 451-9933
Fax: 310 451-0606
URL: http://www.montanaedit.com

Motion City Films

Area(s) of Specialization: Film and Video Production and Post, Interactive Design

Number of Employees: 10+

Motion City Films offers a full range of production services utilizing new media tools. For 3D animation the company uses the Electric Image Animation System, Form-Z, and Extreme 3D. For 2D animation the staff uses the Production Bundle of Adobe After Effects with all of the additional plug-ins. The company also uses several image manipulation packages such as Photoshop, Painter, Illustrator, DeBabelizer, Elastic Reality, and TextureScape. Interactive

Presentations are created using Macromedia's Director.

Motion City Films
1620 Broadway, Suite A
Santa Monica, CA. 90404
Phone: 310 434-1272
Fax: 310 434-1273
URL: http://www.motioncity.com

Motionworks

Area(s) of Specialization: Animation for Computer Software Companies

Number of Employees: 2

Motionworks creates computer graphic animation

Motionworks
953 N. Highland Ave.
Los Angeles CA 90038
Phone: 909 949-1573

Moving Media

Area(s) of Specialization: 2D and 3D Animation for TV corporate web and games

Number of Employees: 2

Moving Media designs and creates computer animation for games and the Web.

Moving Media
1045 17th Street, Studio C
San Francisco, CA 94107

Phone: 415 861-1759
Fax: 415 861-8712
URL: http://www.MovingMedia.com

Net Surf Café

Area(s) of Specialization: Interactive Design

Number of Employees: 3

Net Surf Café provides a full-range of web, e-commerce, and interactive services to companies around the world. The firm specializes in consultation and review of marketing, communication, and e-commerce goals to determine design development for web sites, e-commerce sites, and CD-ROM multimedia products. The company uses technology including streaming video and audio, animation (web, Shockwave, and 3D), Flash, Java and JavaScript programming, HTML, and database integration. The company develops business web sites that utilize secure e-commerce technologies and ASP (Active Server Page), works in interface design, icon development, animation, visual imagery, and special effects. The company offers programming, site maintenance, webmaster services, and content update capabilities.

Net Surf Café
17620 Sonoma Hwy. #4
Sonoma, CA 95476
Phone: 707 938-5988
Toll Free 877 4WEB-DEV (877 493-2338)

Fax: 707 938-1044
URL: http://www.netsurfcafe.com

Netter Digital

Area(s) of Specialization: Animation for Film and Video

Number of Employees: 70+

Located in a 22,000 square foot facility, Netter Digital Animation has 80 3D workstations, 20 2D workstations, 5 Avid Bays, a digital on-line bay and a staff of animators, compositors, designers and editors. The company added a 10-camera high resolution optical motion capture system to further in-house capabilities. The Company has a dedicated render farm that contains over 400 CPU's. The artists work with multiple hardware and software platforms as well as utilize custom programs created for Netter Digital.

Netter Digital
5125 Lankershim Blvd.
North Hollywood, CA 91601
Phone: 818 753-1990
Fax: 818 753-7655
URL: http://www.netterdigital.com

New Hollywood, Inc.

Area(s) of Specialization: Animation Camera Services, Special Effects, Titles, Cinemascope Animation

Number of Employees: 1+

Since 1979, New Hollywood, Inc. has served the animation, Motion Picture, Television, Music Video, and Commercial fields. The areas of participation include: Editorial; Title Design and Execution; Post Production Supervision; Special Effects Supervision and Execution; Animation Production and Camera Service.

New Hollywood, Inc.
1302 N. Cahuenga Blvd.
Hollywood CA 90028.
Phone: 323 466-3686
URL: http://home.sprintmail.com/~ozziez/

Nickelodeon Digital

Area(s) of Specialization: Animation, Film/Video

Number of Employees: 100+

A Viacom International, Inc. company, Nickelodeon Animation Studios produces and creates several cartoon shows. One of the company's feature film is "The Rugrats Movie."

Nickelodeon Digital
231 W. Olive St.
Burbank, CA 91502
Fax: 818 736-3539

Nickelodeon Digital
1515 Broadway, 20th floor
New York, NY 10036-8901
Phone: 212 258-7727
URL: http://www.nick.com

North by Northwest Productions

Area(s) of Specialization: Film and Video Production and Post, Interactive Design

Number of Employees: 35+

North By Northwest Productions is a team of more than 40 people who create, write, shoot, edit, mix, compose, illustrate, animate, create multimedia, produce, direct and consult on film, video and interactive multimedia projects.

North by Northwest Productions/Spokane
903 W. Broadway
Spokane, WA 99201
Phone: 509 324-2949
Fax: 509 324-2959

North by Northwest Productions/Boise
601 W. Broad Street
Boise, ID 83702
Phone: 208 345-7870
Fax: 208 345-7999
URL: http://www.nxnw.net

Northwest Film Center-Portland Art Museum

Area(s) of Specialization: Film/Video, Multimedia

Number of Employees: 9

The Portland Art Museum Northwest Film Center is a regional media arts resource and service organization based in Portland, Oregon founded to encourage the study, appreciation and utilization of the moving image arts, foster artistic and professional excellence, and to help create a climate in which arts may flourish. The Center provides a variety of film and video exhibition, education and information programs primarily directed to the residents of Oregon, Washington, Idaho, Montana and Alaska.

Northwest Film Center
Richmond Communications LLC
1219 SW Park Avenue
Portland, OR 97205
Phone: 503 221-1156
Fax: 503 294-0874
E-mail: info@nwfilm.org
URL: http://www.nwfilm.org

Novocom, Inc.

Area(s) of Specialization: Post Production and Visual Effects

Number of Employees: 15

Novocom provides broadcast branding / identities and design and post-production compositing and visual effects. The company is headquartered in Los Angeles with satellite offices in Hollywood (Paramount Pictures Studios), London, and Singapore. Clients include worldwide television networks, DTH Systems, and cable companies, movie studios, production companies, distributors, advertising agencies, and multimedia content producers, as well as freelance producers, directors, and editors. The company's international staff are from Argentina, Britain, Belgium, Cuba, Germany, Japan, Korea, Russia, Sweden, Singapore, and Taiwan.

Novocom, Inc.
5401 Beethoven St.
Los Angeles, CA 90066
Phone: 310 448-2500
Fax: 310 448-2525
URL: http://www.novo.com

Nx View Technologies

Area(s) of Specialization: 3D Animation, Real-time Programming

Number of Employees: 70

NxView Technologies delivers interactive 3D animation and applications for customer service and support, product training, sales demonstrations and e-commerce. It is based in the Research Triangle Park area of North Carolina and Soquel, CA.

NxView Technologies, Inc.
P.O. Box 1429
Cary, NC 27512-1429
Phone: 919 657-3300
Fax: 919 657-3333

NxView Technologies, Inc.
2425 porter Street, Suite 14
Soquel, CA 95073
Phone: 831 479-8274
Fax: 831 464-8391
URL: http://www.NxView.com

Omni Video

Area(s) of Specialization: Post Production, Graphic Design, Animation Services

Number of Employees: 7

Omni Video offers full-service broadcast equipment rental, as well as comprehensive post-production, graphic design and animation services. The company serves a client base that includes advertising agencies, local production companies, independent producers and corporate communication groups. Located near downtown Portland, Oregon, Omni is a broadcast rental facility specializing in a range of equipment from industrial to electronic cinematography.

Omni Video
911 NE Davis St.
Portland, OR 97232

Phone: 800 258-OMNI
Alt Phone: 503 233-1989
Fax: 503 230-1172
URL: http://www.omni-video.com

Pacific Data Images

Area(s) of Specialization: Visual Effects and Animation for Film and Video

Number of Employees: 350

Founded in 1980 by Carl Rosendahl, PDI started out creating broadcast graphics, and in 1985 expanded into commercials and then to feature film effects. The company provides Hollywood with 3D visual effects and animation. PDI created proprietary software for animation.

Pacific Data Images
3101 Park Boulevard
Palo Alto, CA 94306
Phone: 650 846-8100
Fax: 650 846-8101
PDI Job Hotline-800 655 8779
URL: http://www.pdi.com

Pacific Ocean Post Studios

Area(s) of Specialization: Video Editing and Encoding, Sound, DVD Mastering.

Number of Employees: 150+

Pacific Ocean Post Studios authors DVD disks. The Cinram/Pop DVD Center is equipped to address all the functions necessary to assemble, script, and multiplex elements created by POP Sound and POP Video and transmit data streams directly to Cinram for manufacture. To optimize the DVD creation process, Pacific Ocean Post Video edits the video and format (if necessary) and performs MPEG-2 VBR encoding of video elements.

Pacific Ocean Post Studios
730 Arizona Ave.
Santa Monica, CA 90401
Phone: 310 899-7200
Fax: 310 434-6500
URL: http://www.popstudios.com

Paradesa Media

Area(s) of Specialization: Interactive Design

Number of Employees: 20

The company develops web sites, intranets, extranets and creates multimedia programming for broadcast and cable television, laser disc, CD-ROM and on-line services. Paradesa Media offers development services for both public and private sites, including: interface and graphic design, information design, website development and maintenance, development of intranet applications and databases. Clients include Bank of America, Genstar Instant Space, Piper Jaffray, Thelen, Marin, Johnson & Bridges, The California Trust, West Coast Industries, Bay Area Multimedia Partnership, and Studio Z.

Paradesa Media
375 Alabama Street
San Francisco, CA 94110
Phone: 415 487-2020
Fax: 415 487-2030
URL: http://www.paradesa.com

Paradise F.X.

Area(s) of Specialization: Visual Effects

Number of Employees: 10

Paradise FX develops new technology and applies it to technically challenging projects. Paradise F.X. is committed to developing and photographing the Motion Picture, Theme Park, and Special Venue industries ideas. Paradise FX designed a 3D Dual camera system as well as having several other Large Format 3D systems in development.

Paradise F.X.
3211 S. la Cienega
Los Angeles, CA 90016
Phone: 310 202-6566
Fax: 310 202-1398
URL: http://www.paradisefx.com

Phoenix Editorial Services

Area(s) of Specialization: Post Production for Film and Video

Number of Employees: 12+

Phoenix Editorial is one of San Francisco's editing shops. The company features four creative editors and a graphics artist. Together with its support staff of post-production specialists, producers and editorial assistants, Phoenix provides editing and post-production management on film, video, and computer graphics projects. Most of the company's projects are regional and national television commercials. The company has a client base made up of ad agencies such as Goodby, Silverstein & Partners, Foote, Cone & Belding, Hal Riney & Partners, Young & Rubicam; Butler, and Shine & Stern.

Phoenix Editorial Services
717 Battery Street @ Pacific
San Francisco, CA 94103
Phone: 415 394-7777
Fax: 415 394-8004
URL: http://www.phoenixeditorial.com

Pixar Animation Studios

Area(s) of Specialization: Animated Films

Number of Employees: 475+

Pixar is a high end animation studio based in Northern California. The company creates three dimensional animation shorts and feature films in a partnership with The Walt Disney Company. In collaboration with Disney, the company created such films as

"Toy Story", "A Bug's Life" and other fully computer animated feature films.

Pixar Animation Studios
1200 Park Ave.
Emeryville, CA 94608
Jobs Hotline: 510 752-3017
Phone: 510 752-3000
Fax: 510 752-3151
URL: http://www.pixar.com

Pixel Envy

Area(s) of Specialization: 3D Animation, compositing

Number of Employees: 7

Pixel Envy is a digital facility providing 3D animation, visual effects, compositing, and image processing for broadcast and feature film. Based in Santa Monica, California, Pixel Envy offers services including pre-visualization, visual effects supervision, and complete digital production. Pixel Envy has created digital animation and visual effects sequences for films such as "The X-Files" (Twentieth Century Fox), "Paulie" (DreamWorks), and "Titanic" (Paramount Pictures/Twentieth Century Fox).

Pixel Envy
1540 Seventh St., Ste. 300
Santa Monica, CA 90401
Phone: 310 899-9779.
Fax: 310 899-3113
URL: http://www.pixel-envy.com

Pixel Liberation Front, Inc.

Area(s) of Specialization: Digital Production, Animation, CGI, Visual Effects

Number of Employees: 8

PLF is a visual effects company, offering the specialties of pre-visualization and 3D integration in addition to experience in 3D animation and virtual environments creation. With offices in Los Angeles and New York, and a team of digital artists, PLF offers visual effects production coast to coast.

Pixel Liberation Front/New York
150 W. 28 St. #1003
New York, NY 10001
Phone: 212 239-1455
Fax: 212 239-3201

Pixel Liberation Front/Los Angeles
1316 Abbot Kinney Blvd.
Venice, CA 90291
Phone: 310 396-9854
Fax: 310 396-9874
E-mail: plf@thefront.com
URL: http://www.thefront.com

Planet Blue

Area(s) of Specialization: 3D Animation and Visual Effects

Number of Employees: 12

Since 1988, Planet Blue has been working in the creation and seamless integration of visual effects and animation with live action for commercials, features, television, music videos and the Internet.

Planet Blue
1250 6th Street
Santa Monica, CA 90401-1633
Phone: 310 899-3877
Fax: 310 899-3787
URL: http://www.planetblue.com

P.O.D.

Area(s) of Specialization: Virtual/3D Modeling

Number of Employees: 2

P.O.D. (Promethian Design) creates integrous virtualities (with all its implications) for mental models. The company's services are not limited to virtualization of pre-designed models.

P.O.D
24942 Ravenswood
Lake Forest, CA 92630

P.O.D.
1507 Penmar Ave. #3
Venice CA 90291
Phone: 310 392-9510
URL: http://www.podarts.com

The Portland Post Production and Graphics Company

Area(s) of Specialization: CGI, Multimedia, Film/Video, Animation

Number of Employees: 2

The creative team at Portland Post post produces projects from a 30 seconds TV spot to a seven-minute corporate product roll-out to a ninety-minute feature documentary. The company works in component digital-in standard definition NTSC, in 16:9, or as processes clips for new media application.

The Portland Post Production and Graphics Company
208 SW First Ave.
Suite 200
Portland, OR 97204
Phone: 503 295-0551
Alt Phone: 800 353-0551
Fax: 503 295-0802
URL: http://www.portlandpost.com

Prime Post

Area(s) of Specialization: Film/Video, Sound, Multimedia

Number of Employees: 25-30

Prime Post was established in 1991 to provide post production services to the film and television industries. Prime Post provides on-line & off-line editing, AVID, film to tape transfer, duplication and standards conversion, digital media, motion control, aspect ratio conversion, closed captioning, domestic & international fiber optic and satellite transmission services. Studio clients include Miramax Films, Buena Vista, USA Networks, Universal Studios, CBS, and Showtime Networks. Other clients include DavisGlick Productions, Carsey-Werner Productions, Quentin Tarantino, Tribune Entertainment, Artist View Entertainment, Strom/Magallon Entertainment, Cinequanon Pictures, Tylie Jones and Associates, Gross Productions, Two Headed Monster Productions, Moxie Pictures, Klasky-Csupo Productions, A Band Apart Commercials, Dreamworks SKG, and many others.

Prime Post
3500 Cahuenga Blvd West
Los Angeles, CA 90068
Phone: 323 878-0782
Fax: 323 878-2781
URL: http://www.primepost.com

The Production Group Studios

Area(s) of Specialization: Film/Video, Multimedia

Number of Employees: 12

Located in Hollywood, The Production Group Studios is a full service, turn-key video production facility. The company provides everything from facilities, equipment and crews to production office space, field production packages, coordination service and more.

The Production Group Studios
1330 Vine Street
Hollywood, CA 90028
Phone: 323 469-8111
Fax: 323 962-22182
URL: http://www.production-group.com

Protozoa, Inc.

Area(s) of Specialization: 3D Animation

Number of Employees: 30

Protozoa is a production studio using proprietary performance-animation software, "ALIVE", which is used by broadcasters worldwide, and is suited to 3D on the Web. Protozoa-designed "ALIVE"-driven characters have been seen on television, at live events, and on the Web. The company has over ten years experience in 3D motion-capture animation. The company builds real-time digital puppets for Cartoon Network, Disney, the BBC, MTV.

Protozoa, Inc.
2727 Mariposa St.
Studio 100
San Francisco, CA 94110
Phone: 415 522-6500

Fax: 415 522-6522
URL: http://www.protozoa.com

QB's Computer Animation & Graphics

Area(s) of Specialization: Animation and Still Images

Number of Employees: 2

QB's Computer Animation & Graphics provides broadcast animation and videos for use in television commercials, music videos or industry videos. The company also provides photo realistic still images or animations for multimedia presentations as well as develops computer games for children and adults.

QB's Computer Animation & Graphics
PO Box 185
Kent, WA 98035-0185
Phone: 253 639-1689
URL: http://www.halcyon.com/jpoff/index.htm

Radium

Area(s) of Specialization: Special Effects and Animation

Number of Employees: 30

Radium is a digital visual effects studio based in San Francisco and Los Angeles. Digital artists create for commercials, music videos and feature films, and incorporate digital with organic and analog elements. The company offers complete effects packaging, including creative preproduction consultation and shoot supervision, through effects execution and editorial integration.

Radium
2728 Hyde Street, Suite 200
San Francisco, CA 94110
Phone: 415 674-0674
Fax: 415 674-0675

Radium
2260a South Centinela Ave.
Los Angeles, CA 90064
Phone: 310 979-6467
Fax: 310 979-6496
URL: http://www.radium.com

Random Task

Area(s) of Specialization: Multimedia Design and Production

Number of Employees: 2+

Random Task is a full service design and production company, working with clients in a variety of media.

Random Task
4216 Santa Monica blvd.
Los Angeles, CA 90029
Phone: 323 664-2119
Fax: 323 664-2190
URL: http://www.randomtask.com

Rainmaker Digital Pictures

Area(s) of Specialization: CGI, Animation, Multimedia, DVD

Number of Employees: 12

Rainmaker Digital Pictures is a post production company with a twenty year history from its origins as the west coast post house Gastown Productions. Rainmaker's facility in Vancouver provides producers with an array of post production services ranging from traditional film developing to digital image processing techniques.

Rainmaker Digital Pictures
Los Angeles Office
175 East Olive, Suite 405
Burbank, CA 91502
Phone: 818 526-1500
Fax: 818 953-5051
URL: http://www.rainmaker.com

Raster Ranch, Ltd.

Area(s) of Specialization: Web Design and Development, High-end Imaging, Animation, 3D Environment Design

Number of Employees: 5

Raster Ranch, Ltd. provides creative services and project integration to the multimedia, game, television, and film industries, as well as to companies seeking CD-ROM or presence on the Web. The company worked on projects for Microsoft, Electronic Arts,

Hewlett-Packard, Disney, PBS, National Geographic, General Electric, Hyundai, Nordstrom, Westin Hotels, and many others. Raster offers web design and development, high-end imaging, animation, 3D environment design, art direction, project management, and interactive title development.

Raster Ranch, Ltd.
300 Queen Anne Ave. North
Suite 430
Seattle, WA 98109
Phone: 206 282-5900
Fax: 206 282-5910
URL: http://www.rasterranch.com

Razorfish

Area(s) of Specialization: Web Site Design, Interface Design

Number of Employees: 1,600 (worldwide)

Razorfish provides website and interface design to digital businesses.

Razorfish-San Francisco
169 11th Street
San Francisco, CA 94103
Phone: 415 865-1465
Fax: 415 865-1475
URL: http://www.razorfish.com

Razorfish - San Francisco
340 Main Street
Venice, CA 90291-2524
Phone: 310 581-5599

Fax: 310 581-5598
URL: http://www.razorfish.com

RealNetworks, Inc.

Area(s) of Specialization: Multimedia, Create Software for Streaming Audio and Video.

Number of Employees: 1200

RealNetworks develops and markets software products and services designed to enable users of personal computers and other consumer electronic devices to send and receive audio, video and other multimedia services using the Web. The company developed Realplayer, Realjukebox, and Realsystem software.

RealNetworks, Inc.
2601 Elliott Avenue, Suite 1000
Seattle, WA 98121
Phone: 206 674-2700
Fax: 206 674-2699
URL: http://www.real.com

Reality Check

Area(s) of Specialization: CGI, Multimedia, Animation

Number of Employees: 10-20

Reality Check creates in 3D. Reality Check works with clients from concept and design, to full implementation and integration.

Reality Check
723 Cahuenga Blvd.
Los Angeles, CA 90038
Phone: 323 465-3900
Fax: 323 465-3600
URL: http://www.realityx.com

Red Car

Area(s) of Specialization: Film/Video

Number of Employees: 100+

Red Car Los Angeles is a team of graphics artists, sound designers, type stylists, producers, managers, schedulers, assistants, receptionists, runners, and vault people. Clients include: Wieden & Kennedy, Leo Burnett (leoburnett.com), and Young & Rubicam (yandr.com).

Red Car-Los Angeles
2415 Michigan Ave.
Bergamot Station
Santa Monica, CA 90404
Phone: 310 828-7500
Fax: 310 828-1245
URL: http://www.redcar.com

Rejobi

Area(s) of Specialization: Special Effects for Web, Audio

Number of Employees: 5

Rejobi Interactive Communications, established in February of 1996, work in the area of business development, product marketing, computer-graphics design, applications development, mass-communication technologies, interactive multimedia, CD-ROM and laptop presentation publishing, Internet access technologies and World Wide Web site design and marketing.

Rejobi
908 Lincoln Way
Auburn. CA 95603
Phone: 530 885-8547
Fax: 530 887-3226
URL: http://www.rejobi.com

Renegade Animation, Inc.

Area(s) of Specialization: Traditional Animation, Web-based Animation

Number of Employees: 12+

In 1992, Renegade Animation was created to produce cel animation for the advertising industry. The company's advertising projects have included soft drinks, athletic footwear, breakfast cereals, fast food and toys.

Renegade Animation, Inc.
204 N. San Fernando Blvd.
Burbank, CA 91502
Phone: 818 556-3395
Fax: 818 556-3398
URL: http://www.renegadeanimation.com

ReZ.n8 Productions, Inc.

Area(s) of Specialization: CGI, Animation

Number of Employees: 30

From network branding campaigns to photo-realistic effects, to a treatment of a simple logo, ReZ.n8 creates design and animation.

ReZ.n8 Productions, Inc.
6430 Sunset Blvd., Ste. 100
Los Angeles, CA 90028
Phone: 323 957-2161
Fax: 323 464-8912
URL: http://www.rezn8.com

Rhonda Graphics, Inc.

Area(s) of Specialization: Video/Film Computer Animation and Visual Effects

Number of Employees: 6

Rhonda Graphics is a company of artists and technicians creating computer animation and visual effects for video and film projects. Based in Phoenix, Arizona, the company collaborates with commercial, broadcast and corporate clients to create television commercials, film effects, show opens, broadcast graphics, opens for sporting events and programs, as well as compositing, retouching, and a variety of other visual effects. The company works with advertising agencies, directors, production companies and clients around the world, from Los Angeles to Kansas City, and New York to Tokyo.

Rhonda Graphics Inc.
1730 E. Northern Ave.
Suite 204
Phoenix, AZ 85020
Phone: 602 371-8880
Fax: 602 371-8832
URL: http://www.rhonda.com

Rhythm and Hues

Area(s) of Specialization: 3D Animation and Visual Effects for feature films, television commercials, theme park rides, music videos and interactive games.

Number of Employees: 300+

Founded in 1987, the Commercial Division is well known for its recent work on the Mazda "Cool World" commercials, as well as the ongoing Coca Cola "Polar Bear" campaign. R+H is housed in a 100,000 square foot facilities. The staff includes live action and animation directors, animators, painters, modelers, producers, programmers, writers, technical and production support. The company's space is designed to enhance the creative and collaborative process necessary for computer animation.

Rhythm and Hues Studios, Inc.
5404 Jandy Place
Los Angeles, CA 90066

Phone: 310 448-7619
Fax: 310 448-7600
E-mail: recruitment@rhythm.com
URL: http://www.rhythm.com

Rijn & Reisman

Area(s) of Specialization: 3D Art, Imaging

Number of Employees: 5

Launched in 1992 by artists Leo Rijn and Andy Reisman, Rijn & Reisman work in the specialized area of crafting and producing miniatures, models, sculptures, and maquettes (small, preliminary models of sculptures) for clients such as Universal Studios, Warner Bros., 20th Century Fox, Walt Disney, Paramount Pictures, Tim Burton Productions, Landmark Entertainment Group, and Rhythm & Hues. The staff of artisans create three-dimensional models, sculptures and maquettes. The company resume includes such feature films as "Amistad", "Junior", "Mars Attacks", "An American Werewolf in Paris", and "Wild Wild West."

Rijn & Reisman
10737 Chandler Blvd.
N. Hollywood, CA 91601
Phone: 818 509-0531
Alt Phone: 818 509-0580
Fax: 818 509-1369
URL: http://www.rijnreisman.com

Ring of Fire

Area(s) of Specialization: Animation, Visual Effects

Number of Employees: 16+

A creative digital effects and design studio, Ring of Fire was launched in 1996 to specialize in visual effects supervision, 2D compositing, CGI, and design for commercial, television and feature film projects. Catering to ad agencies, production companies and editorial houses, the Ring of Fire team is made up of visual effects artists and supervisors, using Inferno, Henry and other 3D software.

Ring of Fire
8300 Melrose Avenue, Suite 204
West Hollywood, CA 90069
Phone: 323 966-5410
URL: http://www.ringoffire.com
E-mail: amy@ringoffire.com

Rocket Pictures, Inc.

Area(s) of Specialization: CGI, Multimedia, Film/Video, Animation

Number of Employees: 10

Rocket Pictures is a media production and design firm specializing in film, broadcast, sports, entertainment and corporate communications. The company was founded in 1988 by Les Fitzpatrick and Dan Pepper and has clients such as Airborne Express,

Alaska Airlines, DDB Needham, Microsoft, Millenium Arts, MTV, Fox Searchlight Pictures, Fox Sports, Weyerhaeuser and WongDoody.

Rocket Pictures, Inc.
1114 Post Avenue
Seattle, WA 98101
Phone: 206 623-7678
Fax: 206-623-6349
URL: http://rocket-pictures.com

Route 66 Productions, Inc.

Area(s) of Specialization: Animation, CGI, Multimedia, Film/Video

Number of Employees: 15

Route 66 Productions is a business communications company that produces live events and media for corporate use. The headquarters is located near Los Angeles International Airport and has 8,000 square feet of production workspace. The company has ten years experience producing new product introductions, business meetings, video conferences, interactive training presentations, inspirational videos, and trade show displays and kiosks for companies like Sony, McDonald's, GTE, Microsoft, Lexus, Guess, Apple Computer, Honda, ITT and many more.

Route 66 Productions, Inc.
3215 La Cienega Ave.
Culver City, CA 90232

Phone: 310 815-2424
Fax: 310 815-2420
URL: http://www.digital66.com

San Francisco Production Group

Area(s) of Specialization: Animation, CGI, Multimedia, Film/Video

Number of Employees: 6

SFPG is an animation and special effects service for Web and multimedia developers, video producers and video directors. The company started with HTTP://WWW sites, interactive kiosks, CD-ROM's and interactive television applications. Working entirely on the desktop, the company provides special effects and animations for video producers and directors, and creates content modules for Web and multimedia developers.

San Francisco Production Group
550 Bryant Street
San Francisco, CA 94107
Phone: 415 495-5595
Fax: 415.543-8370
URL: http://www.sfpg.com

Scansite

Area(s) of Specialization: 3D Scanning. Digital Scanning

Number of Employees: 10

In addition to using 3D digitizing technologies, Scansite offers a range of services including scanner sales & training, NURBS model construction, engineering, analysis and verification, rapid prototyping and consulting.

Scansite
1 Madrone Ave.
Woodacre, CA 94973-0695
Phone: 415 472-1073
Fax: 415 472-1074
URL: http://www.scansite.com

Scarlet Letters

Area(s) of Specialization: Titles Design for Motion Pictures

Number of Employees: 5

Working in the motion picture and television title graphics field for over 12 years, Scarlet Letters helps clients with titles from the small screen of the computer to the big screen of the theater.

CIA Creative Group
Scarlet Letters
6430 Sunset Boulevard
Suite 1001
Hollywood, CA 90028
Phone: 323 461-5959
Fax: 323 461-1758
URL: http://www.ciagroup.com/sl.html

Screaming Pixels

Area(s) of Specialization: Animation, Visual Effects, Industrial Design

Number of Employees: 5

Screaming Pixels develops its own production work and is working on a children's CGI series for British Television. The company is equipped with SGI, NT and Macintosh platforms, and runs a suite of top end applications, including Softimage. The company's product design experience runs from ceramics to tightly engineered products; products are shown at photographic levels from the very first stages of development. By developing designs in the CGI environment, the company has the ability to reflect changes in color and form, and give a virtual 360 degree view of the product.

Screaming Pixels
648 Buena Vista Drive
Santa Barbara, CA 93108
Phone: 805 565-0822
Fax: 805 565-4633
URL: http://www.screamingpixels.com

The Secret Lab

Area(s) of Specialization: CGI, Multimedia, Film/Video

Number of Employees: 12

A Disney Company Affiliate, The Secret Lab is the Feature Film Visual Effects Division of The Walt Disney Company. The former Dream Quest Images is now The Secret Lab. Dream Quest is known for its production environment, which combines live-action photography with traditional and digital techniques to achieve images. Dream Quest Images handles all aspects of production, from the initial concept and design of visual effects work for feature films, through the supervision of related live-action photography, to the integration of completed digital and traditional effects.

The Secret Lab
2635 Park Center Drive
Simi Valley, CA 93065
Phone: 805 578-3100
Alt Phone: 310 558-4051
Fax: 805 583-4673

Shadow Caster

Area(s) of Specialization: CGI, Animation.

Number of Employees: 3+

Shadow Caster is a visual effects and entertainment company based in Santa Barbara, California. The company produces imagery for the film, television, and multimedia industries. Shadow Caster was founded by a core group of artists with experience in the design and creation of computer generated visual effects.

Shadow Caster
136 W. Canon Perdido, Ste. B-2
Santa Barbara, CA 93101
Phone: 805 884-1818
Fax: 805 884-9576
URL: http://www.shadowcaster.com

Sierra, Inc.

Area(s) of Specialization: CGI, Multimedia, Animation

Number of Employees: 480+

Sierra, Inc. is one of the developers and publishers of interactive entertainment and productivity software for personal computers. Sierra has been in the computer software field for nearly 20 years.

Sierra, Inc.
3060 139th Ave. SE, Suite 500
Bellevue, WA 98005
Phone: 425 649-9800
Fax: 425 641-7617
E-mail: recruit@sierra.com
URL: http://www.sierra.com

Silicon Graphics, Inc. / Computer Systems Business Unit

Area(s) of Specialization: Multimedia, CGI

Number of Employees: 3000

SGI is one of the leaders in high-performance computing technology. The company's systems, ranging from desktop workstations and servers to supercomputers deliver advanced computing and 3D visualization capabilities to scientific, engineering, and creative professionals and large enterprises. In addition, SGI creates software for design, Internet, and entertainment applications. SGI works in several industries, including manufacturing, government, entertainment, communications, energy, the sciences, and education.

Silicon Graphics, Inc./Computer Systems
Business Unit
2011 Northshoreline Blvd.
Mountain View, CA 94043
Phone: 650 960-1980
Fax: 650 960-0197
Fax: 650 960-3393
URL: http://www.sgi.com

Skywalker Sound

Area(s) of Specialization: Sound, Sound Effects

Number of Employees: 500+

Skywalker Sound is George Lucas's post production company located in Marin County, California. It is a part of Lucas Digital Ltd., a company that includes Industrial Light & Magic. The business of Lucas Digital Ltd. is to provide visual effects and movie sound design to the film industry. Skywalker Sound formerly named Sprockets Systems.

Lucas Digital, Ltd. LLC
P.O. Box 2459
San Rafael, CA 94912
Phone: 415 448-9000
Fax: 415 448-2850
URL: http://www.thx.com/skywalker/skywalker.html

Smashing Ideas Animation

Area(s) of Specialization: Animation for Web, Broadcast Television, Multimedia

Number of Employees: 31

Smashing Ideas Animation creates animation for broadcast television and the web.

Smashing Ideas Animation
1604 Dexter Ave. N.
Seattle, WA 98109
Phone: 206 378-0100
Fax: 206 378-5704
URL: http://www.smashingideas.com
E-mail: evanc@smashingideas.com

Sockeye Creative, Inc.

Area(s) of Specialization: Film/Video, CGI, Multimedia

Number of Employees: 7

Sockeye Creative Inc. is production studio that combines film and video with graphic design. Sockeye is a small studio located in Portland's historic Union Station. The three principles are Tom Sloan, Andy Fraser, and Peter Metz.

Sockeye Creative, Inc.
Union Station
Suite 209
Portland, OR 97209
Phone: 503 226-3843
Fax: 503 227-1135
URL: http://www.sockeyecreative.com

SOL Design FX

Area(s) of Specialization: CGI, Film/Video, Multimedia

Number of Employees: 35+

SOL Design is a small boutique company using a combination of high-tech and traditional methods to create designs and effects works for advertising companies. The company's clients include Janet Jackson, Puff Daddy, and Smashing Pumpkins.

SOL Design FX
120 Broadway, Ste. 260
Santa Monica, CA 90401
Phone: 310 453-6311
Fax: 310 453-6431
E-mail: michele@soldesignfx.com
URL: http://www.soldesignfx.com

Sony Computer Entertainment America

Area(s) of Specialization: Computer Game Console Game and Console Development

Number of Employees: 750

Sony Computer Entertainment America, a division of Sony Computer Entertainment America Inc., distributes and markets the PlayStation game console in North America, develops and publishes software for the PlayStation game console, and manages the U.S. third party licensing program. Based in Foster City, California, Sony Computer Entertainment America Inc. is a wholly-owned subsidiary of Sony Computer Entertainment Inc.

Sony Computer Entertainment America
919 East Hillsdale Blvd., 2nd Floor
Foster City, CA 94404
Phone: 1-800-345-SONY
URL: http://www.scea.com

Sony Pictures Imageworks

Area(s) of Specialization: Film/Video, CGI, Multimedia, Animation

Number of Employees: 350

Sony Pictures Imageworks is a digital production company dedicated to visual effects and computer animation. The company has contributed talent and technology to such films as "Big Daddy", "Patch Adams", "Snow Falling on Cedars", "Godzilla", "City of Angels", "Contact", "Anaconda", "Michael", "The Ghost and the Darkness", "James and the Giant Peach" and "Starship Troopers", Paul Verhoeven's "The Hollow Man"; two films for Robert Zemeckis, "Cast Away" and "What Lies Beneath"; Mike Nichols' "What Planet Are You From?" and Imageworks President Ken Ralston's directorial debut, "Jumanji II."

Sony Pictures Imageworks
9050 West Washington Blvd.
Culver City, CA 90232
Phone: 310 840-8000
Fax: 310 840-8888
URL: http://www.spiw.com

Southern Exposure

Area(s) of Specialization: Multimedia

Number of Employees: 4

An artist-run organization, Southern Exposure reaches out to diverse audiences, and serves as a forum and resource center that provides support to the Bay Area's arts and educational communities.

Southern Exposure
401 Alabama Street
San Francisco, CA 94110
Phone: 415 863-2141
Fax: 415 863-1841

E-mail: soex@soex.org
URL: http://www.soex.org

Spaff Animation

Area(s) of Specialization: 2D Animation

Number of Employees: 100

The company produces animation. The company's clients include Walt Disney Company, Universal, MTV, Warner Bros and many others. The studio works in the style of traditional animation.

Spaff Animation
10843 Magnolia Blvd., Ste. 1
North Hollywood, CA 91601
Phone: 818 761-6744
Fax: 818 761-9608
URL: http://www.spaffanimation.com

Spank Interactive

Area(s) of Specialization: Animation, Modeling, Digital Video, Special Effects, Simulations, Web Design

Number of Employees: 2

Spank Interactive specializes in creating work that interactively draws on the senses and personifies information. The staff believes communication of ideas and information must be immediate, accessible and coherent. The company offers a cohesive approach to helping clients explore and utilize new media opportunities.

Spank Interactive
4041 Damant Court
North Highlands, CA 95660
Phone: 916 334-8385
Fax: 916 334-8385
URL: http://www.spank.com

Spazzco

Area(s) of Specialization: Animation, web design

Number of Employees: 3

Spazzco specializes in animation using traditional techniques as well as 2D and 3D digital character animation tools, such as Flash Animation, Traditional Cel Animation, and 3D Max Character Studio animation. Other services include: storyboards and background studies.

Spazzco
1620 Folsom
San Francisco, CA 94103
Phone: 415 551-2692
Fax: 415 551-1080
URL: http://www.spazzco.com

Special Designs Animation Studio

Area(s) of Specialization: Animation, CGI, Multimedia

Number of Employees: 1

Special Designs began in 1993 providing 3D modeling and animation services to the entertainment industry. Special Designs Studios is a complete 3D digital effects studio for the feature film, commercial and game industries, also the host to a creative content team providing story development, character design and development for a variety of other projects. The company handles a variety of media, including feature film visual effects, commercials, corporate video, educational multimedia, video games and more.

Special Designs Animation Studio
4628.5 Radford Ave.
North Hollywood, CA 91607
Phone: 818 766-9766
Fax: 818 766-9716
URL: http://www.sdas.com

Spicy Cricket Animation

Area(s) of Specialization: 3D Animation for Film/Video/Games

Number of Employees: 1

Spicy Cricket Animation is a 3D animation site for beginners and industry professionals alike. With easy-to-use links and reference pages, Angie Jones, the site's creator, offers case-study instruction on 3D character design and an insider's suggestions on career advancement.

Spicy Cricket Animation
3189 Shearer Ave.
Cayucos, CA 93430-1856
URL: http://www.spicycricket.com
E-mail: ajones@spicycricket.com

Spumco, Inc.

Area(s) of Specialization: Animation

Number of Employees: 100+

Spumco is a production company founded by John Kricfalusi, who was once the understudy of Ralph Bakshi, working as creative director on the rejuvenated Mighty Mouse series. John Kricfalusi also worked on the original animation series "Ren and Stimpy." With his Spumco teammates, he created multimedia projects such as the rock video for Bjork's "I Miss You" and the cartoon series made exclusively for the Internet, with characters: George Liquor, Jimmy The Idiot Boy, and Sody Pop. The company markets comic books, dolls, and novelty products from this series, and also other work, exclusively through the web site.

Spumco, Inc.
415 E. Harvard Street, Ste. 204
Glendale, CA 91205
Phone: 818 550-5960
Fax: 818 550-0320
URL: http://www.spumco.com

Spyglass, Inc.

Area(s) of Specialization: Multimedia, CGI

Number of Employees: 25

Strategic Internet Solutions Spyglass is a provider of strategic Internet consulting, software and professional services to content providers, service operators and device manufacturers to capitalize on the use of the Internet. The company's technologies enable Web conductivity through embedded browsers and servers, and provide performance enhancements, content conversion and extraction through server-based solutions. Spyglass Professional Services provides consulting for defining, developing and delivering complete, end-to-end project solutions.

Spyglass, Inc./ Los Gatos
16795 Lark Avenue
2nd Floor
Los Gatos, CA 95032
Phone: 408 399-8800
Fax: 408 399-4395
URL: http://www.spyglass.com

Spyglass, Inc./ Menlo Park
1100 Marsh Rd.
Menlo Park, CA 94025
Phone: 650 462-9171
Fax: 650 462-9174

Stan Winston Studio

Area(s) of Specialization: Special Effect
Model Making

Number of Employees: 100

For 25 years, Stan Winston and a team of
artists and technicians have been creating
characters, creatures and monsters for
motion pictures and television. Live action
character and make-up effects have been
used in films such as: "The Lost World:
Jurassic Park", "Terminator", "Predator",
"Aliens" and "Interview with the Vampire".
The company's illustrators, sculptors,
technicians, painters, engineers and
fabricators have created everything from
dinosaurs and gorillas to alien life forms
from the other side of the universe.

Stan Winston Studio
7904 Van Nuys Blvd. Suite 501
Van Nuys, CA 91406
Phone: 818 782-0870 Ext. 132
Fax: 818 782-0807
URL: http://www.swfx.com

Stargate Films, Inc.

Area(s) of Specialization: Animation, CGI,
Film/Video, Multimedia

Number of Employees: 25-30

Stargate Films studio works in film, video,
and computer technologies in a totally
integrated multimedia production studio.

The company integrates technical
filmmaking with special effects and live
action production.

Stargate Films, Inc.
1103 W. Isabel St.
Burbank, CA 91506
Phone: 818 972-1100
Fax: 818 972-9411
URL: http://www.stargatefilms.com

Station X Studios, LLC

Area(s) of Specialization: CGI, Animation,
Multimedia, Film/Video

Number of Employees: 66+

Station X Studios, LLC was founded in 1997
by a team of animators, programmers,
systems administrators, and production
personnel to create a complete entertainment
studio. The company creates visual effects for
film, TV, and commercials, develops new
software for the visual effects industry, and
develops and produces film and television
projects. Besides various commercials and
in-house productions, the company created
over 200 shots for the feature film "Dungeons
and Dragons," which the company is co-
producing.

Station X Studios
1717 Stewart Street
Santa Monica, CA 90404
Phone: 310 828-6460

Fax: 310 828-4101
URL: http://www.stationxstudios.com

Swankytown

Area(s) of Specialization: Animation, Multimedia, CGI

Number of Employees: 10+

Swankytown.com is a digital media company creating customized comedy advertainment. The company licenses original Flash animation, streaming video content, animated interactive games, e-cards as well as provides traditional media support. Swankytown Partners was officially formed in 1998 to create comedic entertainment. Swankytown.com was formed in 1999 as a virtual studio, creating digitally produced comedy content for web-sites and other media. Swankytown's first endeavor, the digital short comedy film, "New Testament", was released worldwide in 1998.

Swankytown
4470 Sunset Blvd. Ste. 300
Los Angeles, CA 90027
Phone: 323 466-8600
Fax: 323 466-8800
URL: http://www.swankytown.com

T-Bone Films, Inc.

Area(s) of Specialization: Film/Video, Multimedia, CGI

Number of Employees: 2+

Formed in 1993 by Executive Producer Craig Caryl and Director Evan Stone, T-Bone Films has evolved from sports filmmaking roots into a full service creative shop. The company has collaborated with MTV to produce shows including the 1996 #1 MTV Sports Segment "Junk State". Channel One News hired T-Bone to produce documentaries for an in school programming Network. T-bone provides services to clients from Airwalk to Disney Interactive.

T-Bone Films, Inc.
225 Santa Monica Blvd. Suite 207
Santa Monica, CA 90401
Phone: 310 451-1775
Alt. Phone: 888 813-0219
Fax: 310 451-1969
URL: http://www.t-bone.com

TFX, Inc.

Area(s) of Specialization: CGI, Multimedia

Number of Employees: 20-35

In 1992 Allen Pike and Charley Zurian founded a fully integrated automotive and product prototyping facility in Southern California using digital technologies as well as traditional design approaches. Employees at TFX are experienced in the fields of design, engineering, sculpting, and the visual arts.

TRANSFX a.k.a. TFX
8300 Waters Rd.
Moorpark, CA 93021
Phone: 805 532-1526
Fax: 805 532-1645
URL: http://www.transfx.com

Tigar Hare Studios

Area(s) of Specialization: 2D and 3D Computer Animation/Special Effects for Film/Commercials/Television

Number of Employees: 16

Tigar Hare Studios is a high-end 3D computer animation and graphics design studio. The company services clients in commercial, broadcast, feature film, special venue markets, computer gaming, convergence media, and web animation.

Tigar Hare Studios
4735 N. Sepulveda Blvd.
Suite 426
Sherman Oaks, CA 91403
Phone: 818 907-6663
Fax: 818 907-0693
URL: http://www.tigarhare.com

Tippet Studios

Area(s) of Specialization: CGI, Film/Video, Multimedia, Animation

Number of Employees: 125+

With sixteen years and over fifteen feature films, Tippet Studios has a staff of more than 125 artists, designers, engineers and animators. Tippett Studios is an animation and visual effects studio under the guidance of Phil and his partners, Jules Roman (Vice President and Executive Producer) and Craig Hayes (Creative Director and Visual Effects Supervisor).

Tippet Studios
2741 Tenth St.
Berkeley, CA 94710
Phone: 510 649-9711
Fax: 510 649-9399
URL: http://www.tippet.com

Tooned In

Area(s) of Specialization: 3D computer and Cel Animation

Number of Employees: 12+

Tooned In is an animation studio located in Seattle, Washington. The company specializes in melding technology with traditional animation techniques, and maintains a small permanent staff of artists and technologists, and employs a large number of freelance artists from the Seattle, Los Angeles, and other parts of the country. In addition to the U.S. based animation team, the company has a software consulting and animation production partnership with Wang Film Productions in Taipei, Taiwan.

Tooned In
218 Broadway East, Suite 202
Seattle, WA 98102
Phone: (206) 323-1426
Fax: (206) 323-1427
URL: http://www.toonedin.com
E-mail: info@toonedin.com

Tooniversal

Area(s) of Specialization: Cel Animation, Live Action Film, Special Effects

Number of Employees: 50

The Tooniversal Company is an independent producer and distributor of motion pictures, both live-action and animated. Tooniversal also has a live-action production and distribution division, Premiere Pictures International. The company represents both animation and live-action production facilities, and also distributes films from various countries in a number of territories worldwide including the United States. For many years, Tooniversal has been a producer of limited edition animation art. Clients include the Warner Bros. Studio Stores and more than 150 animation art galleries in the U.S. and Canada.

The Tooniversal Company
21755 Ventura Blvd., #101
Woodland Hills, CA 91364
Phone: 310 230-7684
Fax: 801 365-7267
URL: http://www.tooniversal.com

Total Video Co.

Area(s) of Specialization: Film/Video, Multimedia, CGI

Number of Employees: 25

Total Video Co has been creating videos for more than 20 years serving its corporate and broadcast clients. The company creates video news releases, new product roll-outs, national sales meetings, commercials, and corporate documentaries; Total Video's staff aids clients with sending messages to target audiences.

Total Video
432 North Canal Street, Suite 12
South San Francisco, CA 94080
Phone: 650 583-8236
Fax: 650 583-4708
URL: http://www.totalvideo.com

The Truly Dangerous Company

Area(s) of Specialization: Motion Simulator, Puppets, Creature Effects

Number of Employees: 2

The Truly Dangerous Company is two people - Trey Stokes and Maija Beeton- who provide production and design services to the entertainment industry.

The Truly Dangerous Company
9818 Commerce Ave.
Tujunga, CA 91042
Phone: 818 353-5556
Fax: 818 353-4140
URL: http://www.trudang.com

Urban Vision Entertainment

Area(s) of Specialization: Japanese Animation

Number of Employees: 9

Urban Vision Entertainment, Inc., a production/distribution company based in Los Angeles, formed in July, 1996 to help introduce the alternative animation genre known as anime or Japanimation to mainstream media. The company primarily produces/acquires Japanese animation for direct-to-home video release and distributes to the home video market. The company also has a broad-based licensing division which includes such endeavors as theatrical and television releases and interactive games. Urban Vision unites the Japanese style of animation with the American style of storytelling to create a contemporary form of animated releases geared for a world market.

Urban Vision Entertainment
5120 Goldleaf Circle
Los Angeles, CA 90056
Phone: 323 292-0147
URL: http://www.urban-vision.com

Valve Software

Area(s) of Specialization: CGI, Multimedia, Animation

Number of Employees: 40+

Valve is an entertainment software company founded by Gabe Newell and Mike Harrington and based in Kirkland, Washington. Valve's debut product was a PC game called "Half-Life," released in November, 1998.

Valve Software
520 Kirkland Way #201
Kirkland, WA 98033
Phone: 425 889-9642
Fax: 425 889-9642
URL: http://www.valvesoftware.com

The Video Agency, Inc./TVA

Area(s) of Specialization: Film/Video, Animation, Multimedia

Number of Employees: 23+

TVA is a full service film / video production and duplication company close to Universal Studios. Housed in a 17,500 sq. ft. facility with blue screen sound stages, motion control, digital editing bays, audio recording studio, TVA produces (from script to screen, dubs to distribution) television programs, corporate motion pictures, computer animation and visual effects, special venue films, WaterScreen attractions, TV commercials, direct-mail video, etc., in every major language. The company specializes in traditional film/video uses as well as other emerging technologies 3D reflective videography, 70 mm WaterScreen attractions, motion control, special formats (including 12/15 perf), digital animation and interactive programming.

The Video Agency Inc./TVA Productions
10900 Ventura Blvd.
Studio City, CA 91604
Phone: 818 505-8300
Fax: 818 505-8370
URL: http://www.tvaproductions.com

Video Arts, Inc.

Area(s) of Specialization: Film/Video, CGI, Animation, Multimedia

Number of Employees: 15+

Video Arts is a digital studio providing for clients' production needs. The company specializes in design, animation, editing and special effects for advertising, corporate communications and broadcast clients.

Video Arts, Inc.
724 Battery St., Ste. 5400
San Francisco, CA 94111
Phone: 415 788-0300
Fax: 415 788-3331
URL http://www.vidarts.com

Viewpoint

Area(s) of Specialization: 3D Modeling

Number of Employees: 300

Viewpoint Digital is recognized for creating and publishing a library of 3D digital content, and providing custom modeling services-helping create digital effects for films, television programs, advertisements, games and Web sites. Viewpoint's work is featured in motion pictures including "The World Is Not Enough", "Mystery Men" and "Pushing Tin," and has had roles in numerous films such as "Antz", "Star Trek: Insurrection", "Independence Day", "Air Force One" and "Godzilla." Viewpoint's work can also be seen in characters and props for game titles including Interstate '82, Pandora's Box, Civilization: Call to Power and Gauntlet: Legends; television programs such as "Star Trek Voyager" and "Jonny Quest;" advertisements for Dodge, McDonalds, Taco Bell and Nike; and 3D-enabled Web sites for The Sharper Image, Autobytel.com and Ticketmaster.com.

Viewpoint
13348 Beach Ave.
Marina Del Rey, CA 90292
Phone: 310 280-2000
Alt. Phone: 800-328-2738
Fax: 310 845-9412
URL: http://www.viewpoint.com

Viewport Images

Area(s) of Specialization: Computer
Graphics, Animation

Number of Employees: 5

Viewport Images is a computer graphics and
animation production facility specializing in
3D/2D graphics and effects for the
entertainment, interactive, multimedia and
visualization industries. Viewport Images
was established in 1986 by John Howard with
experience in the design and production of
computer graphics and visual effects for
feature films, video, theatrical ID's, cable and
network broadcast graphics packages.
Viewport Images uses the Softimage
Extreme Creative Environment on Silicon
Graphics Workstations to produce computer
graphics and animation. All projects are
mastered in-house on a Abekas Digital Disk
Recorder and can be output to all NTSC
formats including D1, D2, D3, Digital
Betacam & Beta SP. Projects have also been
delivered in several digital media formats
including SyQuest, Optical cartridge,

Recordable CD-ROM's, DAT and Exabyte
tape.

Viewport Images
109 N Naomi St.
Burbank, CA 91505
Phone: 818 559-8705
URL: http://www.pacificnet.net/vimages
E-mail: jhoward@vimages.com

Virtualmagic Animation

Area(s) of Specialization: Animation, CGI,
Multimedia

Number of Employees: 20-30

VirtualMagic Animation is a service for 2D
digital ink, paint and compositing
production. Founded in 1992, the company
is a resource for television and film
production companies, major studios and ad
agencies. Working with USAnimation,
Softimage Toonz, Media Pegs and other
software packages on Hewlett-Packard,
Silicon Graphics and Windows NT platform,
the company provides clients with digital ink
& paint services.

Virtualmagic Animation
4640 Lankershim Blvd.
Suite 201
North Hollywood, CA 91602
Phone: 818 623-1866
Fax: 818 623-1868
URL: http://www.virtualmagic.com

Visible Productions

Area(s) of Specialization: CGI, Multimedia, Animation

Number of Employees: 20

Visible Productions develops custom biomedical animations, illustrations, and interactive multimedia for the healthcare and educational markets. Based on the National Library of Medicines' "Visible Human Project", VP's anatomical content can be used to create: anatomical imagery that is used to conduct biomedical research, simulate surgical procedures, and educate students, patients, and healthcare professionals.

Visible Productions
116 N. College Ave.
Suite 7
Fort Collins, CO 80524
Phone: 970 407-7240
Fax: 970 407-7248
URL: http://www.visiblep.com

Visionary Studio

Area(s) of Specialization: Digital Animation, Illustration

Number of Employees: 5

Visionary Studio was founded by Tim Haskins to do illustration of books. The company offers one-on-one classes in drawing, animation, web design, and digital coloring/special fx.

Visionary Studio
3535 NE 141st
Portland, OR 97230
Fax: 503 256-4578
URL: http://www.visionarystudio.com

Vision Crew Unlimited

Area(s) of Specialization: Animation, CGI, Multimedia, Film/Video

Number of Employees: 10

Vision Crew Unlimited was founded in 1994 to provide visual effects for feature films, commercials, and television. Building miniature fabrication and mechanical effects, VCU has expanded into a full service visual effects facility.

Vision Crew Unlimited
5939 Rodeo Rd.
Los Angeles, CA 90016
Phone: 310 558-0450
Fax: 310 558-0437
URL: http://www.visioncrew.com

Vision Scape Imaging, Inc.

Area(s) of Specialization: 3D Animation, Digital Effects

Number of Employees: 30

Vision Scape Imaging, Inc. is a production studio dedicated to creating 3D animation and digital effects for the feature film, commercial and electronic game industries. The company's staff writes code, creates software plug-ins and explores new applications if necessary.

Vision Scape Imaging, Inc.
5125 Convoy St., Ste. 121
San Diego, CA 92111
Phone: 858 391-1300
Alt Phone: 800 507-5678
Fax: 858 391-1301
URL: http://www.thelab3d.com

Visual Concept Engineering, Inc./VCE

Area(s) of Specialization: Film/Video, CGI, Multimedia

Number of Employees: 10-12

VCE (Visual Concept Entertainment) began in 1982 after founder Peter Kuran finished work as animation supervisor for Industrial Light and Magic (ILM) on George Lucas' "The Empire Strikes Back." VCE has worked on over 200 theatrical motion pictures including both "Addams Family" films and all three "Robocop" features. The latest feature work from VCE was seen in "Idle Hands", "Starship Troopers", "Courage Under Fire", and "Nixon".

Visual Concept Engineering, Inc./VCE
13300 Ralston Ave.
Sylmar, CA 91342
Phone: 818 367-9187

Fax: 818 362-3490
URL: http://www.vce.com

Visual Magic Images, Inc.

Area(s) of Specialization: 3D Computer Animation, Digital Visual Effects

Number of Employees: 8+

VMI is a boutique visual effects production studio specializing in high end digital animation and effects. The company provides a range of computer generated and digital effects services for the producers of: Feature Films, Ride Films, Commercial, Multimedia, Ride Film Libraries, Theme Parks and Theater Design. Whether a simple logo treatment or complex visual effects for a feature film or interactive game, the VMI creative team works with a client from the creative concept to the final project completion.

Visual Magic Images
929 E. 2nd Street, Ste.# 201
Los Angeles, CA 90012
Phone: 213 680-3336
Fax : 213 628-2111
URL: http://www.visual-magic.com
E-mail: info@visual-magic.com

Wallace Creative, Inc.

Area(s) of Specialization: 3D Animation

Number of Employees: 2

Wallace Creative Inc provides concept and content development, directorial and full production capabilities, 2D and CGI character and graphic animation, design and art direction and cinematic storyboarding. The company creates work for the Internet, commercial broadcast, video, multimedia, music videos, gaming, film and print.

Wallace Creative, Inc.
1705 NW 25th. Ave.
Portland, OR 97210
Phone: 503 224-9660
Fax: 503 224-9667
URL: http://www.wallyhood.com

Walt Disney Feature Animation

Area(s) of Specialization: Animation, Multimedia, Film/Video, CGI

Number of Employees: 1,000+

More than 75 years ago, Walt Disney led a crew of artists to create 37 full-length animated films. Walt Disney Feature Animation has a library of classics. Through the collaborative efforts of 2,000 artists and crew members at animation studios in Los Angeles, Orlando, and Paris, the Feature Animation groups are creating ten new stories. Walt Disney Animation combines traditional and digital artists with

technology, administration, and production management teams.

Walt Disney Feature Animation
500 South Buena Vista Street
Burbank, CA 91521-7454
Phone: 407-828-3110
Fax: 818 558 2547
URL http://disney.go.com

Warner Bros. Television & Classic Animation

Area(s) of Specialization: Feature Films to Television, Home Video, Animation, Comic Books.

Number of Employees: 9000

Warner Bros., is a fully integrated, broad-based entertainment company, involved in the creation, production, distribution, licensing and marketing of all forms of entertainment and attendant businesses. Warner Bros., a Time Warner Entertainment Company, works in every aspect of the entertainment industry from feature films to television, home video, animation, comic books, product and brand licensing, retail stores and international theaters. With the acquisition of Turner Entertainment by Time Warner in October 1996, the classic MGM (pre-1986) and RKO titles, as well as animation from Hanna-Barbera, Ruby-Spears and MGM, were added to the Warner Bros.-managed library.

Warner Brothers
4000 Warner Blvd
Burbank, CA 91522
Phone: 818 954- 6000
URL: http://www.warnerbros.com

Western Images

Area(s) of Specialization: CGI, Multimedia, Animation, Film/Video

Number of Employees: 40

Western Images, a digital production and design studio, handles projects ranging from commercial to theatrical, music video, long-form and broadcast design. Western's animators, artists, designers, editors and colorists are accessible as resources from the early stages of project planning through delivery, collaborating with clients (and each other) to produce multimedia and animation.

Western Images
600 Townsend St., Ste. 300W
San Francisco, CA 94103
Phone: 415 252-6000
Fax: 415 621-6780
URL: http://www.westernimages.com

Wild Brain, Inc.

Area(s) of Specialization: Multimedia, Animation, CGI

Number of Employees: 300

Founded in 1994, Wild Brain, Inc. is an animation studio in the heart of the San Francisco Bay Area. Wild Brain's client list includes names in entertainment and advertising: Universal, Microsoft, Twentieth Century Fox, Coca-Cola, Disney, Nike, Warner Bros., Levi Strauss, LucasArts, Nickelodeon and HBO.

Wild Brain, Inc.
2650 18th Street
San Francisco, CA 94110
Phone: 415 553-8000
Fax: 415 553-8009
URL: http://www.wildbraininc.com

William Moffitt Associates

Area(s) of Specialization: Film/Video, Digital Production

Number of Employees: 4

William Moffitt Associates is a full-service communications company specializing in film, video and digital production for clients world wide. The company services a client's company or organization in the boardroom, on TV, or over the Internet.

William Moffitt Associates
747 North Lake Avenue
Pasadena, CA 91104
Phone: 626 791-2559
Fax: 626 791-3092
URL: http://www.lonehorse.com

Will Vinton Studio

Area(s) of Specialization: Dimensional Animation

Number of Employees: 400

Will Vinton Studio id a production studio that was founded in 1975 by Will Vinton and Bob Gardiner. The studio worked on "Rip Van Winkle", "Creation", "The Great Cognito" and created special visual effects in the Disney feature "Return to Oz." The studio has also done work on such films as "The Little Prince", "Martin the Cobbler" and "Dinosaur." In the studio is credited for producing the first feature-length clay animation called "The Adventures of Mark Twain." In addition the studio has produced popular animation such as The California Raisins, animation effects for the series "Moonlighting" and most recently for the "PJs."

Will Vinton Studio
1400 NW 22ND Ave.
Portland, OR 97210
Phone: 503 225-1130
Fax: 503 226-3746
URL: http://www.vinton.com

Wired Digital

Area(s) of Specialization: CGI, Multimedia

Number of Employees: 170+

Wired Digital creates a range of on-line products that help people put technologies to use in the company's personal and professional lives. Their on-line services provide technology-oriented information and tools that people can use day to day. Wired Digital is headquartered in San Francisco with satellite offices in New York, Chicago, and Los Angeles.

Wired Digital
660 Third Street
Fourth Floor
San Francisco, CA 94107
Phone: 415 276 8400
Fax: 415 276 8499
URL: http://hotwired.lycos.com/home/digital

Xaos, Inc.

Area(s) of Specialization: Multimedia, Film/Video, CGI

Number of Employees: 20-25

Xaos is an artist driven boutique facility. The staff wrote a body of software with which to create imagery. The company's facility offers opportunities to work on diverse projects including commercials, broadcast IDs, feature films, special venue and large-format cinema.

Xaos, Inc.
444 De Haro St.
San Francisco, CA 94107
Phone: 415 558-9267
Fax: 415 558-9160
URL: http://www.xaos.com

Zona Productions, Inc.

Area(s) of Specialization: Multi Camera Productions

Number of Employees: 5

Zona Production works in multi-camera production.

Zona Productions, Inc.
215 S. La Cienega Blvd. #204
Beverly Hills, CA 90211
Phone: 310 652-4070
Fax: 310 652-0390

Zooma Zooma

Area(s) of Specialization: Film/Video

Number of Employees: 7

A bi-coastal production company specializing in commercials, music videos and short films. Established 8 years ago, Zooma Zooma's goal is to create a production company for young filmmakers to showcase talent.

Zooma Zooma
804 Main St., Suite 200
Venice, CA 90291
Phone: 310 392-8676
Fax: 310392-0636
URL: http://www.zoomazooma.com

Zygote Media Group

Area(s) of Specialization: 3D Modelers

Number of Employees: 15-25

Zygote Media Group, Inc. is a Utah-based company providing 3D computer data (models and texture maps) for use in commercial 3D modeling, rendering, and animation software packages (3D applications). The name "Zygote" signifies the first stage of life, just as computer modeling is the first stage of a 3D computer animation.

Zygote Media Group
679 N. 1890 West, Suite 45A
Provo, UT 84601
Phone: 801 375-7220
Alt Phone: 800 267-5170
Fax: 801 375-7389
URL: http://www.zygote.com

168 Design Group

Area(s) of Specialization: Computer graphics and design

Number of Employees: 20

The company creates design packages for television.

168 Design Group
60 Broadway
San Francisco, CA 94111
Phone: 415 837-0168
Fax: 415 693-4203
URL: http://www.168designgroup.com

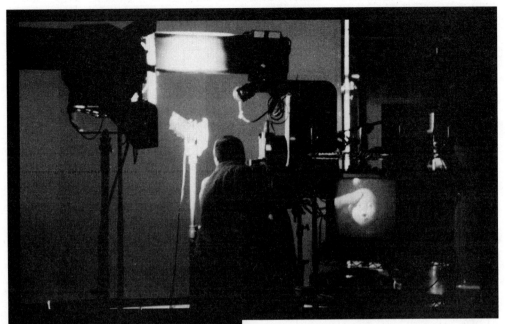

Stopmotion animator at Curious Pictures works on animating a head for a scene in HBO's "A Little Curious." Courtesy of Garth Gardner Photography Archive.

Canada

Alias-Wavefront

Area(s) of Specialization: CGI, Multimedia, Animation

Number of Employees: 500+

As the one of the world's creators of 2D and 3D graphics technology, Alias|Wavefront develops advanced software for the film and video, games and interactive media, industrial design and visualization markets. Based in Toronto, Alias|Wavefront is a wholly owned, independent software subsidiary of Silicon Graphics, Inc.

Alias-Wavefront
Global Headquarters - Toronto
210 King Street East
Toronto, Ontario, Canada M5A 1J7
Phone: 800 447-2542
416 362-9181
Fax: 416 369-6140
URL: http://www.aw.sgi.com

Audio Visions Productions

Area(s) of Specialization: Film/Video, Multimedia, Sound, Animation

Number of Employees: 1

MPSL is Toronto's full service video and digital media production center. Since 1981, MPSL has provided video production services to the broadcast and corporate television production industries. Production, video editing, computer animation, duplication, standards conversion, teleprompting services and CD-ROM/DVD production are all carried out in the six-thousand square foot facility, which is located near the center of Toronto. Linear and non-linear off-line edit suites, video duplication and international standards conversion facilities, and digital workstations for animation, CD-ROM / DVD production, video capture and multimedia file conversion to video provide all the services required by video and multimedia producers.

Audio Visions Productions
885 Don Mills Rd.
Suite 208
Toronto, ON Canada M3C 1V9
Phone: 416 449-7614
Fax: 416 449-9239
URL: http://www.mpsl.com

Bardel Animation, Ltd.

Area(s) of Specialization: 2D Traditional Animation.

Number of Employees: 12+

Bardel Animation, a Western Canadian 2D animation house produces everything from festival shorts to feature films. Founded in 1987, Bardel develops and creates its own projects as well as producing animation for North American studios. Phases of production, from design and storyboarding to AVID editing and digital ink and paint, are done in-house.

Bardel Animation, Ltd.
509 Richards St.
Ground Floor
Vancouver, BC
Canada V6B 2Z6
Phone: 604 669-5589
Fax: 604 669-9079
URL: http://www.bardelanimation.com

Barking Bullfrog Cartoon Company, Inc.

Area(s) of Specialization: Multimedia

Number of Employees: 2

Barking Bullfrog Cartoon Company Inc. is a multifaceted animation company providing production services for television and multimedia programming. The company was established in 1996 by partners Ian Freedman and Mark Freedman, who had been providing animation from their own respective companies.

Barking Bullfrog Cartoon Company, Inc.
#101-480 Smithe St.
Vancouver, B.C
Canada V6B 5E4

Phone: 604 689-0702
Fax: 604 689-0715
URL: http://www.barkingbullfrog.com

Boomstone Entertainment, Inc.

Area(s) of Specialization: Pre-Production

Number of Employees: 5

Boomstone has worked on a number of animated productions. The company creates in a variety of animation styles. Mr. Dodo can be found on the end credits of the Stellar Entertainment Inc. live action feature film, "Undercover Angel."

Boomstone Entertainment, Inc.
311 Richmond Rd., Suite #302
Ottawa, ON Canada
K1Z 6X3
Phone: 613 725-3843
Fax: 613 725-9327
URL: http://www.boomstone.com
E-mail: info@boomstone.com

Bone Digital Effects

Area(s) of Specialization: Animation & Digital Compositing

Number of Employees: 4

Since 1997, Bone Digital Effects has provided 3D animation, visual effects, video production, multimedia and internet related services to producers of film, television, and corporate communications. The company provides high end post production and communication development. The studio operates from a 28,000 sq. ft. production facility located in Toronto's film district. Production resources consist of: Silicon Graphic computers running 2D/3D software, and a Mac/NT network for nonlinear editing, multimedia, and internet publishing applications.

Bone Digital Effects
33 Villiers Street suite 107
Toronto, ON M5A 1A9
Phone: 416 469-3406
Fax: 416 469-3506
URL: http://www.bonefx.com

Bowes Production, Inc.

Area(s) of Specialization: Stop-motion animation

Number of Employees: 5

Created to specialize in Clay Animation, Bowes Production Inc. has expanded to cover a variety of stop-motion techniques, using mediums such as clay, rubber foam latex, silicones, foam core, sand, nuts, bolts, and found objects. Bowes Productions is a stop-motion animation studio in Western Canada, producing commercials, television productions, children's programming, station

IDs, short films, music videos and various other specialized projects. Clients include: McDonalds, Milton Bradley, General Mills, Mattel, CBC Canada, YTV Canada, and Fuji Television Corporation Japan.

Bowes Production, Inc.
4776 Buxton St.
Burnaby, Vancouver B.C. V5H 1J3
Canada
Phone: 604 871-0338
Fax: 604 433-0340

Brainchild Studios

Area(s) of Specialization: Interactive Games, Animation

Number of Employees: 4

Brainchild Studios creates animation and digital effects for Film, Video, Interactive Media and the Internet.

Brainchild Studios
Suite 15 - 15531 24th Ave.
Surrey, BC CANADA V4A-2J4
Phone: 604 541-1315
Fax: 604 541-9975
URL: http://www.brainchildstudios.com

Buzz Image Group, Inc.

Area(s) of Specialization: Post Multimedia

Number of Employees: 15

Since its establishment in 1988, Buzz Image Group has been creating and processing visual imagery, offering services in video post production, animation and 2D/3D visual effects for the film and television industries.

Buzz Image Group, Inc.
Groupe Image Buzz Inc.
312 Sherbrooke Street East
Montréal, Québec
Canada H2X 1E6
Phone: 514 848-0579
800 567-0200
Fax: 514 848-6371
URL: http://www.buzzimage.com

C.O.R.E. Digital Pictures

Area(s) of Specialization: Film/Video, CGI, Multimedia, Animation

Number of Employees: 30+

C.O.R.E. is a digital animation and special effects company with studios in Toronto, Canada. They design and produce digital visual effects for feature films, television series, commercials, and movies of the week. The company worked on the television series TekWar the "Upload Sequence", "Mimic", and "Fly Away Home." Their artists are equipped with Silicon Graphics hardware running a variety of 2D and 3D animation software including Prisms, Houdini, Alias Power Animator, Flint, Renderman, Amazon Paint.

C.O.R.E. Digital Pictures
488 Wellington St. W.
Suite 600
Toronto, Ontario M5V 1E3
Phone: 416 599-2673
Fax: 416 599-1212
URL: http://www.coredp.com

Cuppa Coffee Animation

Area(s) of Specialization: Animation, Multimedia, Film/Video

Number of Employees: (on contract, number varies)

Cuppa Coffee is an experimental animation company based in Toronto. Owner and Executive Producer Adam Shaheen founded the company in 1992.

Cuppa Coffee Animation
401 Richmond St. West
Ste. 104
Toronto, ON
Canada M5V 1X3
Phone: 416 340-8869
Fax: 416 340-9819
URL: http://www.cuppacoffee.com

Digital Animatics

Area(s) of Specialization: 3D Modeling

Number of Employees: 10

Digital Animatics provides family programming for Television, PC and the Internet. MHDA.COM is in its fourth year on the Internet and backed by a staff spanning over 25 years. The company specializes in media concepts and solutions for corporate communication. MHDA.COM provides ready made models and meshes for 3D in every form, from CGI For Television and Film, VRML for the Internet and Virtual Software creations. The company also offers custom modeling on a per project basis.

Digital Animatics
Suite 101-4180 Nanaimo Street
Vancouver, British Columbia
CANADA, V5N 5H7
Phone: 604 879-1001
Fax: 604 879-1001
URL: http://www.mhda.com

DKP/Dan Krech Productions, Inc.

Area(s) of Specialization: CGI, Multimedia, Animation, Film/Video, Sound

Number of Employees: 24

DKP is a fully-equipped visual-effects and animation facility whose head office and main facility are located in Toronto. Operating as a boutique, DKP has expertise in high-end visual effects for the commercial and feature film markets. Recent projects include a 48 minute all computer generated

direct to video title, "The Nuttiest Nutcracker" for Columbia Tri-Star and approximately two minutes of 3D stereo IMAX for Siegfried and Roy "The Magic Box". DKP provided CG and 2D effects and compositing for DreamWorks SKG's "Joseph" (prequel to "Prince of Egypt"). The staff experience in effects design ranges from character creation for classical and CGI animation to full in camera effects to multi-layer cross platform effects and animation compositing.

DKP/Dan Krech Productions, Inc.
48 River Street
Toronto, ON
M5A 3N9 Canada
Phone: 416 861-9269
Fax: 416 363-3301
URL: http://www.dkp.com

DKP Effects

Area(s) of Specialization: Visual Effects, Animation

Number of Employees: 22+

DKP is a fully-equipped visual-effects and animation facility. Since its inception, DKP has created imagery through animation and digital effects based the philosophy of founder, Dan Krech. Building on experience and expertise, DKP is producing effects and animation out of three distinct divisions: Commercial, Long Form, and Multi-Media creative groups. Technical directors and creative teams pool resources to form partnerships, to expedite the work.

DKP Effects
48 River Street
Toronto, ON M5A 3N9 Canada
Phone: 416 861-9269
Fax: 416 363-3301
URL: http://www.dkp.com
e-mail: effects@dkp.com

Gajdecki Visual Effects

Area(s) of Specialization: Film/Video, Multimedia, CGI, Animation

Number of Employees: 15

GVFX is a visual effects company servicing the motion picture, commercial, television and special venue industries. Based in Toronto and Vancouver, the company offers visual effects supervision, digital compositing and animation, physical production facilities including motion control systems, a model shop, insert stage and pyro team. GVFX has created effects for over 150 major International motion picture and television productions. GVFX staff are encouraged to broaden their experience and knowledge by working in different departments and disciplines. The company's committed to training at all levels so that employees throughout the company can

understand the entire VFX and film making process.

Gajdecki Visual Effects
1145 West 7th Ave.
Vancouver, British Columbia
Canada V6H 1B5
Phone: 604 736-4839
Fax: 604 736-4838
URL: http://www.gvfx.com

Grafixation

Area(s) of Specialization: Graphics, Web Design, Web Hosting

Number of Employees: 10

Grafixation provides small to medium sized companies with web and e-commerce solutions. Regular web sites to custom java based shopping cart sites are available at reasonable costs.

Grafixation
6810 Simpson Pioneer Trail
Mississauga, Ontario
L5W 1A6
Phone: 416 817-0828
Fax: 905 565-9395
URL: http://www.grafixation.com

Head Gear Animation

Area(s) of Specialization: Stop-Motion, Cel Animation, Mixed Media

Number of Employees: 3

Head Gear was launched in July, 1997, after three years of building an extensive reel of unique animation work at Toronto production house Cuppa Coffee. The company creates various styles of 2D animation. The company's clients include: General Motors, Sundance Channel, and Nickelodeon.

Head Gear Animation
35 McCaul, Suite 301
Toronto, Ontario
Phone: 416 408-2020
Fax: 416 408-2011
URL: http://www.headgearanimation.com

Loop Media Inc.

Area(s) of Specialization: Computer Animation

Number of Employees: 9

Loop Media Inc. is a 2D and 3D computer animation studio, offering a variety of high-end production services. Using Silicon Graphics workstations with Prisms, Houdini and Renderman software, Loop provides character and corporate animation in addition to visual effects for film and television.

Loop Media Inc.
401 Richmond St. West
Ste. 243
Toronto, ON Canada M5V 3A8

Phone: 416 595-6496
Fax: 416 595-0306
URL: http://www.loopmedia.com

Lost Boys Studios

Area(s) of Specialization: Design and Consulting, Video/ Film Production and Post Production

Number of Employees: 12

Lost Boys Studios was formed in the winter of 1997 through an alliance of the Vancouver based Solstice Digital Imaging and LA-based Virgin Digital Studios. Lost Boys Studios is a creative house specializing in the design and execution of DFX. The company is involved in pre-production DFX design and budgeting consulting, On-set DFX Supervision, DFX execution, and approvals.

Lost Boys Studios
Suite 210 - 1737 West Third Avenue
Vancouver BC, Canada V6J 1K7
Phone: 604 738-1805
Fax: 604 738-1806
URL: http://www.lostboys-studios.com

Mainframe Entertainment, Inc.

Area(s) of Specialization: Long Form 3D Animation

Number of Employees: 330

Mainframe Entertainment, Inc. creates 3D generated imagery for film, and television. Mainframe is a Canadian-owned company based in Vancouver. The company has evolved from a small crew of animators in 1993 to a staff of over 300 today. In 1993 Mainframe created "Reboot" a 100 percent CGI television series. The company also develops and owns a number of proprietary software programs that enhance and accelerate animation production processes, and manages a Merchandising and Licensing program based on its properties.

Mainframe Entertainment, Inc.
Suite 500 - 2025 West Broadway
Vancouver BC, Canada, V6J 1Z6
Phone: 604 714-2600
Fax: 604 714-2641
URL: http://www.mainframe.ca

Mercury Filmworks

Area(s) of Specialization: 3D Animation, Digital on-line Editing

Number of Employees: 40

Located in a 8,000 sq. ft. facility in Vancouver, Mercury Filmworks is a fully equipped digital animation facility. From feature quality digital paint, special effects, 3D animation, and compositing, to uncompressed digital on-line editing, mastering, and network packaging, Mercury Filmworks services clients world wide via high-speed wireless to fiber optic connections. Clients include studio B, Nelvana, Fox, Teletoon, the Sony ANIMAX, Network, Harvey Entertainment Co., Wild Brain, Pearson Entertainment, Fun Bag Animation, Bardel Animation, Bardel Animation, Curious Pictures, and ECODE Entertainment.

Mercury Filmworks
190 Alexander Street
Suite 500
Vancouver, B.C.
V6A 1B5
Phone: 604 684-9117
Fax: 604 684 8339
URL: http://www.mercuryfilmworks.com

Nelvana Limited

Area(s) of Specialization: Animation Production

Number of Employees: 700

A producer and distributor of animated children's and family entertainment, Nelvana's areas of programming include animated television series, specials and feature films. Nelvana's Toronto head office houses one of North America's large animation studios. The Company also has operations in Los Angeles, London and Paris. As an international distributor to the global television marketplace, the Company has licensed its programming to more than 160 countries.

Nelvana Limited
32 Atlantic Ave.
Toronto, Ontario M6K 1X8
Phone: 416 588-5571
Fax: 416 588-5252
URL: http://www.nelvana.com

Northwest Imaging and FX

Area(s) of Specialization: Post Production

Number of Employees: 40

Ten Years ago, the Northwest Imaging and FX began as a fully digital visual effects edit suite evolving to a full service post production facility. Services include visual effects supervision, 3D animation, compositing, digital matte painting, morphing, image tracking, film transfer (35mm and 16mm), tape to tape color correction, on-line picture finishing, off-line editing, and tape duplication.

Northwest Imaging and FX
2339 Columbia
Ste. 100
Vancouver, BC
Canada V5Y 3Y3
Phone: 604 873-9330
Fax: 604 873-9339
URL: http://www.nwfx.com

The Post Group

Area(s) of Specialization: Post Production

Number of Employees: 14+

Over the past five years The Post Group has been providing its clients with post production technology and a team of artists – providing both on-line and off-line editing.

The Post Group
411 Richmond Street East
Suite 205
Toronto, Ontario
Canada M5A 3S5
Phone: 416 363-3004
Fax: 416 363-8960
URL: http://www.thepostgroup.com

Rainmaker Digital Pictures

Area(s) of Specialization: Film/Video, Multimedia, Animation, CGI

Number Of Employees: 150

Rainmaker Digital Pictures is a post production company with a twenty year history. Rainmaker's facility in Vancouver provides producers with an array of post production services ranging from traditional film developing to the digital image processing techniques.

Rainmaker Digital Pictures
Vancouver Office
50 West 2nd Ave.
Vancouver, British Columbia

Canada V5Y 1B3
Phone: 604 874-8700
Fax: 604 874-1719
URL: http://www.rainmaker.com

Relic Entertainment, Inc.

Area(s) of Specialization: Game Developer

Number of Employees: 43

Relic Entertainment Inc. is a developer of electronic entertainment software. The company is developing other types of electronic entertainment such as on-line gaming, arcade, and location-based media. Relic has also developed technologies in the area of 3D imagery and sound systems to expand through licensing agreements with studios looking to save on development costs.

Relic Entertainment, Inc.
400-948 Horner St.
Vancouver, BC
Canada V6B 2W7
Phone: 604 801-6577
Fax: 604 801-6578
URL: http://www.relic.com

Sarco Studios

Area(s) of Specialization: Animation for Broadcast

Number of Employees: 6

Sarco is a content producer that creates custom projects for the Internet using Flash and Shockwave. The studio also produces original 3D content for media as diverse as video games and short films.

Sarco Studios
312 Adelaide St. W.
Suite 406
Toronto, ON
Canada M5V 1R2
Phone: 416 977-3450
Alt Phone: 888 346-6630
Fax: 416 597-8591
URL: http://www.sarcostudios.com
E-mail: info@sarcostudios.com

Sundog Films

Area(s) of Specialization: Special Effects

Number of Employees: 20

Sundog Films Inc. is a full production and post-production company, offering facilities for live-action video and motion picture development. Credits include films such as: "Starship Troopers", "Independence Day", "Batman and Robin", "Titanic" and "Alien 4." The company's creative team includes visionary Designers, Art directors, CGI Operators, MAC artists and Animators. Sundog provides expertise in Domino, Henry, Flint/Flame, Alias/Wavefront, Softimage, Lightwave, Mobile Motion Control Rigs, Camera/Grip/Gaffer Packages, and 2nd Unit

Photography Experience and Expertise in Film and Digital Visual FX, Design and Animation, Film Input/Output Services, Titles, Compositing, Rig Removal. The company creates various styles of animation using the 3D Computer Animation, Claymation, Stop/Go Motion, Computer Logos and Graphics, Traditional Cel, and 2D Paintbox Design.

Sundog Films Toronto
530 Richmond St. West
Rear Bldg.
Toronto, ON Canada M5V 1Y4
Phone: 416 504-5335
Fax: 416 504-4545
URL: http://www.sundogfilms.ca

Topix/Mad Dog

Area(s) of Specialization: Special Effects

Number of Employees: 20

Founded in September 1987, Toronto-based TOPIX is a Canadian computer graphics and animation facility. Specializing in character animation, special effects, film titling, type and broadcast design, the company creates photo-realistic, computer-generated animation for the advertising, feature film, broadcast and music video industries. Clients include: Coca Cola, Kraft Foods, Chrysler, Budweiser, Playtex, Discover Card and Post Cereals, among others; international campaigns for Alka Seltzer, Pepsi Cola and

Honda, McDonald's, Nescafe, Ford, Molson's, and Labatt's. The company collaborated on rock videos including David Bowie's "Little Wonder", Sheryl Crow's "Anything But Down", Sarah McLachlan's "Sweet Surrender", The Tragically Hip's "Ahead by a Century", The Barenaked Ladies' "Brian Wilson", Amel Larrieux "Get Up", and Mary J. Blige "All That I Can Say." Another TOPIX · Mad Dog co-venture: Red Giant, a television production company that has co-created the magazine-style television series, "Splat," a half hour live action show.

Topix/Mad Dog
35 McCaul St.
Toronto, ON
Canada M5T 1V7
Phone: 416 971-7711
Fax: 416 971-9277
URL: http://www.topix.com

Vivid Group Inc.

Area(s) of Specialization: Multimedia, CGI, Film/Video, Animation

Number of Employees: 20

Vivid Group creates and develops interactive arenas used in the Museum, Science Center and Hall of Fame Industry. The company uses patented Gesture Xtreme (GX) technology allows for custom programming of Corporate Communication packages using the clients' logo and/or theme objective. Originally created for use as a performance medium, GX technology branched out and quickly caught on as an education and entertainment instrument. GX is in the rehabilitation and physiotherapy industry, as well as virtual reality entertainment.

Vivid Group Inc.
317 Adelaide Street West
Suite 302
Toronto, Ontario
Canada, M5V 1P9
Phone: 416 340-9290
Fax: 416 348-9809
URL: http://www.vividgroup.com

Index – Listed by State or Province

Alabama

Anivision 41

Arizona

Creative Industries and Technology 147
Fox Animation Studios 161
Green Rabbit Design Studio, Inc. 109
Jamaica Bay 171
Laredo Productions, Inc. 113
Master Designs Computer Graphics 182
MDFX 186
Mirage Digital 116
Rhonda Graphics Inc. 202
Virtual Pictures Company 122

California

168 Design Group 224
525 Studios 127
A.D.2, Inc. 128
A.I. Effects, Inc. 130
Academy of Television Arts & Sciences 127
Aces Research, Inc. 127
Acme Filmworks Animation 128
Adobe Systems Inc. 128
Advantage Audio 129
Advox 129
Aftershock Digital 129
Alias-Wavefront 130
An-Amaze-Tion 131
Angel Studios 131
Animalu Productions 132
Animation and Effects 132

Artichoke Productions 134
ATV - All Things Video 134
Available Light Ltd. 135
Ayres Group 135
Baer Animation Company, Inc. 135
Banned From the Ranch 136
BearByte Animation 136
Bill Melendez Production 137
Blizzard Entertainment 137
Bluelight Animation 137
Blur Studio, Inc. 138
Brilliant Digital Entertainment 138
Calico Creations LTD 138
California Image Associates 139
Camera Control, Inc. 139
Catalyst Productions 139
Centropolis Effects 140
Chandler Group, The 140
Chiodo Brothers Productions, Inc. 141
Cinema Now 142
Cinema Production Service 142
Cinema Research 142
CinePartners Entertainment 143
Cinesite Film Scanning and Recording 143
Click 3x 143
Communication Bridges 145
Component Post 145
Composite Image Systems/CIS 145
Computer Café 145
Computer Graphics Systems Development 146
Continuity Studios 146
Crazy Horse Editorial, Inc. 147
Cruse & Company 147
Curious Pictures - San Francisco 147
Cyber F/X, Inc. 148
David Allen Productions 148
Debut Entertainment, Inc. 148
Design Visualization Partners 149

Digiscope 149
Digital Capture 149
Digital Domain 150
Digital Factory 150
Digital Firepower 151
Digital Imagination 151
Digital Muse 151
Digital Visionaries 1 151
Dimensions 3 152
DJN Studios Inc. 152
DMK Productions, Inc. 153
Dream Theater 154
DreamWorks SKG 154
Duck Soup Produckions 154
EdgeX Studio 155
Effects/Gene Young 155
Elektrashock, Inc. 156
Encore Visual Effects 156
Epoch Ink Corp. 156
Europa Films 157
Excite@Home 157
Eye Candy Post 157
Fat Box, Inc. 158
Film Roman 158
Flash Film Works 158
Flint & Steel Productions, Inc. 159
Flip Your Lid Animation Studios 159
Flying Rhino Productions 160
Foundation Imaging 160
Four Media Company 161
Fred Wolf Films 161
Fusionworks, Inc. 162
Gentle Giant Studios 162
Giant Killer Robots 163
Gigawatt Studios 163
Gosch Productions 163
Grafx 164
H-gun Labs-Unplugged 164
Hammerhead Productions 164

Hansard Vision Productions-FX 165
Helium Productions, Inc. 165
Hornet Animation 166
House Film Design 166
House of Moves Motion Capture Studios 166
Howard A. Anderson Company 167
Human Code, Inc. 167
Image G/ Ikongraphics 168
Imaginary Forces 168
Imagination Workshop 168
Industrial Light And Magic 168
Inertia Pictures, Inc. 169
Infinite Dimensions Studios 169
International Cartoons and Animation
    Center, Inc. 169
Intrepidus Worldwide 170
Introvision International 170
Island Fever Productions, Inc. 171
Jim Henson Company, The 171
Jim Keeshen Productions 172
Joseph Abbati 172
K & J Design 172
Kenimaiton Animation Services 173
Klasky Csupo Inc. 173
Kleiser-Walczak Construction Co. 173
Krakatoa Digital Post, Inc. 173
Krell Wonders 174
Kurtz & Friends Films 174
L@it2D 174
Landmark Entertainment Group 175
Landor Associates 175
Laser Media, Inc. 175
Launch Media, Inc. 176
Leprevost Corp., The 176
Liquid Light Studios 177
Little Fluffy Clouds 177
Loko Pictures 177
LOOK! Effects, Inc. 178
Lucas-THX 179

LucasArts Entertainment Co. 178
Lucasfilm Ltd. And Lucas Licensing Ltd. 179
Lumeni Productions, Inc. 179
Lumens 180
Lunarfish 180
Lyric Media 180
M80 Interactive Marketing 180
MacLeod Productions 181
Macromedia, Inc. 181
Magic Box Productions, Inc. 181
Manex Entertainment 182
Matte World Digital 183
Media Staff, The 183
Media X 183
Mesmer Animation Labs 184
Method 185
Metrolight Studios 185
Metropolis Digital, Inc. 185
Metropolis Editorial 186
Midway Games West, Inc. 186
Mirage Media 186
Mixin Pixls 187
Mobility Inc. 187
Modern VideoFilm 188
Mondo Media 188
Montana Edit, Inc. 188
Motion City Films 189
Motionworks 189
Moving Media 189
Net Surf Café 190
Netter Digital 190
New Hollywood, Inc. 190
Nickelodeon Digital 191
Novocom, Inc. 192
NxView Technologies, Inc. 192
Pacific Data Images 193
Pacific Ocean Post Studios 193
Paradesa Media 194
Paradise F.X. 194

Phoenix Editorial Services 194
Pixar Animation Studios 195
Pixel Envy 195
Pixel Liberation Front, Inc. 195
Planet Blue 196
POD 196
Prime Post 197
Production Group, The 197
Protozoa, Inc. 198
Radium 198
Rainmaker Digital Pictures 199
Random Task 198
Razorfish 200
Reality Check 200
Red Car 201
Rejobi 201
Renegade Animation, Inc. 201
ReZ.n8 Productions, Inc. 201
Rhythm and Hues 202
Rijn & Reisman 202
Ring of Fire 203
Route 66 Productions, Inc. 204
San Francisco Production Group 204
Scansite 204
Scarlet Letters 205
Screaming Pixels 205
Secret Lab, The 205
Shadow Caster 206
Silicon Graphics, Inc. /Computer Systems Business
    Unit 206
Skywalker Sound 207
SOL Design FX 208
Sony Computer Entertainment America 208
Sony Pictures Imageworks 208
Southern Exposure 209
Spaff Animation 209
Spank Interactive 209
Spazzco 210
Special Designs Animation Studio 210

Spicy Cricket Animation 210
Spumco, Inc. 211
Spyglass, Inc. 211
Spyglass, Inc. 211
Stan Winston Studio 211
Stargate Films, Inc. 212
Station X Studios, LLC 212
Swankytown 212
T-Bone Films, Inc. 213
TFX, Inc. 213
The Video Agency, Inc. / TVA 216
Tigar Hare Studios 214
Tippet Studios 214
Tooniversal 215
Total Video Co. 215
Truly Dangerous Company, The 215
Urban Vision Entertainment 216
Video Arts, Inc. 217
Viewpoint 217
Viewport Images 218
Virtualmagic Animation 218
Vision Crew Unlimited 219
Vision Scape Imaging, Inc. 219
Visual Concept Engineering, Inc. / VCE 220
Visual Magic Images, Inc. 220
Walt Disney Feature Animation 221
Warner Bros. Television & Classic Animation 221
Western Images 222
Wild Brain, Inc. 222
William Moffitt Associates 222
Wired Digital 223
Xaos, Inc. 223
Zona Productions, Inc. 224
Zooma Zooma 224

Colorado

All Video Production 131
ARG Cartoon Animation Studio 133
Base2 Studios 136

Celluloid Studios 140
Colorado Studios 144
Visible Productions 218

Connecticut

Impact Studios 69
Palace Production Center 82
Service Group, Inc. 88
Sonalysts Studios, Inc. 88
Wreckless Abandon 96

Delaware

Teleduction, Inc. 91

Florida

AARGH Animation, Inc. 37
Animatic And Storyboards Inc 39
APA Studios 42
AVC 44
Boca Entertainment 48
Broadcast Video, Inc. 49
Bush Entertainment, Inc. 49
Century III at Universal Studios 51
Deep Blue Sea 59
Dynacs Digital Studios 60
M&M Creative Services 76
Mindvisions (3d Studios) 78
Motion Image 79
Pixel Factory, Inc., The 83
Royal Vision Productions 87
Successful Images 89
Universal Studios 93
Venture Productions 93

Georgia

APC Studios 42
Atlanta Video 43
Click 3X - Atlanta 54

Crawford Digital 56
Dzignlight Studios 60
Engineered Multimedia, Inc. 62
Fathom Studios 64
Giant Studios 67
Macquarium, Inc. 74
Magick Lantern 74
Post Modern Editorial, Inc. 84
Video Tape Associates 94

Idaho

North by Northwest Productions/Boise 191
Omni Studio, Inc. 117

Illinois

Astropolitan Pictures, Inc. 102
Atomic Imaging 102
Big Idea 102
Broadview Media 103
Calabash Animation, Inc. 103
Dreamscape Design, Inc. 106
GenneX Health Technologies 108
Midway Games Inc. 115
Network Century /Cinema Video 116
Red Car - Chicago 118
Spyglass, Inc. 119
Strictly FX 120
There TV 120
Tribune Broadcasting 92
Tribune Media Services 121
Tricky Pictures 121

Indiana

Advanced Architectual Concepts and
    TGWB, Inc. 101
TUV Productions RRR by ABC of Film 122

Iowa

Hellman Associates, Inc. 110

Louisiana

Vidox Image and Data 122

Maryland

3DVisual.com 37
EPI 63
Spicer Productions 89
XL Translab Animations 97
ZKAD Productions 98

Massachusetts

Activeworlds.com 37
Animation Technologies 40
Borris FX 48
Cole and Company 55
Cosmic Blender 57
Envision Group, The 62
Fablevision Animation Studios 63
Finish 65
Ingalls 70
Kleiser-Walczak Construction Co. 73
Media Education Foundation 77
Multimedia Productions 80
Olive Jar Studios, Inc. 81
Pixel Soup 83
Razorfish-Boston 85
Spot 89
Universal Studios 93
ViewPoint Studios 94
Weber Group, The 95

Michigan

Grace & Wild Digital Studios 109
Leaping Lizards, Ltd. 114

Minnesota

Adtech Animation and Graphic Design 101
Alec Syme Illustration 101
Broadview Media, Minneapolis 49
Capstone Multimedia, Inc. 103
Fischer Edit 107
Ghost Productions, Inc. 108
HDMG Digital Post & Effects 110
Juntunen Media Group 112
Lamb and Company 113
Oops Animation, Inc. 117
Pixel Farm 118
Reelworks Animation Studio 119

Missouri

Fearless Eye, Inc. 107
Innervision Productions, Inc. 111
LiveWire Marketing, Inc. 114
Maximillion Zillion Animation 115
PopTop Software Inc. 118
Technisonic Studios 120
Trinity Animation & Visual Effects 121

Nebraska

Gourmet Images 108

Nevada

CHOPS & Associates Live Animation 141
Lighthouse Graphics, Inc. 176

New Jersey

Aspen, Inc. 43
Effects House Corporation, The - New Jersey 61
Intoons 71
O'Plenty Animation Studios 82
Rab-Byte Computer Graphics, Inc. 84
Susan Brand Studio Inc./Animation 91

New Mexico

Bandelier, EFX 135
Flamdoodle Animation Inc. 158

New York

4-Front Video Design, Inc. 66
AFCG 38
Animagination, Ltd. 39
Animated, Inc. 39
Animation NYC 40
Animus Films 41
Artbear Pigmation, Inc. 42
Association for Independent Video
   & Filmmakers 43
Atlantic Motion Pictures 44
Avekta Productions 44
Balsmeyer & Everett, Inc. 45
Betelguese Productions, Inc. 45
Big Sky Editorial 46
Bill Feigenbaum Designs Inc. 46
Black Logic 46
Blue Rock Editing Co. 47
Blue Sky Studios 47
BNN 47
Broadway Video Design 49
Buzzco Associates, Inc. 50
BXB, Inc. 50
Cabana Corporation 50
Charlex 52
Children's Television Workshop 52
Cineframe Animation 52
Cineric 53
Cinnesite Film, Scanning and Recording 53
City Lights Media Group 54
Click 3X - New York 54
Continuity 57
Continuity Studios 55
Corey Design Studios Inc. 56

Creative Time 56
Crush Digital Video 57
Curious Pictures - New York 58
Cutting Vision, Inc. 58
Cyclotron 58
Data Motion Arts 59
Effects House Corporation, The 61
F-Stop Studio 63
Fantasimation Classic Animation 63
Film East 64
Film/Video Arts 64
Funny Garbage 66
GLC Productions 68
GTV 68
Image Group Design 69
Improv Technologies 70
Ink Tank, The 70
Jim Henson Company, The 71
Judson Rosebush Company 72
Kleiser-Walczak Construction Co. - New York 73
L.A. Bruell 73
Loop Filmworks 74
Lovett Productions, Inc. 74
Magnetic Image Video 75
Manhattan Transfer 76
Marvel Entertainment Group, Inc. 76
Mechanism Digital 77
Metastream (View Point) 77
Mitch Butler Company, Inc. 78
Modern Uprising Stuios 79
Muffin-Head Productions 79
Nick Ericson Studio 80
Oculus 81
Outpost, The 82
Pixel Liberation Front, Inc. 83
R/GA Digital Studio 86
Razorfish 85
Redcar - New York 85
Registered Films 86

REI Media Group 85
Replica Technology 86
Rhinoceros Visual Effects 87
Rhinodesign 87
Sunbow Entertainment 90
Sunburst Technology 90
TZ-NY 92
Unbound Studios 92
WDDG 95
Women Make Movies, Inc. 96
Zander's Animation Parlour 97
Zero Degrees Kelvin 97
Zooma Zooma 98

North Carolina

Communications Group, Inc. 55
Flying Foto Factory, Inc. 66
John Lemmon Films 72
MindWorks Multimedia 78
Nx View Technologies 192
Planet Three Animation Studio 84
Terminal Side F/X Studios 92

North Dakota

Level 5 114

Ohio

Character Builders, Inc. 104
Creegan Company, The 105
EDR Media 106
Kaleidoscope Animation, Inc. 113

Oklahoma

Da Vinci Motion Graphics, LLC 105
Digital DK Studios 105
Winner Communications Inc. 123

Oregon

Artbeats Software Inc. 133
COBI Digital 143
Digital Wave Productions 151
Downstream 153
Happy Trails Animation 165
Northwest Film Center-
    Portland Art Museum 191
Omni Video 192
Portland Post Production and
    Graphics Company 196
Sockeye Creative, Inc. 207
Visionary Studio 219
Wallace Creative, Inc. 220
Will Vinton Studio 222

Pennsylvania

Amalgamation House 38
Camp Chaos Animation Studio 51
Cartoon Tycoon, The 51
Fire Mist Media 65
Home Run Pictures 69
MBC Teleproductions 75
Source W Media 89
Summer Kitchen Studio 90

South Carolina

Digital Animation Corporation 59

Tennessee

Paradigm Productions 117
ZFx, Inc. 97

Texas

Charlie Uniform Tango 104
DNA Productions, Inc. 106
Gathering Of Developers, Inc. 107

HD Vision, Inc. 110
Human Code, Inc. 111
Imageworks Computer
    Graphics Imaging, Inc. 111
Intelecon 112
Janimation, Inc. 112
Match Frame Post Production 115
Mere Productions, Inc. 235
Nvision, Inc. 116
Picturestart 118
Red Car - Dallas 118
Reel FX Creative Solutions 119
VT/TV Graphics and Post 123

U.S. Virgin Islands

Sam and Vick's Café 88

Utah

Zygote Media Group 224

Virginia

Animators at Law, Inc. 41
Digital Bunker 60
Eagle Films 60
Empire Video, Inc. 61
Frank Beach and Associates, Inc. 66
Garth Gardner Company, Inc. 67
Gearboxx 67
Henninger Productions 68
Olympus Group, Inc 81
Video Solutions 93
Vorizon Video Services 94
Wave Works Digital Media 95
Weber Group, The 95

Washington

Adobe Systems Inc. - Seattle 129
American Production Services 131

Arkiteck, Inc. 133
Atom Films 134
BLADE Simulation 137
Digital Farm 150
Dreadnought Pictures 153
Edmark Corporation 155
Encore Productions 156
Flying Spot, Inc. 160
Merwin Creative 115
Mesmer Animation Labs 184
Modern Digital 188
North by Northwest Productions 191
QB's Computer Animaiton & Graphics 198
Raster Ranch, Ltd. 199
RealNetworks, Inc. 200
Rocket Pictures, Inc. 203
Sierra, Inc. 206
Smashing Ideas Amimatinon 207
Tooned In 214
Valve Software 216

Washington D.C.

Interface Media Group 70
Wave Works 95

Wisconsin

Visuality LLC 122
Webpromotions, Inc. 123

Canada

British Columbia

Bardel Animation, Ltd. 227
Barking Bullfrog Cartoon Company, Inc. 228

Bowes Production, Inc. 229
Brainchild Studios 229
Digital Animatics 230
Gajdecki Visual Effects 232
Lost Boys Studios 233
Mainframe Entertainment, Inc. 234
Mercury Filmworks 234
Northwest Imaging and FX 235
Rainmaker Digital Pictures 235
Relic Entertainment, Inc. 235
168 Design Group 192

Ontario

Alias-Wavefront 227
Audio Visions Productions 227
Bone Digital Effects 228
Boomstone Entertainment, Inc. 228
C.O.R.E. Digital Pictures 230
Cuppa Coffee Animation 230
DKP Effects 232
DKP/Dan Krech Productions, Inc. 231
Grafixation 232
Head Gear Animation 232
Loop Media Inc. 233
Nelvana Limited 234
Post Group, The 235
Sarco Studios 236
Sundog Films 236
Topix/Mad Dog 237
Vivid Group Inc. 237

Québec

Buzz Image Group, Inc. 229

Index –Listed by Company Name

Symbols

168 Design Group 224
3DVisual.com 37
4-Front Video Design, Inc. 66
525 Studios 127

A

A.D.2, Inc. 128
A.I. Effects, Inc. 130
AARGH Animation, Inc. 37
Academy of Television Arts & Sciences 127
Aces Research, Inc. 128
Acme Filmworks Animation 128
Activeworlds.com, Inc. 37
Adobe Systems, Inc. 129
Adtech Animation and Graphic Design 101
Advanced Architectual Concepts and TGWB, Inc. 101
Advantage Audio 129
Advox 129
AFCG, Inc. 38
Aftershock Digital 130
Alec Syme Illustration 101
Alias-Wavefront 130, 227
All Video Production 131
Amalgamation House 38
American Production Services 131
An-Amaze-Tion 131
Angel Studios 132
Animagicians 38
Animagination, Ltd. 39
Animalu Productions 132
Animated, Inc. 39
Animatic and Storyboards, Inc. 39
Animation and Effects 132
Animation NYC 40
Animation Technologies 40
Animators at Law, Inc. 41
Animus Films 41
Anivision, Inc. 41
APA Studios 42
APC Studios 42
ARG Cartoon Animation Studio 133
Arkiteck, Inc. 133
Artbear Pigmation, Inc. 42
Artbeats Software Inc. 133
Artichoke Productions 134
Aspen, Inc. 43
Association for Independent Video & Filmmakers 43
Astropolitan Pictures, Inc. 102
Atlanta Video 43
Atlantic Motion Pictures 44
Atom Films 134
Atomic Imaging 102
ATV-All Things Video 134
Audio Visions Productions 227
Available Light, Ltd. 135
AVC 44
Avekta Productions 44
Ayres Group 135

B

Baer Animation Company, Inc. 135
Balsmeyer & Everett, Inc. 45
Bandelier, EFX 135
Banned from the Ranch 136
Bardel Animation, Ltd. 228
Base2 Studios 136
BearByte Animation 136
Betelguese Productions, Inc. 45
Big Idea Production 102
Big Sky Editorial 46
Bill Feigenbaum Designs, Inc. 46

Bill Melendez Production 137
Black Logic 46
BLADE Simulation 137
Blizzard Entertainment 137
Blue Rock Editing Co. 47
Blue Sky Studios 47
Bluelight Animation 137
Blur Studio, Inc. 138
BNN 47
Boca Entertainment 48
Boomstone Entertainment, Inc. 228
Borris FX 48
Bowes Production, Inc. 229
Brainchild Studios 229
Brilliant Digital Entertainment 138
Broadcast Video, Inc. 49
Broadview Media 103
Broadway Video Design 49
Bush Entertainment, Inc. 49
Buzzco Associates, Inc. 50
BXB, Inc. 50

C

Cabana Corporation 50
Calabash Animation, Inc. 103
Calico Creations, Ltd. 138
California Image Associates 139
Camera Control, Inc. 139
Camp Chaos Animation Studio 51
Capstone Multimedia, Inc. 104
Cartoon Tycoon, The 51
Catalyst Productions 139
Celluloid Studios 140
Centropolis Effects 140
Century III at Universal Studios 51
Chandler Group, The 140
Character Builders, Inc. 104
Charlex 52
Charlie Uniform Tango 104

Children's Television Workshop 52
Chiodo Brothers Productions, Inc. 141
CHOPS & Associates Live Animation 141
Cineframe Animation 52
Cinema Now 142
Cinema Production Service 142
Cinema Research 142
CinePartners Entertainment 143
Cineric 53
Cinesite Film Scanning and Recording 143
Cinesite Film, Scanning and Recording 53
City Lights Media Group 54
Click 3X 54
Click 3x 143
COBI Digital 144
Cole and Company 55
Colorado Studios 144
Communication Bridges 145
Communications Group, Inc. 55
Component Post 145
Composite Image Systems/CIS 145
Computer Café 145
Computer Graphics Systems Development 146
Continuity Studios 55, 146
Corey Design Studios, Inc. 56
Cosmic Blender 56
Crawford Digital 56
Crazy Horse Editorial, Inc. 147
Creative Industries and Technology 147
Creative Time 57
Creegan Company, The 105
Cruse & Company 147
Crush Digital Video 57
Curious Pictures 57, 148
Cutting Vision, Inc. 58
Cyber F/X, Inc. 148
Cyclotron 58

D

Da Vinci Motion Graphics, LLC 105
Data Motion Arts 58
David Allen Productions 148
Debut Entertainment, Inc. 148
Deep Blue Sea 59
Design Visualization Partners 149
Digiscope 149
Digital Animatics 231
Digital Animation Corporation 59
Digital Bunker 60
Digital Capture 149
Digital DK Studios 105
Digital Domain 150
Digital Factory 150
Digital Farm 150
Digital Firepower 151
Digital Imagination 151
Digital Muse 151
Digital Visionaries 1 152
Digital Wave Productions 152
Dimensions 3 153
DJN Studios Inc. 153
DKP Effects 231
DMK Productions, Inc. 153
DNA Productions, Inc. 106
Downstream 154
Dreadnought Pictures 154
Dream Theater 154
Dreamscape Design, Inc. 106
DreamWorks SKG 154
Duck Soup Produckions 155
Dynacs Digital Studios 60
Dzignlight Studios 60

E

Eagle Films 60
EdgeX Studio 155
Edmark Corporation 156
EDR Media 106
Effects House Corporation, The 61
Effects/Gene Young 156
Elektrashock, Inc. 156
Empire Video, Inc. 61
Encore Productions 156
Encore Visual Effects 157
Engineered Multimedia, Inc. 62
Envision Group, The 62
EPI 62
Epoch Ink Corp. 157
Europa Films 158
Excite@Home 158
Eye Candy Post 157

F

F-Stop Studio 63
Fablevision Animation Studios 63
Fantasimation Classic Animation 63
Fat Box, Inc. 158
Fathom Studios 64
Fearless Eye, Inc. 107
Film East 64
Film Roman 159
Film/Video Arts 64
Finish 65
Fire Mist Media 65
Fischer Edit 107
Flamdoodle Animation, Inc. 159
Flash Film Works 159
Flint & Steel Productions, Inc. 160
Flip Your Lid Animation Studios 160
Flying Foto Factory, Inc. 65
Flying Rhino Productions 160
Flying Spot, Inc. 161
Foundation Imaging 161
Four Media Company 161
Fox Animation Studios 162

Frank Beach and Associates, Inc. 66
Fred Wolf Films 162
Funny Garbage 66
Fusionworks, Inc. 162

G

Gajdecki Visual Effects 232
Garth Gardner Company, Inc. 67
Gathering of Developers, Inc. 107
Gearboxx 67
GenneX Health Technologies 108
Gentle Giant Studios 162, 163
Ghost Productions, Inc. 108
Giant Killer Robots 163
Giant Studios 67
Gigawatt Studios 163
GLC Productions 68
Gosch Productions 164
Gourmet Images 108
Grace & Wild Digital Studios 109
Grafixation 232
Grafx 164
Green Rabbit Design Studio, Inc. 109
GTV 68

H

H-gun Labs-Unplugged 164
Hammerhead Productions 164
Hansard Vision Productions-FX 165
Happy Trails Animation llc 165
HD Vision, Inc. 110
HDMG Digital Post & Effects 110
Helium Productions, Inc. 166
Hellman Associates, Inc. 110
Henninger video 68
Home Run Pictures 69
Hornet Animation 166
House Film Design 166
House of Moves Motion Capture Studios 167

Howard A. Anderson Company 167
Human Code, Inc. 111, 168

I

Image G/Ikongraphics 168
Image Group Design 69
Imageworks Computer Graphics Imaging, Inc. 111
Imaginary Forces 168
Imagination Workshop 169
Impact Studios 69
Improv Technologies 69
Industrial Light And Magic 169
Inertia Pictures, Inc. 169
Infinite Dimensions Studios 169
Ingalls 70
Ink Tank, The 70
Innervision Productions, Inc. 111
Intelecon 112
Interface Media Group 70
International Cartoons and
    Animation Center, Inc. 170
Intoons 71
Intrepidus Worldwide 170
Introvision International 170
Island Fever Productions, Inc. 171

J

Jamaica Bay 171
Janimation, Inc. 112
Jim Henson Company, The 71, 171
Jim Keeshen Productions 172
John Lemmon Films 71
Judson Rosebush Company 72
Juntunen Media Group 112

K

K & J Design 172
Kaleidoscope Animation, Inc. 113

Kenimatlon Animation Services 173
Klasky Csupo, Inc. 173
Kleiser-Walczak Construction Co. 72, 173
Krakatoa Digital Post, Inc. 174
Krell Wonders 174
Kurtz & Friends Films 174

L

L.A. Bruell 73
L@it2D 175
Lamb and Company 113
Landmark Entertainment Group 175
Landor Associates 175
Laredo Productions, Inc. 113
Laser Media, Inc. 176
LaserPacific Media Corporation 176
Launch Media, Inc. 176
Leaping Lizards, Ltd. 114
Leprevost Corp., The 176
Lighthouse Graphics, Inc. 177
Liquid Light Studios 177
Little Fluffy Clouds, Inc. 177
LiveWire Marketing, Inc. 114
Loko Pictures 178
LOOK! Effects, Inc. 178
Loop Filmworks 73
Loop Media Inc. 233
Lost Boys Studios 233
Lovett Productions, Inc. 74
Lucas-THX 179
LucasArts Entertainment Co. 178
Lucasfilm Ltd. and Lucas Licensing Ltd. 179
Lumeni Productions, Inc. 180
Lumens 180
Lunarfish 180
Lyric Media 180

M

M&M Creative Services 75

M80 Interactive Marketing 181
MacLeod Productions 181
Macquarium, Inc. 74
Macromedia, Inc. 181
Magic Box Productions, Inc. 182
Magick Lantern 74
Magico 182
Magnetic Image Video 74
Manex Entertainment 182
Manhattan Transfer 75
Marvel Entertainment Group, Inc. 76
Master Designs Computer Graphics 183
Match Frame Post Production 114
Matte World Digital 183
Maximillion Zillion Animation 115
MBC Teleproductions 75
MDFX 186
Mechanism Digital 76
Media Education Foundation 76
Media Staff, The 183
Media X 184
Mercury Filmworks 234
Mere Productions, Inc. 115
Merwin Creative 184
Mesmer Animatinon Labs 184
Metastream (View Point) 77
Method 185
Metrolight Studios 185
Metropolis Digital, Inc. 185
Metropolis Editorial 186
Midway Games Inc. 115
Midway Games, Inc. 186
Mike's Miniature Movies 77
Mindvisions (3d Studios) 77
MindWorks Multimedia 78
Mirage Digital 116
Mirage Media 187
Mitch Butler Company, Inc. 78
Mixin Pixls 187
Mobility, Inc. 187

Modern Uprising Stuios 78
Modern VideoFilm 188
Mondo Media 188
Montana Edit, Inc. 189
Motion City Films 189
Motion Image 79
Motionworks 189
Moving Media 190
Muffin-Head Productions 79
Multimedia Productions 79

N

Nelvana Limited 234
Net Surf Café' 190
Netter Digital 190
Network Century / Cinema Video 116
New Hollywood, Inc. 191
Nick Ericson Studio 80
Nickelodeon Digital 191
North by Northwest Productions 191
Northwest Film Center- Portland Art Museum
    192
Northwest Imaging and FX 235
Novocom, Inc. 192
Nvision, Inc. 116
Nx View Technologies 193
Nx View Technologies, Inc. 80

O

Oculus 80
Olive Jar Studios, Inc. 81
Olympus Group, Inc 81
Omni Studio, Inc. 117
Omni Video 193
Oops Animation, Inc. 117
O'Plenty Animation Studios 81
Outpost, The 82

P

P.O.D. 196
Pacific Data Images 193
Pacific Ocean Post Studios 193
Palace Production Center 82
Paradesa Media 194
Paradigm Productions 117
Paradise F.X. 194
Phoenix Editorial Services 194
Picturestart 118
Pixar Animation Studios 195
Pixel Envy 195
Pixel Factory, Inc., The 82
Pixel Farm 118
Pixel Liberation Front, Inc. 83, 196
Pixel Soup 83
Planet Blue 196
Planet Three Animation Studio 83
PopTop Software, Inc. 118
Portland Post Production and
    Graphics Company, The 197
Post Modern Editorial, Inc. 84
Prime Post 197
Production Group, The 197
Protozoa, Inc. 198

Q

QB's Computer Animaiton & Graphics 198

R

R/GA Digital Studio 86
Rab-Byte Computer Graphics, Inc. 84
Radium 198
Rainmaker Digital Pictures 199, 235
Random Task 199
Raster Ranch, Ltd. 199
Razorfish 84, 200
Reality Check 200

RealNetworks, Inc. 200
Red Car 118, 201
Red Car New York 85
Reel FX Creative Solutions 119
Reelworks Animation Studio 119
Registered Films 86
REI Media Group 85
Rejobi 201
Relic Entertainment, Inc. 236
Renegade Animation, Inc. 201
Replica Technology 86
ReZ.n8 Productions, Inc. 202
Rhinoceros Visual Effects 87
Rhinodesign 87
Rhonda Graphics, Inc. 202
Rhythm and Hues 202
Rijn & Reisman 203
Ring of Fire 203
Rocket Pictures, Inc. 203
Route 66 Productions, Inc. 204
Royal Vision Productions 87

S

Sam and Vick's Café 88
San Francisco Production Group 204
Sarco Studios 236
Scansite 204
Scarlet Letters 205
Screaming Pixels 205
Secret Lab, The 205
Service Group, Inc. 88
Shadow Caster 206
Sierra, Inc. 206
Silicon Graphics, Inc. /Computer Systems Business
    206
Skywalker Sound 207
Smashing Ideas Amimatinon 207
Sockeye Creative, Inc. 207
SOL Design FX 208

Sonalysts Studios, Inc. 88
Sony Computer Entertainment America 208
Sony Pictures Imageworks 208
Source W Media 89
Southern Exposure 209
Spaff Animation 209
Spank Interactive 209
Spazzco 210
Special Designs Animation Studio 210
Spicer Productions 89
Spicy Cricket Animation 210
Spot 89
Spumco, Inc. 211
Spyglass, Inc. 119, 211
Stan Winston Studio 212
Stargate Films, Inc. 212
Station X Studios, LLC 212
Strictly FX 120
Successful Images 89
Summer Kitchen Studio 90
Sunbow Entertainment 90
Sunburst Technology 90
Sundog Films 236
Susan Brand Studio, Inc./Animation 91
Swankytown 213

T

T-Bone Films, Inc. 213
Technisonic Studios 120
Teleduction, Inc. 91
Terminal Side F/X Studios 92
TFX, Inc. 213
The Video Agency, Inc./TVA 216
There TV 120
Tigar Hare Studios 214
Tippet Studios 214
Tooned In 214
Tooniversal 215
Topix/Mad Dog 237

Total Video Co. 215
Tribune Broadcasting 92
Tribune Media Services 121
Tricky Pictures 121
Trinity Animation & Visual Effects 121
Truly Dangerous Company, The 215
TUV Productions RRR by ABC of Film 122
TZ-NY 92

U

Unbound Studios 92
Universal Studios 93
Urban Vision Entertainment 216

V

Valve Software 216
Venture Productions 93
Video Arts, Inc. 217
Video Solutions 93
Video Tape Associates 94
Vidox Image and Data 122
Viewpoint 217
ViewPoint Studios 94
Viewport Images 218
Virtual Pictures Company 122
Virtualmagic Animation 218
Visible Productions 219
Vision Crew Unlimited 219
Vision Scape Imaging, Inc. 219
Visionary Studio 219
Visual Concept Engineering, Inc./VCE 220
Visual Magic Images, Inc. 220
Visuality LLC 122
Vivid Group Inc. 238
Vorizon Video Services 94
VT/TV Graphics and Post 123

W

Wallace Creative, Inc. 220
Walt Disney Feature Animation 221
Warner Bros. Television & Classic Animation 221
Wave Works Digital Media 95
WDDG 95
Weber Group, The 95
Webpromotions, Inc. 123
Western Images 222
Wild Brain, Inc. 222
Will Vinton Studio 223
William Moffitt Associates 222
Winner Communications, Inc. 123
Wired Digital 223
Women Make Movies, Inc. 96
Wreckless Abandon 96

X

Xaos, Inc. 223
XL Translab Animations 97

Z

Zander's Animation Parlour 97
Zero Degrees Kelvin 97
ZFx, Inc. 97
ZKAD Productions 98
Zona Productions, Inc. 224
Zooma Zooma 98, 224
Zygote Media Group 224

Order Form for GARDNER'S Guides

Phone 1-800-968-9622

Please send me the following books/videos	ISBN/UPC	Price

Special Request

Shipping: $5.00 for the first book and $2.00 for each additional book.

Payment type   ○ Cheque   ○ Credit card   ○ VISA   ○ MasterCard

Card Number

Name on Card   Exp. Date (mm/yy)   /

Your Name   Phone Number

Street Billing Address

City, State, Zip Code

Fax Orders
440-895-6003
703-354-8279

Book Orders
4602 John Hancock Ct.
Suite 302
Annandale, VA 22003
703-354-8278
703-354-8279 fax
www.gogardner.com

GGC publishing